REPAIRING AND RESTORING FURNITURE

THE COMPLETE MANUAL
17th - 20th CENTURY

REPAIRING AND RESTORING FURNITURE

THE COMPLETE MANUAL
17th - 20th CENTURY

V.J. TAYLOR

BCA

LONDON · NEW YORK · SYDNEY · TORONTO

Frontispiece: Selection of antique chairs of the period 1780–1810, taken from *The Antique Furniture Trail,* also by V. J. Taylor (David & Charles, 1989)

This edition published 1992 by BCA by arrangement with David & Charles plc

CN 5333

Copyright text and illustrations © V. J. Taylor 1992

Typeset by ICON, Exeter
and printed in Great Britain by Butler & Tanner Ltd
for David & Charles plc
Brunel House Newton Abbot Devon

Contents

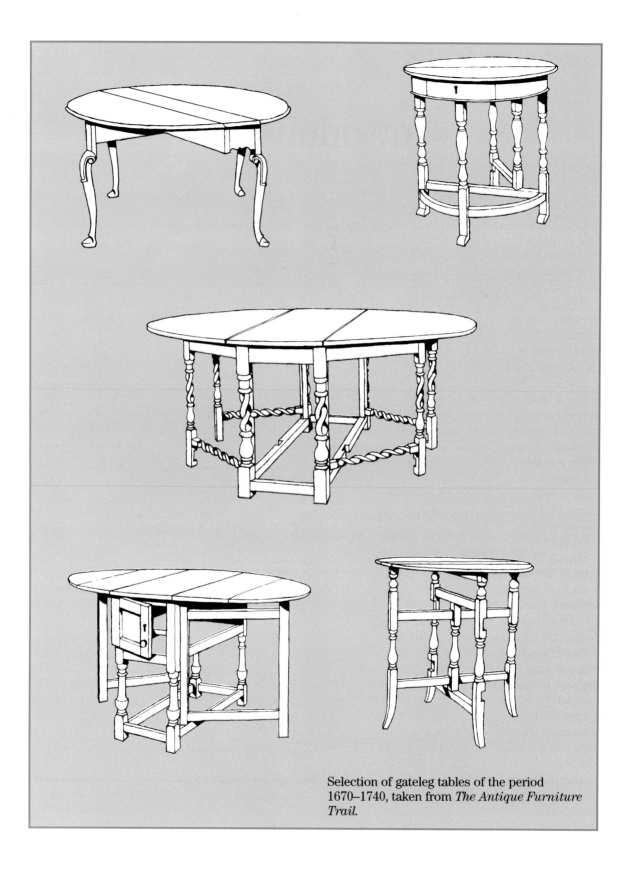

Selection of gateleg tables of the period 1670–1740, taken from *The Antique Furniture Trail*.

Introduction

This book deals with three kinds of woodwork, namely, reviving, repairing, and restoring furniture, so it will be helpful at this juncture to define what work each category includes.

'Reviving' is usually confined to furniture from the 1950s onwards which can loosely be described as 'non-period', bearing in mind that the most recent recognised period is the Art Deco of the 1930s, which was followed by Utility Furniture during World War II and for a few years afterwards. Reviving such pieces is usually not too difficult because any repairs are generally minor, and it is mainly a matter of updating the appearance by stripping off an old finish and re-finishing with either a modern polish, paint, or varnish. Replacing old handles and fittings with up-to-date ones, or using plastic carvings as decoration, are other quick ways to smarten up shabby furniture that still has plenty of life left in it from a constructional point of view.

Sprung furniture such as easy chairs, sofas, and beds of the same age are often perfectly sound apart from damaged or worn covers, which can be replaced. There is, too, always the possibility of re-springing them with resilient rubber webbing in conjunction with latex or plastic foam cushions.

'Repairing' involves making good breakages as a result of misuse, dealing with troubles caused by warping, remaking loose joints, and touching up or completely repolishing faulty polished surfaces. Such work is bound to be more difficult and time-consuming than reviving. Repairs of this kind may have to be carried out on furniture belonging to any style or period but it is permissible to use modern materials.

As an example, let us suppose that you have acquired an old oak settle that is in a sorry state, having been stored in an attic for many years. The repairs to this could well include stripping off what remains of the old finish and repolishing, remaking the joints and dealing with any other damage. You can use a modern plastic lacquer for the new finish, wood filler to fill in any small splits or blemishes, and a PVA or epoxy resin adhesive for the joints.

On the other hand, all of the materials used in 'restoration' (or 'conservation' as some experts prefer to call it) must be traditional and of the type used when the piece was first made. It should also be capable of being reversed and removed so that any future restoration may be undertaken without further damage. This means, for instance, that the glue must be an animal one such as Scotch glue which can readily be dissolved, and the finish must be wax, or traditional varnish, or French polish, all of which can be easily stripped and renewed. It is recommended that a professional restorer should make a note of the work he has done, and this should accompany the piece throughout its life. One last point – restoration should never seek to modify, alter, or conceal the true nature of the piece.

Fuller details of the true aims of restoration or conservation may be obtained from: The United Kingdom for Conservation, c/o Conservation Dept, Tate Gallery, Millbank, London, SW1 4RG.

Obviously, when planning a book of this nature, a start has to be made somewhere, and the logical assumption is that the reader has already reached a level in woodworking skill higher than that required for straightforward DIY jobs.

As well as basic cabinet-making, there are the related crafts of polishing, upholstering, and veneering which need to be described, and this has been done to the degree that they are required in repair and restoration. Those who would like to study them more fully will find a list of practical handbooks in the Bibliography. The same remarks apply to the skills of woodcarving, woodturning, and sharpening tools, which (in some books at least) receive poor coverage of only two or three pages per subject.

Should you have to work on period furniture, sooner or later you will need to check constructional or decorative details, and some of the commonest of these are included in Chapter 13, although the list is by no means comprehensive. There are always museums and stately homes where you can study authentic period pieces, and there are also plenty of books available, although those of the 'coffee table' kind are rarely of much use because small details are too vague to be seen clearly. The Bibliography, therefore, includes a section of books with plans and working drawings indispensable for practical work.

1 The tools you will need

The professional will have not only a full kit of woodworking tools but also those required for upholstery, polishing, and for special finishes such as gilding. He will also have a few metalworking tools which are handy for repairing locks, handles, and the occasional job of metalwork. Such a wide range of tools takes time and money to assemble and, because many professionals come into restoration work from cabinet-making, they already possess a good basic kit to build on.

Similarly, their workshops and equipment such as benches, shelving, etc, are all arranged to be as convenient as possible: here, I am irritated by those writers of books on woodworking who glibly assume that their readers have roomy workshops. The majority of us have to push the car out of the garage before we can start work, and there are many enthusiasts who are even worse off and have to make do with the spare room.

Among these less fortunate woodworkers are those who anticipate doing repairs and renovations on a fairly large scale for themselves or their friends, and also those who only undertake occasional jobs as and when necessary. All of them will almost certainly have only the few tools that comprise the usual household DIY kit, so the following is a list of extra tools that should be most useful. Tools and equipment for special jobs such as polishing, gilding, veneering, upholstery, etc, are described in the chapters dealing with those particular jobs.

SAWS (Fig 1:1)

You will need a saw for general cutting purposes. The best choice is a panel saw (A) with either 8 or 10 teeth per inch (25mm) – sometimes abbreviated to TPI – and preferably with a skew back slightly curved to lessen the chance of the saw's binding in the cut. A 20in (508mm) or 22in (559mm) blade length is suitable for most people. Such a saw will cut both across or with the grain, although in the latter case the work can be tiring and you would be well advised to use a portable power saw instead, or a motorised saw bench if you are fortunate enough to have one. There are rip saws that are specially made for cutting with the grain, but unless you are likely to have a lot of this to do, the extra expense is not worthwhile.

The saw you will probably use more than any other is a tenon saw (B) which, as its name implies, is primarily designed to cut tenons. It is also ideal for cutting across the grain when trimming pieces to length, and for sawing mitres and other joints. A 10in (254mm) blade is about right, with 12 teeth per inch (25mm).

Both the tenon saw and the 'gent's' saw (C), which is the next one to consider, are called 'back saws', which means that they have a solid metal spine along the back which stiffens the blade. The gent's saw is the one to use for sawing dovetails. Its peculiar name derives from the time when 'gentlemen' pursued woodworking as a hobby and this small saw was designed for them. You will find that one with a 6in (152mm) blade length will cut dovetails and many other small joints.

A coping saw (D) with blade holders that rotate a full 360° can be invaluable for cutting curves, circles, and scrolls if you do not already have a powered jigsaw which does the same kind of work. If you do have such a jigsaw, a hand fretsaw would be more useful than a coping saw.

A saw for cutting holes that are too small for a powered jigsaw to negotiate is the padsaw (E). Choose one that has a separate handle into which either fine or coarse-toothed blades can be inserted.

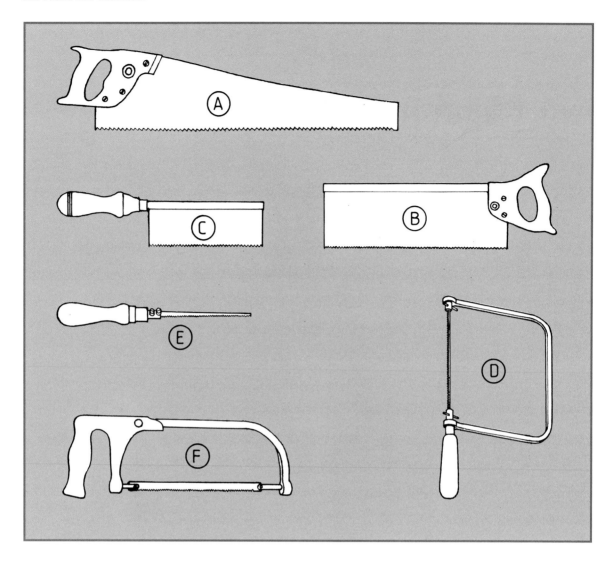

Fig 1:1 Various types of saws

Finally, a hacksaw (F) is a necessary tool for the occasions when you have to cut metal and it is indispensable for cutting through stubborn nails and screws.

PLANES (Fig 1:2)

Although the more of these you have the better, you will certainly need a minimum of two. The first should be a smoothing plane (A) about 10in (254mm) long with a 2in (51mm) or 2⅜in (61mm) wide cutting iron. The second should be a block plane about 6in (152mm) long with a 1⅜in (35mm) wide cutting iron.

Smoothing planes are used for truing up and smoothing along the grain. The length recommended is the maximum for this type of plane and some woodworkers would no doubt consider that such work is better done with either a jack plane or a jointer plane, both of which are much longer. But generally, they are considered to be tools for the professional cabinet-maker who uses them all the time, rather than the restorer.

A small block plane (B) is almost essential. Choose one that has its cutting iron set at the low angle of 12½° because this will enable you to plane awkward end grain and man-made boards.

A shoulder rebate plane (C) is also desirable. The usual size is about 8in (200mm) long with a 1¼in (32mm) wide cutting iron that cuts its full

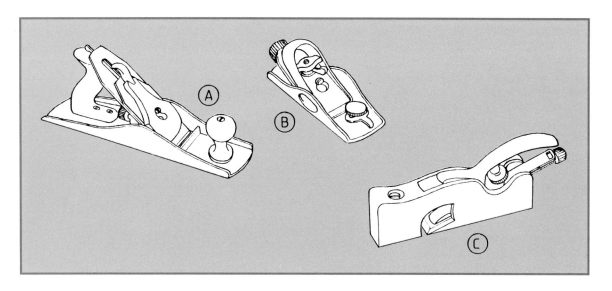

Fig 1:2 Planes for different purposes

width. The iron is set very near to the front so that it can plane close to an end. Two more advantages are that it can be operated with one hand, and can be used in either the normal position or laid flat on its side.

You can choose either wooden or metal smoothing planes. Some craftsmen swear by wooden planes, but it's a matter of whether you like the feel of wood or metal. You can also buy a plane with a wooden body which is fitted with the same adjusting mechanism as a metal one.

Fig 1:3 Various spokeshaves

SPOKESHAVES (Fig 1:3)

These are used for smoothing and rounding off curved surfaces. You'll need one for convex and one for concave surfaces. Those made of metal with adjustable cutters are best.

SCRAPERS

The cabinet scraper is an ideal tool for smooothing flat surfaces prior to glasspapering and polishing, and also for removing blemishes. It is one of the simplest tools there are, because it consists of a rectangular piece of tempered steel about 6in (150mm) long by 2½in (65mm) wide, and it can be bought at most tool shops.

Fig 1:4 shows how it is used. Your thumbs should press the blade into a slight curve and push it forward. The angle at which you hold it can only

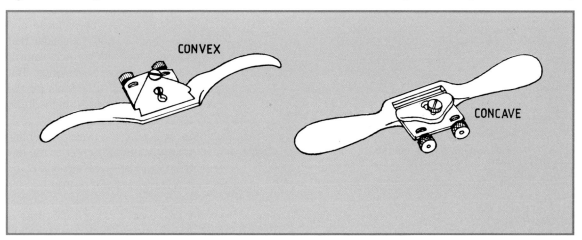

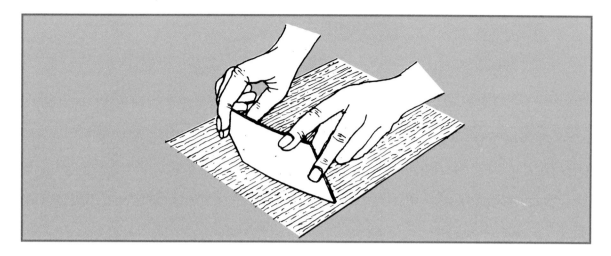

Fig 1:4 Showing how the cabinet scraper is pushed forward, being bent by the fingers at the same time

be found by experiment because it depends largely on how the scraper has been sharpened. It gets hot in use, and if you find this unpleasant you could buy one or other of the several proprietary scraper planes. Most cabinet-makers, however, find that the simple scraper blade is a more sensitive and efficient tool.

ABRADING TOOLS

From our point of view, these are rasps, files, and a wire brush. A kit of 'handyman's' files, consisting of a flat file with one smooth face and a coarse face on the reverse side, a round ⁵⁄₁₆in (8mm) diameter file for enlarging holes, and a half-round file with a smooth face, is worth buying and should be sufficient. You may care to supplement the kit at a later date by obtaining one or other of the several scraper tools of the Surform type, which are always useful.

Also, it's worthwhile investing in a small wire brush of the kind used for cleaning suede shoes. The larger ones used by engineers and mechanics are too fierce for our purposes.

CHISELS AND GOUGES (Fig 1:5)

There are three types of chisels and two gouges to be considered. These are the mortise (A), the bevelled-edge (B), and the firmer chisels (C); and the firmer and the scribing gouges (D) and (E).

Let us deal with the chisels first. The mortise chisel, as is obvious from its name, is used to chop out mortises and is robustly made to withstand heavy blows from a mallet. A set of three in ⅛in (3mm), ¼in (6mm), and ⅜in (10mm) widths should meet most of your requirements, and other sizes can be added later.

Bevelled-edge (or paring) chisels are intended for light work and are meant to be hit only with the hand. Firmer chisels are the ones to use for heavier jobs. Lately, however, a new pattern of chisel (F) has been introduced which, although it has bevelled edges, has a spine in its blade that is strong enough to withstand blows from a mallet. The extra strength is created by reducing the widths of the bevelled edges as they approach the top of the blade. The result is that you will only need one set of the new chisels instead of one set of firmer plus one set of bevelled. Three widths of blade – ⅜in (10mm), ½in (12mm), and ¾in (19mm) – should be enough to start with.

Now to consider the gouges. The difference between the two kinds is that the firmer gouge has its bevel on the outside of the curve (consequently it is often referred to as 'out-cannel'), and the scribing gouge has its bevel on the inside ('in-cannel'). Both are best acquired when the need arises. If you have a powered router, you will find that when you use it with the appropriate cutters it will, to a large extent, replace the firmer gouge.

BITS AND DRILLS (Fig 1:6)

Your choice of these depends upon whether you have hand or electric power, and may therefore

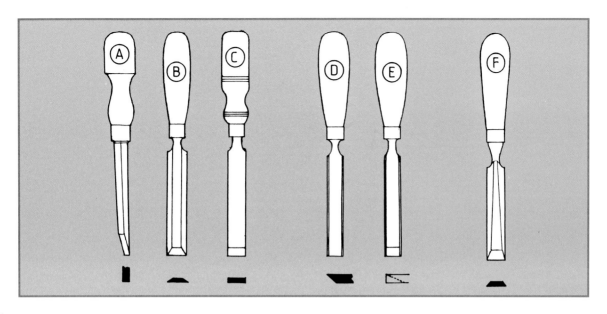

Fig 1:5 Various kinds of chisels and gouges

Fig 1:6 Showing the wide range of bits and drills available

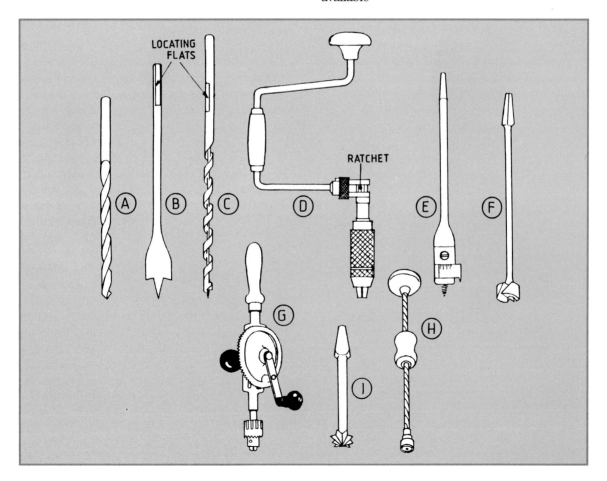

include power drills, carpenters' braces, or hand drills. Most households now have at least one power drill but, if you are thinking of buying one, make sure it has at least two speeds. Twist drills (A) are the only ones suitable for the higher speed of the power drill, while the lower speed can be used for flat bits (B) and the auger bits (C) specially made for the purpose.

The carpenter's brace (D) is an optional extra even though it has several facilities that supplement the other types of drills. These facilities are that you can use it with the special auger bits mentioned above and there are turnscrew (screwdriver) bits, too, which enable you to exert really powerful leverage on stubborn screws. There is also an expansive bit (E) that has a cutter which can be expanded to bore holes from ½in (12mm) to 1½in (38mm) diameters, plus another that expands from ⅞in (22mm) to 3in (76mm).

Finally, the brace can be used with the Forstner bit (F) which is specially designed to bore flat-bottomed holes. This can be an advantage in certain circumstances – for instance, when boring the holes in Windsor chair seats for the legs. All other bits rely on a central screw point to draw the cutters (or 'nickers') into the wood before they can start cutting, but the Forstner bit is guided by its circular rim. This means that you can bore a hole to its full depth with no fear that the point of the bit will break through.

The hand drill (G) is used with twist drills. You will probably find yourself employing it rather than the power drill on many occasions because you don't have to keep switching off and on every time you change drills. Make sure you buy a good quality drill because the teeth of the gear wheels on cheap models will soon slip or lose their alignment.

An Archimedean drill (H) can drill only tiny holes and is used in fretwork and very delicate woodwork. It is not expensive and is well worth having. You can buy drills for them. You can also make your own drills from panel or veneer pins by cutting off their heads and sharp ends, and grinding or filing one end to a chisel point with approximately a 20° angle.

Obviously, the more bits and drills of various types and sizes you have the better. One more thing you will need is a set of rose countersink bits (I). These are used to splay out the end of a hole so that a screw with a countersunk head can be driven home for its head to be flush with the surrounding wood surface.

SCREWDRIVERS (Fig 1:7)

Most homes will already contain a selection of these and they are such well known tools that there is no need to give detailed descriptions.

There are, however, two types that are relatively little known. The first is the turnscrew bit (A), which has already been mentioned. When it is

Fig 1:7 Different kinds of screwdrivers

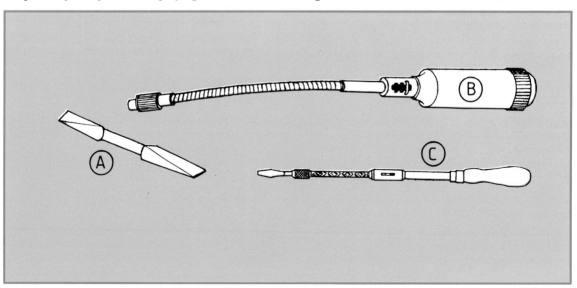

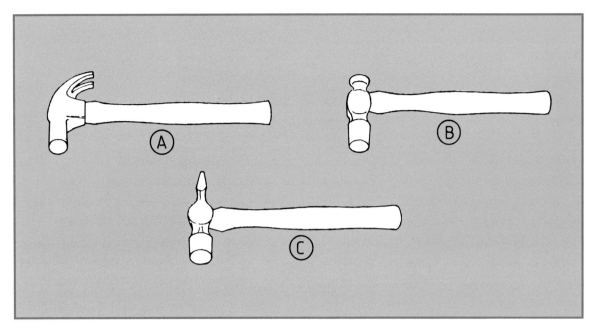

Fig 1:8 Hammers and mallets

fitted into a carpenter's brace it will give you a really strong leverage that will loosen the most stubborn screw. The second is the flexible shaft screwdriver (B). You will find this a godsend because it enables you to get into the most awkward places. It is fitted with a chuck into which you can fit different sizes of screwdriver bits for both slotted and cruciform screw heads.

You may be tempted to buy a 'Yankee' spiral ratchet screwdriver (C) but try to resist the temptation. It is an admirable tool for driving large numbers of screws into pre-drilled holes, because instead of having to twist the handle, you simply pump it up and down. This takes little effort and spares your wrist. But it is not the kind of job you are ever likely to do. And unless the pre-drilled hole is exactly the right size for the screw, the screwdriver blade may jump out of the slot and damage the work.

HAMMERS AND MALLETS (Fig 1:8)

As with screwdrivers, most homes contain a hammer or two. A 16oz (0.45kg) claw hammer (A) is useful for general work and also for extracting nails; and a 12oz (0.34kg) ball pein hammer (B) and a 12oz (0.34kg) cross pein hammer (C) are useful additions. The pein of a hammer is the part opposite to the striking face of the head. A ball pein is handy for rounding off metal studs or pins if you are doing simple metalwork, and a cross pein is useful for starting small nails or panel pins. You will need two mallets: an all-wood carpenter's 5in (127mm) one for use with chisels, and a soft-faced one for dismantling furniture without bruising the wood. The latter can have either a rubber or a nylon-faced head.

MARKING, GAUGING, AND MEASURING APPLIANCES (Fig 1:9)

Chief among these are measuring tools which, from our point of view, consist of a flexible metal rule, and a 36in (or 1m) wooden folding rule. Other essentials are a try square (A); a sliding bevel (B); and a marking/cutting gauge (C) for marking out mortises – its cutter can also be used for trimming thin material such as veneer.

Although it is rather expensive, a steel straight-edge can be a valuable piece of equipment when you need a precise guide for making straight cuts with a craft knife. It can also serve as a guide for power routers and portable saws.

A moulding profile gauge (D) is useful although not essential. In principle it consists of a number of thin metal or plastic leaves clamped together: when their edges are pushed against a moulding they assume the reverse of its profile, from which you can make an exact copy.

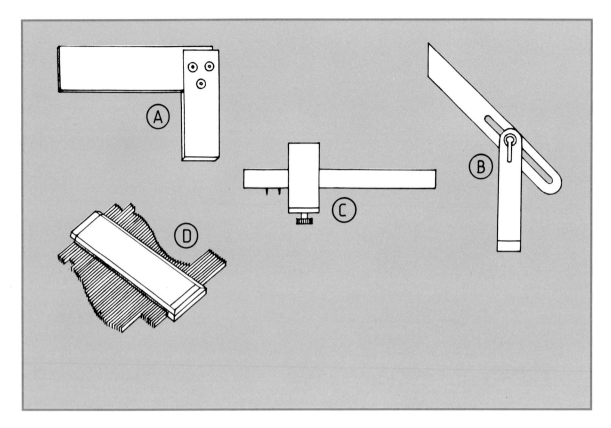

Fig 1:9 Types of marking, gauging, and measuring appliances

SHARPENING EQUIPMENT

Keeping your tools razor sharp is one of the keys to efficient work and good results. To describe the actual methods of sharpening the various kinds of tools would need a whole book. In any case, the subject is frequently dealt with in woodworking books and magazines so we will confine ourselves to the equipment available.

The best grinders are those which have sandstone wheels that run at a slow speed in a water trough. This means that there is no danger of drawing the temper of the steel, which can happen all too easily on a grinder fitted with carborundum wheels running at high speed.

You'll need an oilstone for putting edges on your chisels and plane irons, and while there is a wide variety available, the best choice to start with is a combination (fine/coarse) stone about 8in (200mm) by 2in (50mm) by 1in (25mm) thick, preferably mounted in its own protective box.

If you have any scribing or carving gouges that have their bevels ground on the inside, you will also need some oilstone slips of the correct curvature to fit them.

SUNDRY TOOLS

You will probably already have several of these in your household tool kit, but a useful range should include:
Two pairs of pliers (1 combination and 1 long-nosed)
A pair of pincers
A bradawl
A stout craft knife with a blade which will not break under pressure
A soldering iron (optional but desirable)
A hair drier, which you will find handy for warming joints before applying Scotch glue, and for the many occasions when you need to concentrate heat on a localised area

CRAMPING APPLIANCES (Fig 1:10)

These can be divided into two categories, namely the ones you have to buy and those you can make

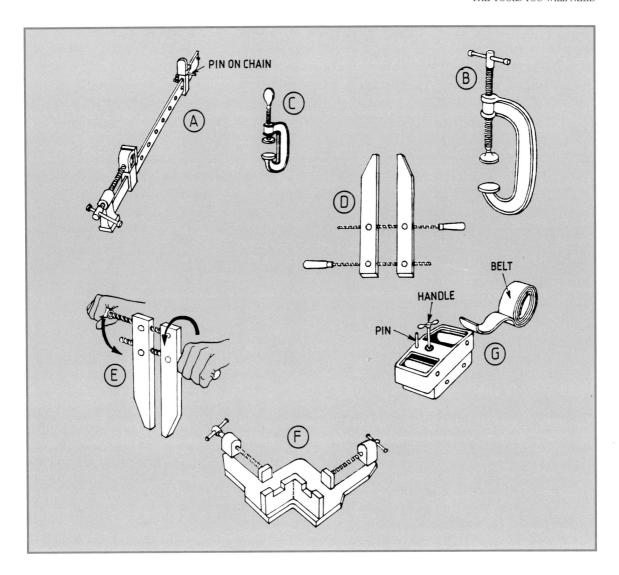

PIN ON CHAIN

A

C

B

D

BELT

HANDLE

PIN

G

E

F

yourself, which are dealt with in Chapter 2.

You can never have too many cramps, and the ones described below are essential for serious work:

Two sash cramps (A), preferably 36in (1m) long, for cramping up large work (you could, however, make yourself a cramping board as shown in Chapter 2, which fulfils many of the same functions).

As many G-cramps (B) as possible, from 6in (152mm) size upwards.

Three or four small thumbscrew cramps (C) (they are sometimes called fretworkers' cramps).

Two handscrews (D). These exert considerable pressure which is spread over a wider area than a

Fig 1:10 Showing a range of commonly used cramps

G-cramp; furthermore the jaws can be slightly out of parallel and they will still operate. To use them, grasp a handle in each hand and revolve one about the other as shown in (E).

A corner cramp (F). This is handy for cramping up mitred corners.

A band cramp (G) (sometimes called a 'webbing' cramp). It makes easy work of cramping up curved, round, or elliptical shapes. You could, however, make one for yourself as shown in Chapter 2.

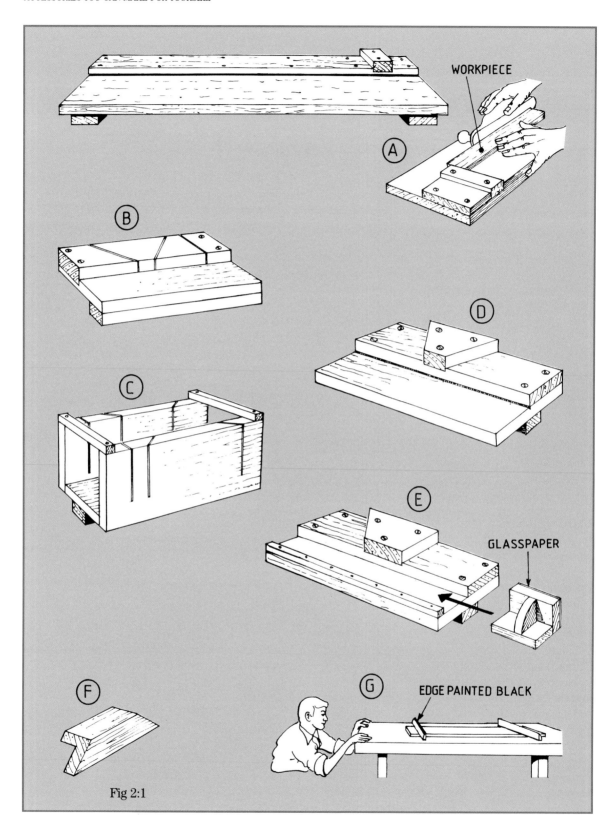

WORKPIECE

A

B

C

D

E

GLASSPAPER

F

G

EDGE PAINTED BLACK

Fig 2:1

2 Accessories you can make for yourself

You can greatly increase the scope and usefulness of your workshop by using some of the devices described and illustrated in Fig 2:1 and throughout this chapter. Most of them are continually employed by professional cabinet-makers and, as a result, there can be no doubt that they earn their keep. None of them costs much to make; indeed, some of them can be made from oddments that would otherwise be thrown away, so you will be saving money as well.

Because solid hardwood of a width of 6in (150mm) or more is very expensive, you can utilise medium density fibreboard, which is abbreviated to the initials MDF in the trade. It is available in the same large sizes as chipboard, and in ⅝in (16mm) and ¾in (19mm) thicknesses. Unlike chipboard, it can be sawn, machined, and jointed without any danger of crumbling. The edges can be moulded or shaped in the same way as a good quality hardwood, and it takes screws perfectly. As a result, it is ideal for constructing any accessory which incorporates large, flat, and absolutely true surfaces.

SHOOTING BOARD (Fig 2:1)(A)

A handy size for this would be about 30in (760mm) long. The method of construction should be clear from the illustrations, which also show how the board is used, with the workpiece being held against the stop block and the plane slid along on its side. Note the small groove that serves to collect any sawdust and small shavings that may accumulate during use.

As with many of these devices, it's a good idea to screw a strip to the underside so that it can be held in a bench vice.

BENCH HOOK AND MITRE-CUTTING BLOCK (Fig 2:1)(B)

This can be about 9in (230mm) long, and the cutting guide slots must be perfectly accurate. In use, the strip fixed to the underside of the front edge laps over the edge of the workbench and is held against it with your free hand.

MITRE BOX (Fig 2:1)(C)

Again, this should be about 9in (230mm) long and large enough to accept 3in (76mm) square mouldings. The cramping strip on the underside can be fixed in the bench vice and will hold it steady for you.

MITRE SHOOTING BOARD (Fig 2:1)(D)

Make this about 18in (450mm) long and use it, in conjunction with a block plane, for trimming the mitred ends of rails – always an awkward job. Note the cramping strip underneath.

MITRE AND SQUARE GLASSPAPERING BOARD (Fig 2:1)(E)

This resembles the mitre shooting board (D). However, a block with glasspaper glued to its face takes the place of a plane for truing up the squared or mitred ends of such small parts as mouldings, beadings, and the like once they have been planed.

A length of 18in (450mm) should be about right – the other dimensions can be made to suit your own purposes and the material available. It would be a good plan to make up two or three sliding

Fig 2:1 Constructional details of several handy devices you can make for yourself

blocks with a different grade of glasspaper on each. Some candle wax smeared along the trough in which the block slides will make things easier.

MITRE TEMPLATE (Fig 2:1)(F)

This is a small device that can be cramped over a moulding to guide the chisel when trimming a mitre.

WINDING STRIPS (Fig 2:1)(G)

These are two strips of hardwood which must be parallel throughout their lengths and identical in size and shape. Make them out of 1½in (38mm) by ¾in (19mm) thick hardwood, and about 12in (305mm) long. They should be slightly tapered in section so that they will stand upright. Paint the top edge of one of them black for about ½in (12mm) downwards. This will ensure that when you sight across them as in G, the amount of wind will be apparent. The word 'wind' is pronounced to rhyme with 'bind'.

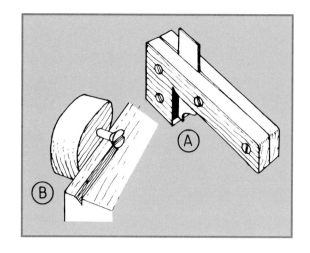

Fig 2:2 Tools you can make for scratching mouldings

Fig 2:3 Cramping equipment that can be built in the workshop

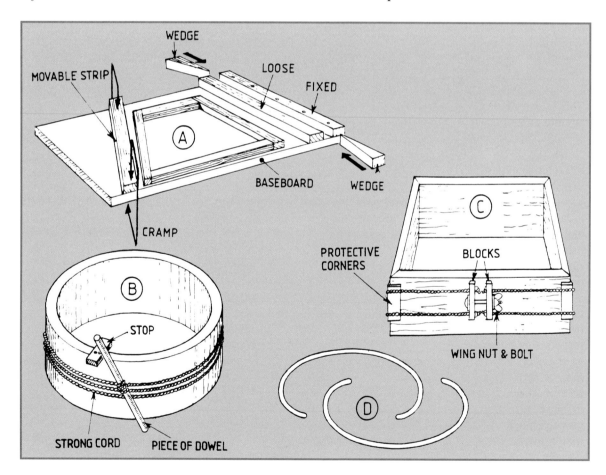

SCRATCH STOCK (Fig 2:2)

One of the chief differences between a cabinet-maker and a restorer is that the latter often has to make up parts to match or replace those that are either damaged or missing – something a cabinet-maker never has to do. This is particularly true of mouldings, and frequently the only way to work the replacement pieces is by means of a scratch stock (A). This consists of a piece of steel mounted in a conveniently shaped handle called the 'stock', with one edge ground or filed to a reverse profile of the required moulding.

The steel can be a piece of bought-in scraper steel, or a broken section of a bandsaw blade. As you can see, the stock is a block of wood with a notch cut out of it, the whole thing then being cut in half lengthwise. A handy size is 8in (203mm) long by 2½in (64mm) deep by 1¼in (32mm) thick.

Round off the edges of the notch slightly so that it runs freely along the workpiece. The screws simply hold the two halves together with the steel cutter between them. By using a cutter of the appropriate size you can use the tool to cut grooves for inlays as well.

SCRATCH (B)

This is simplicity itself to make. It consists of a countersunk-head wood screw driven partway into a piece of hardwood shaped to fit your hand comfortably. Use it to form edge beadings or scratch decoration, as shown.

ROUTER TABLE

As already mentioned, a powered plunge router is just about the most versatile woodworking tool you can have, and its scope is vastly increased if you can arrange for it to be inverted and used upside down in a specially designed table.

There are several proprietary patterns of these tables, but it's quite straightforward to make your own. Regrettably, there is insufficient space to reproduce it here, but a design which can be made in the workshop is contained in a book called *Router Projects for the Woodworker,* published by Stobart & Son Ltd, Hertford. As well as projects to make, it contains much useful information on how to operate the router, the various accessories that are available, and several proprietary table designs.

CRAMPING EQUIPMENT (Fig 2:3)

The cramping board (A) is used for the same purposes as sash cramps. Its main advantage is that the cramping action is spread over its entire length instead of being confined to one area, as is the case with sash cramps.

Make it as large as you can, bearing in mind that you may need to cramp up such large pieces as chairs, table tops, etc. You will find that ¾in (19mm) thick MDF board is an ideal material to use. The movable block can be held in whatever position you want by G-cramps, even to accommodating a slanting workpiece, which is sometimes necessary. The wedges should be tapered at a slope of about 1 in 8.

'SPANISH WINDLASS' OR 'TOURNIQUET' (B)

This device is as old as the hills but is nonetheless very effective for shaped work. The illustration should be self-explanatory.

BAND CRAMP (C)

This is a more sophisticated version of the Spanish Windlass, but you can nevertheless make one up quite easily in the workshop. If you are going to use it to cramp up a square or rectangular frame you will need some small corner pieces to protect the corners. Many DIY stores stock an L-shaped right-angled moulding, and pieces cut from it do the job perfectly.

SMALL CRAMPS

You can use C-shaped pieces (D) cut from worn-out upholstery springs to hold small parts in place while the glue sets. These are also useful for holding the corners of picture or mirror frames – their holding power is increased if you file the ends to sharp points.

Ordinary spring clothes pegs, stout rubber bands, and even inner tubes from bicycle tyres will all come in handy sooner or later as unconventional but effective cramps. Obviously, restorers never throw anything away if it has the slightest potential as a workshop aid.

TRESTLES

As these are so well known, I have not illustrated them. They are invaluable for supporting work-pieces, particularly if your bench is not large.

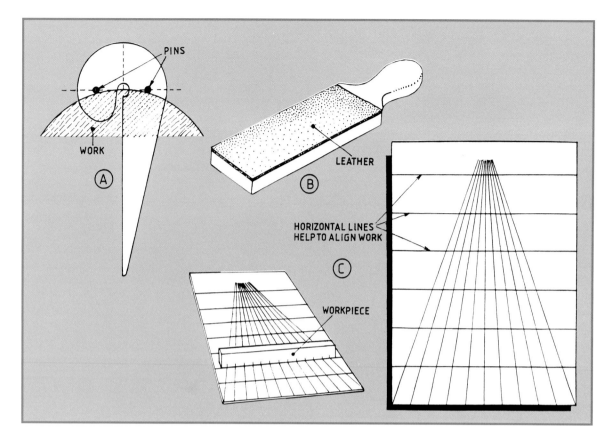

Fig 2:4 Miscellaneous home-made devices for the workshop

SUNDRY EQUIPMENT (Fig 2:4)

You can make the Centre Finder (A) out of hardboard, thin plywood, or acrylic sheet, and the drawing should be self-explanatory. A diameter of about 2½in (65mm) for the basic circle will give a handy size for most jobs, although smaller or larger ones may be needed to suit your purposes.

To use it, push both dowel pins against the workpiece and draw a line along the straightedge. Then move the dowels round to another position and draw another line. Repeat the process until you have three lines. Where they intersect is the central point.

SHARPENING STROP (B)

This is a flat piece of wood about 10in (250mm) long by 3in (75mm) wide by ¾in (19mm) thick, with a handle fashioned on one end and a piece of leather glued to one side. Use 1 part water to 5 parts PVA adhesive, or a stiff mixture of cold water wallpaper-hanging paste for the glue. Dress it with a paste of fine emery powder mixed with oil (see below) and strop your chisel on it, keeping the same angle on the bevelled edge as when it was being sharpened. This will remove the wire edge without having to resort to the oilstone.

There are three types of oil which are suitable for oilstones. You can use one of the several proprietary brands; or neat's-foot oil (neat is the old-fashioned name for cattle); or a half-and-half mixture of paraffin and light machine oil of the kind used for bicycles and sewing machines. Never use linseed oil because it is much too thick and will clog the pores of the stone.

Their usefulness is enhanced if you make up a few wooden bearers, say 24in (610mm) long by 4in (100mm) wide by 1in (25mm) thick, and fix strips of old carpet to one side of each of them. They can then be used in conjunction with the trestles to prevent the work from being marked and also stop it sliding around.

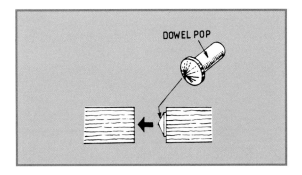

Fig 2:5 Dowel 'pops'

EQUAL SPACE CALCULATOR (C)

This is a simple aid that will soon become invaluable. It consists of a piece of white plastic-faced hardboard (although you could use painted hardboard, plywood, or acrylic sheet instead) on which you draw accurately as large a rectangle as possible. From the exact centre point of the top, draw diverging lines to equally spaced points along the bottom, so that wherever you position a piece of wood at right angles across the board, the lines will indicate points that are equally spaced along it.

Use it to work out the centres for dovetails or the fingers of finger joints, for repeat patterns of woodcarving, and for many other similar jobs.

DOUBLE-SIDED ADHESIVE TAPE

When I read in a book on routing that this kind of tape could be used to hold wooden parts in place while being routed I found it hard to believe. I have used it in this way many times since, however, and it does work. Similarly, it can be used to join any parts that have to be held together temporarily.

There is one small disadvantage – the tape is so sticky that if you remove it quickly it is liable to pull tiny splinters of wood with it. As a result it usually is advisable not to use it on any polished or finished surfaces.

DOWEL-LOCATING DEVICES

There will be many occasions when making dowelled joints on which you will need some means of transferring the centres for the dowels from one part to another, bearing in mind that it must be done with precision to avoid a badly fitting joint.

There are several proprietary devices that will do the job, but they tend to be awkward to use on furniture which is partly framed up because things get in the way of each other. You can also buy sets of dowel centres – 'dowel pops' or 'pips' as they are sometimes called. Each set contains centres of different diameters that match those of the most commonly used dowels. Fig 2:5 shows a typical dowel centre. The cylindrical end is inserted in a pre-bored hole in the rail and the part to be joined is held firmly in position against it. A light tap with a hammer on the end of the rail will cause the pointed end to make a tiny dimple that can be used as a centre for drilling the matching hole.

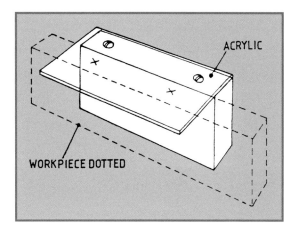

Fig 2:6 A simple dowelling jig that can be made in the workshop

A home-made marker is shown in Fig 2:6. It simply consists of a small rectangle of transparent plastic sheet, say 4in (102mm) by 2in (51mm) screwed to a handy-sized block. Acrylic sheet is ideal. Failing this, any suitable transparent stiff piece cut, for example, from a used plastic bottle will do. Hold it against the piece to be marked with the plastic lapping over the end of it (or the side, as the case may be), and the dowel-hole centres marked on it with crosses. You then drill tiny holes at each cross, transfer the whole marker to the other piece to be dowelled, and then pencil through the holes to locate the centres for the matching dowels.

In conclusion, most of this equipment is for general work and you will be using it all the time. More specialised devices and gadgets are described in the relevant chapters or sections.

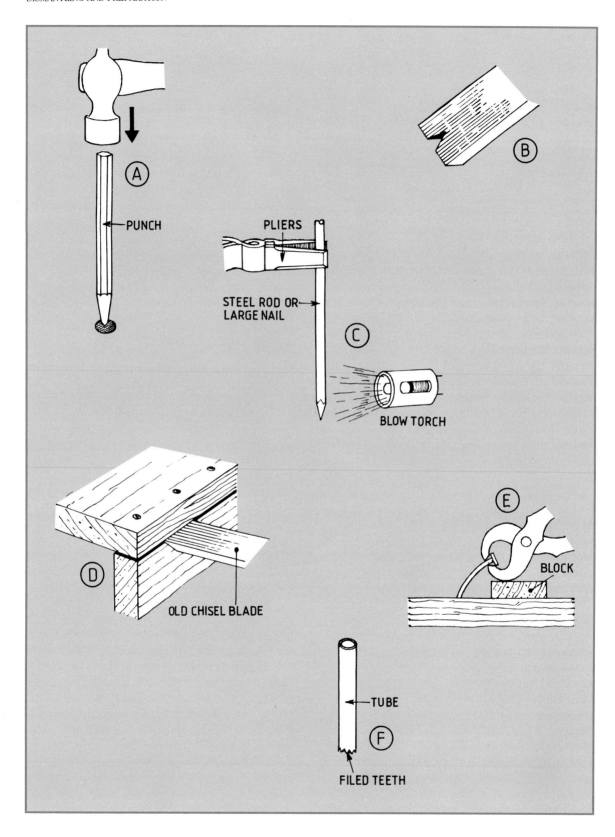

A PUNCH

B

PLIERS

STEEL ROD OR
LARGE NAIL

C

BLOW TORCH

D

OLD CHISEL BLADE

E

BLOCK

TUBE

F

FILED TEETH

3 Dismantling and preparation

Dismantling furniture for repair is like going to law; if you can possibly avoid it, do so. There is a further similarity, which is that if you have to do either, be sure that you have a plan of action firmly in mind so that you don't bite off more than you can chew. When applied to dismantling furniture, this means spending time studying the construction of the piece and working out how best to take it apart without damaging it more than is necessary. Be prepared to be either exasperated or fascinated; exasperated because removing one awkward nail can sometimes take hours; and fascinated because you will often have to devise some bizarre methods of your own to solve a particular problem. As an example of the latter, it has been known for a scissors-type car jack to be used to force joints apart!

The ageing process of many an antique piece will have done much of the work for you because old glue perishes and allows a joint to loosen. This leads to other joints becoming loose. Often someone has tried to remedy this state of affairs by hammering in nails indiscriminately, and removing them can be annoying and time-consuming.

REMOVING NAILS AND SCREWS
Fig 3:1 shows some ways to extract them. Whichever subsequent method you intend to employ, as a preliminary step it's worth using a nail punch and hammer (A) to give the head of the nail a smart blow. This can often loosen its grip in the wood and you can then try prising the head out of the wood. You can buy proprietary nail extractors to do the job but often they only work if the head is already proud of the wood.

Fig 3:1 Methods for extracting difficult nails

A good tool for the job is an old ¾in (19mm) or 1in (25mm) wide chisel with a vee-shaped nick ground into its end (B); note that the chisel should be used upside down with the bevel underneath. Because the edge is sharp, you will be able to dig it into the wood on either side of the nail head until you can get the nick under it. Then by levering the chisel upwards on its bevel you should be able to withdraw the nail quite easily. It also makes a handy tack-lifter when you are dealing with upholstered furniture.

The next method (C) can be used for stubborn steel screws as well as nails, and relies on the well known fact that iron and steel expand when heated. It involves applying heat to the nail or screw head so that when hot it will expand right down its length, forcing the fibres of the timber apart. When it cools, it will contract to its original size and thus become loose. You can apply heat with the tip of a soldering iron (although it's a slow job), or by heating a piece of steel rod with a blowlamp and touching the nail head with it.

Where you can get at the joint, as in (D), try forcing the two pieces apart by inserting and hammering an old chisel, an old plane iron, or a wide-bladed screwdriver into the joint and levering it apart. You should then be able to use a hacksaw blade to saw through the shank of the nail so that the joint will come apart completely allowing you to use pincers to pull the shank out. Remember to use a block under the pincers as shown at (E), because this not only protects the wood but also affords greater leverage. The nail head can be punched through from the underside.

The tool shown at (F) can, again, be used for both nails and screws. It consists of a short length of iron or steel tubing, say about 3in (75mm) long and ⅜in (10mm) to ½in (12mm) diameter. You'll need to file small teeth round the bottom edge. Try to get a piece which will fit into the chuck of your brace or hand drill, but if you can only find one that is too big, don't despair. To get over the problem, whittle or rasp a piece of dowel to fit firmly into the end of the tube. Then drill a small hole for a nail to penetrate both the tube and the dowel, ensuring that they rotate together. Finally, reduce the end of the dowel so that it fits the chuck. You will probably find that it will only last for two or three jobs before you have to remake it; even so, it is well worth the trouble.

It usually happens that by the time you have drilled part way, the nail is loose enough to be pulled out with a pair of long-nosed pliers. The process will obviously leave a hole to be filled by either plugging or pelleting, both of which are easier and neater than trying to restore bruised and gashed wood with a filler of some kind.

There are three more ways to deal with obstinate woodscrews as well as those already mentioned, and they are illustrated in Fig 3:2. The first (A) shows how a smallish screwdriver blade can be located at one corner of the slot in the screw head so that, by tapping the end of the screwdriver, you can try to force the screw to begin unwinding. The disadvantage is that it does not take long for the slot to become so mangled that it is useless, and you should stop if this begins to happen.

You can apply extra torsion to the screwdriver blade if you cramp a small thumbcramp to the flat part of the shank as at (B) and push on it for greater leverage. The same effect can be achieved if you use a screwdriver (turnscrew) bit in a brace.

The proprietary screw extractor (C) often gives good results. Use a centre punch to make a starting dimple in the exact centre of the screw head, then drill a pilot hole – usually about $\frac{1}{8}$in (3mm) diameter – down into the screwshank. Insert the extractor, which has a self-tapping thread, and screw it down into the hole until it is wedged tightly; then unscrew the extractor and screw together. It's all rather like using a corkscrew.

You will find the extractor is often the only way to remove solid brass screws because after some years they crystallise and shatter easily, or the

Fig 3:2 Dealing with difficult woodscrews

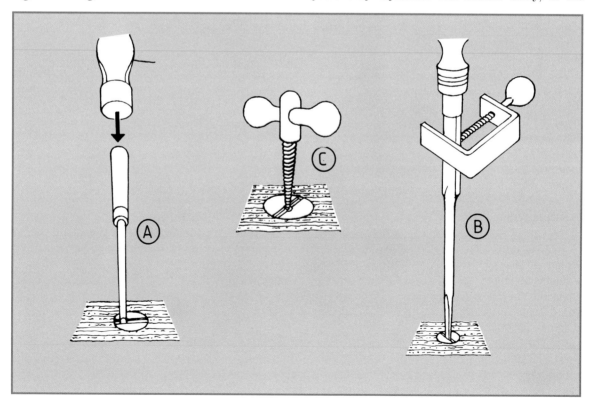

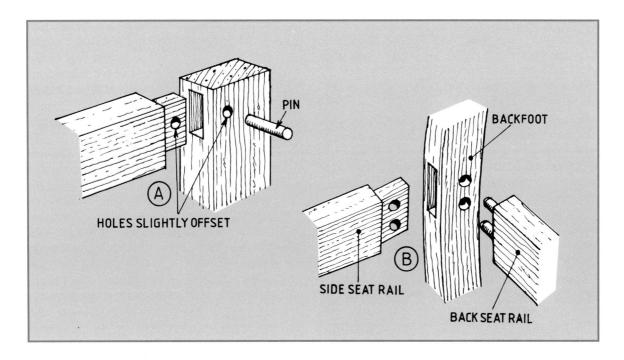

PIN

HOLES SLIGHTLY OFFSET

A

BACKFOOT

SIDE SEAT RAIL

B

BACK SEAT RAIL

Fig 3:3 How to tackle pegged or pinned mortised and tenoned joints

head twists off completely when you try to unscrew it. When you have dealt with a few problems such as these you will remember in future never to drive in a screw without first rubbing its thread with wax or candle grease. Not only does this make your job easier as you drive the screw in, but it may also cause someone in the years to come to bless you when he has the job of unscrewing it. When using solid brass screws it's good practice to insert a steel screw first to act as a 'pilot'. When it has been removed, a brass screw can be driven in the same hole without any risk of its snapping off.

DEALING WITH TENONS

Sooner or later, you will be confronted with the problems of pinned tenons, as illustrated in Fig 3:3. The kind shown at (A) is a 'draw-bored' tenon as used on sixteenth- and seventeenth-century furniture, or on reproductions of it. The procedure was to bore holes in the tenon and through the leg or rail into which it went.

These holes were not bored to coincide because the one on the tenon was offset very slightly by

about ¹⁄₁₆in (2mm) or so. As a result, when the pin was driven in it pulled the tenon tightly against the leg or rail, creating a strong joint without using glue.

You can often see the heads of the pins protruding on genuinely old pieces, and it's a period feature gratefully copied by reproduction furniture makers. Removing the pins should be easy because they normally penetrate the whole thickness and emerge on the other side, making it easy to tap them back through. The important point is that you should mark each pin and joint so that you can reassemble them in their proper order and original positions. If you do have to replace any, bear in mind that they were whittled and therefore are not, like dowels, perfectly cylindrical.

Illustration (B) shows another kind of pinned joint, sometimes called a 'locked' joint, which is frequently found on modern chairs where the seat rails are joined to the back legs ('backfeet' in the chair trade). This joint is the one most likely to break because some people tilt the chair backwards while sitting, imposing an enormous strain on it. In particular, you will often find such joints used on the frames of upholstered armchairs and settees.

It is usually the back seat rail that is fitted with

dowels, and they are located to penetrate the tenons on the side seat rails, thus resisting the strain as far as possible. Such joints are glued together, so you must first find out what kind of glue was used. Animal or Scotch glues were employed until about thirty years ago when they were superseded by synthetic adhesives, which have now taken over completely.

Luckily, animal glues can be re-liquefied by applying heat, preferably in the form of steam, although the glue resets once it cools. As a result, you will need some way of applying steam to the joint. Probably the simplest is the arrangement shown in Fig 3:4. It consists of a tin kettle (as sold by most camping equipment shops), with a length of tubing fixed to its spout by means of a hose clip. A camping cooker boils the water, and the steam can be directed by means of the tubing. A further refinement is to wedge a metal nozzle from a cake-icing set on to the end of the tube so that the steam can be concentrated into the crevices.

Wear gloves to protect your hands, and top up

Fig 3:4 A primitive but effective way of applying steam to glued joints

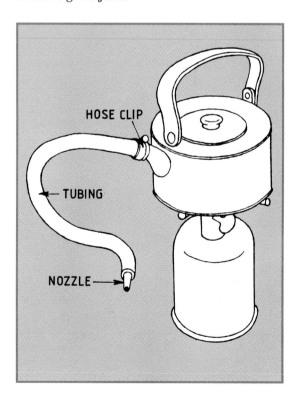

the water in the kettle from time to time. Don't expect the job to be too easy, however. You will probably have to open up the joint a little before you can get the steam into it, and even then it will probably be a matter of repeated steaming and levering until the joint is really loosened. If, for one reason or another, you cannot adopt the kettle-steaming method, you can try wrapping the joint with cloths wrung out in boiling water, renewing them frequently as they cool, but this is a heartbreakingly slow process.

Recently an apparatus for steam-shampooing carpets at home has appeared on the DIY market. It has an accessory consisting of a flexible tube fitted with a nozzle that can direct steam on to small areas and, although I have not tried it yet, it would seem ideal for steaming joints.

Neither method does any good at all to polish, finish, or veneer on the wood, and you will have to decide before you start whether you can accept having to make good the surface. Also, because the steam or hot water liquefies the glue in the joint, it will do the same to the glue holding down any veneer, but this need not be detrimental. The glue resets as it cools and will re-establish the bond between the veneer and its groundwork. But you may have to put weights on the veneer to hold it down until this happens.

If you wish to preserve the original finish you must use a completely different method. You can also use this for joints that have been bonded with synthetic adhesives.

From Fig 3:5 you will see that you have a choice of two tools to carry out the process: a coping saw, or alternatively, a hacksaw blade mounted in a handle (which can be workshop-made). As the coping saw frame can be adjusted to any convenient angle to the saw blade, it need not get in the way, but sawing through a rail that may be about 2in (50mm) deep by ¾in (19mm) thick is likely to snap the blade unless you are very careful. For this reason, you may find it more practical to use the more robust hacksaw blade. You can wrap adhesive plastic tape round the parts close to the work to keep scratches to a minimum.

Once the parts are separated, you still have work to do on them. First of all, the ends of the dowels have to be dealt with, and because there is no way they can be pulled or prised out you will have to drill them out before making the holes into which the new dowels can be glued. The end of the tenon in the backfoot will also need to be drilled out, and a new mortise chopped out. Once you have done this, you can reassemble the parts with new dowels and a loose tenon, the latter being illustrated in Chapter 4, Fig 4:7.

There are two kinds of tenons that are specially designed to withstand great strain. Although it is unlikely that the joints themselves will break, you may have to separate them in the course of dealing with some other damage. They are the wedged-through tenon, and the fox-wedged tenon, shown at (A) and (B) respectively in Fig 3:6. Generally, the wedged-through tenon is used where it is unlikely to be seen, while the tenon of the fox-wedged pattern is completely hidden – a fact which makes it impossible to identify.

Hopefully, dismantling the wedged-through tenon will be straightforward. Start by drilling a series of pin holes into each wedge, using an Archimedean drill for preference, although the finest drills that fit in the chuck of a hand drill will also do the job. Then use the steaming device already described to get steam into the joint and liquefy the glue. It will help if you can arrange for

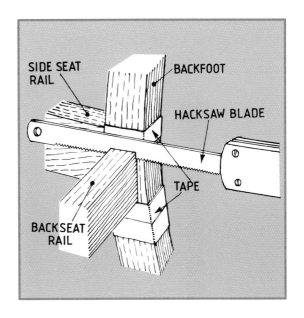

Fig 3:5 Using a hacksaw blade to saw through a tenon

Fig 3:6 Wedged through-tenon (A); and the fox-wedged tenon (B)

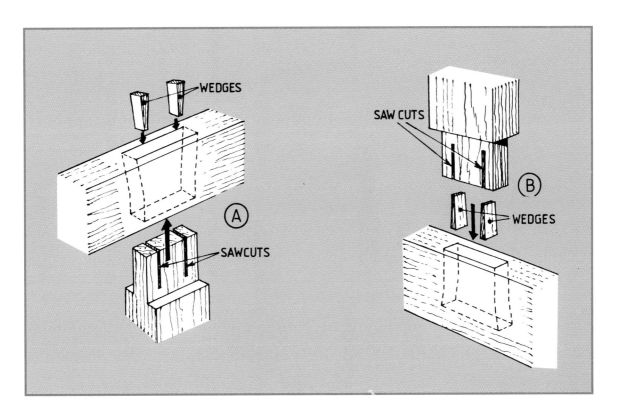

the joint to be positioned so that the steam rises into it. Eventually you should be able to prise out the wedges and tap the joint apart.

As already mentioned, the fox-wedged tenon cannot easily be recognised as such and, frankly, the only way is to saw through it. Fortunately, you are unlikely to meet either joint very often unless you are a professional restorer, because both were used only in the best class of furniture, usually Victorian or Edwardian.

DISMANTLING DOVETAILS

We come now to the joint that is just as popular today as it was three hundred years ago – the dovetail. Although it is, in modern furniture, usually restricted to the joints on drawer fronts, it

Fig 3:7 The through dovetailed joint and its variations

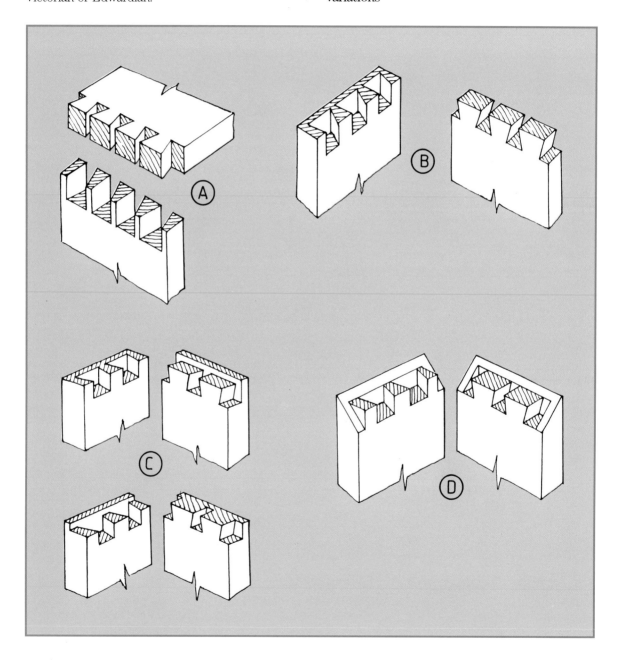

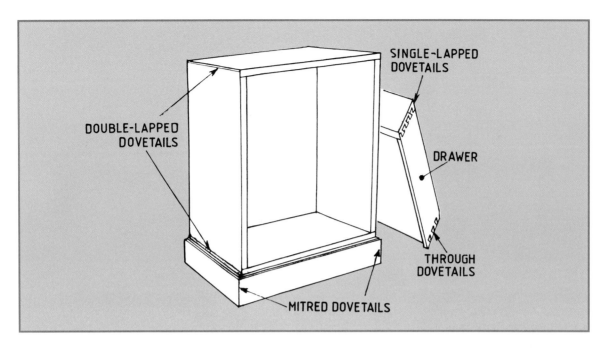

SINGLE-LAPPED
DOVETAILS

DRAWER

DOUBLE-LAPPED
DOVETAILS

THROUGH
DOVETAILS

MITRED DOVETAILS

Fig 3:8 Sketch showing probable location of
dovetailed joints on a cupboard

was also used to joint up 'carcase furniture' until
the 1930s. Carcase furniture is furniture built up
from solid panels as distinct from that constructed
by means of a framework fitted with panels.

The through dovetail, (A) in Fig 3:7 is the basic
pattern from which three commonly used variations are derived: the single-lapped (B); the
double-lapped (C); and the mitred (D). Fig 3:8 is a
sketch of a cabinet with a drawer, and shows the
joints where the different kinds of dovetails would
most likely be used.

Separating through and single-lapped dovetails
is usually straightforward because you can see
what is happening while you are working. A few
blows with a mallet on a block of wood held against
the joint will start it moving. Use a block with the
mallet to ensure that you spread the force of the
blows across the width of the joint. Before using
the mallet, cut round the outlines of the dovetails
with the point of a craft knife to loosen any glue on
the surface.

The two other dovetails are more difficult to
deal with. Assuming they have been used to joint a
carcase, it is often necessary to remove its back
and any transverse rails to leave an open box with

no back or front. By gently rocking it from side to
side you should be able to open the joints enough
to introduce some steam into them, or you could
lay hot wet cloths in the angle between the two
parts to soften the glue.

Fortunately, most dovetail joints were put
together with animal glue which, as we know, can
be re-liquefied. If you are unlucky enough to have
to deal with joints that were bonded with a
synthetic adhesive (such as in the drawers of a
modern kitchen cabinet) there is little you can do
other than to saw them apart. Trying to force them
will result in certain damage, because the wood
will split before the adhesive bond can be broken.

LEGS OF TRIPOD TABLES

One of the jobs that turns up regularly in a
restorer's workshop is the repair of broken legs on
a tripod table. The trouble is usually that the joint
between the leg and the pillar has been damaged.

The conventional (and best) method of making
the original joint was by means of a tapered
dovetail on the leg which fitted into a matching
socket on the pillar; this is shown at (A), Fig 3:9. In
the same illustration, at (B), is a drawing of a
typical metal reinforcing plate. These were often
fitted when the table was made. Obviously, this
plate has to be removed, and then the glue in the
joint can be softened by steam or hot wet cloths.

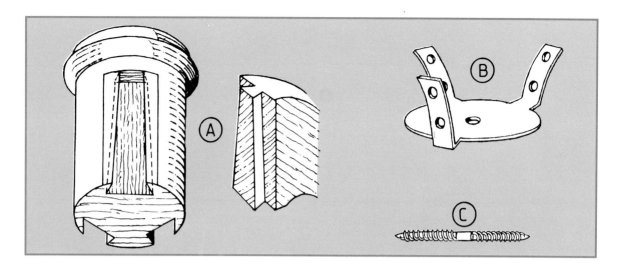

Finally, the leg can be knocked downwards to separate it. With cheaper examples, the legs have sometimes merely been dowelled on, and clearly this makes a very weak joint. Others, including many which have been repaired by well-meaning but unskilled enthusiasts, have the legs fixed on with double-ended dowel screws of the kind shown at (C), Fig 3:9. The offending leg can be unscrewed by turning it anticlockwise, but this leaves half the screw still embedded in the wood, making it extremely difficult to remove. You will have to try pliers, pincers, or Mole grips to move it. If these fail, a series of small-diameter holes drilled closely round it should loosen it enough for you to try them again.

KNOBS AND FINIALS

Many turned knobs and finials, and especially the knob handles beloved by the Victorians, were screwed on by means of threads worked on their shanks. Try gently to unscrew them before resorting to more drastic measures.

BARRED DOORS

These are tricky but interesting to dismantle. The first task is to remove the door and lay it carefully down on a perfectly flat surface. Antique doors had the glass panes puttied in, and often the putty was mixed with gold size which makes it rock hard. The safest and most effective way to remove it is by softening it with the tip of an electric soldering iron. Start at one corner and press the tip gently

Fig 3:9 Methods of repairing broken leg on a tripod table

but firmly on to the putty. As soon as it begins to sizzle and smoke, remove the tip and prise the putty away. Do not be surprised if some strips of linen appear underneath. These were stuck to the glazing bars as reinforcement and will have to be replaced.

Modern barred doors will probably have small-sectioned beadings to hold the glass in place. These are easily removable because they are only pinned on and never glued. No matter what kind of door is being repaired, always mark the various parts as you dismantle them, because even with modern factory-made doors some variations in length are bound to occur. A good idea is to make a sketch of the door before starting, and to letter each part so that matching identifying letters can be marked on the actual pieces.

SAVING THE ODDMENTS

When you dismantle any piece of furniture, keep a box handy into which you can place any chipped parts, screws, nails, and all the other oddments that are bound to accumulate. Mark them if necessary, so that you know where they came from. If you are working with an exotic or unusually coloured wood, save some of the sawdust as well; mixed with glue it can make a good matching filler.

4 Repairs to cabinets

From the previous chapter it will be clear that there are many occasions when it is necessary to fill a hole neatly before carrying on with further work. As examples, there is the hole that results from extracting a nail or screw, those that remain after you have removed an unwanted handle, or after you have drilled out unsightly knots or blemishes.

There are three ways to fill these easily and unobtrusively, and they are shown in Fig 4:1. The first and most obvious one (A) is to cut off a short length of dowel of a suitable diameter and glue it in the hole. This is an acceptable practice if out of sight, but as the end of the dowel is crossgrained, it will stick out like the proverbial sore thumb on any surface that can be seen. Furthermore, any stain or polish you may subsequently apply will sink into the crossgrain much more than on the surrounding area and it will be a real eyesore. It might be possible to sink it slightly below the surface and fill the depression with a small disc of veneer glued in, but again, the end grain may absorb glue so greedily that it could be difficult to achieve a good bond.

The second way is to use a pellet (B). These are turned up in the lathe three or four at a time, and then sawn off. You can arrange the grain on the head of the pellet to match that of the part being worked on, or you can countersink it below the surface and glue in a patch of matching veneer.

The last method is to glue in a plug that can be produced by using a special plug cutter in the chuck of a power drill, which is itself mounted in a vertical drill stand. Plug cutters are available in various diameters to match those of standard bits and drills, and the grain of a plug can be matched to the grain of the surrounding area.

FAULTS IN PANELS

These occur in furniture of the post-and-panel type and are invariably splits resulting from shrinkage of the timber which takes place across the width of the grain. Shrinkage in length is so small as to be negligible. This problem was known from the earliest times and consequently panels

Fig 4:1 Different ways to plug holes

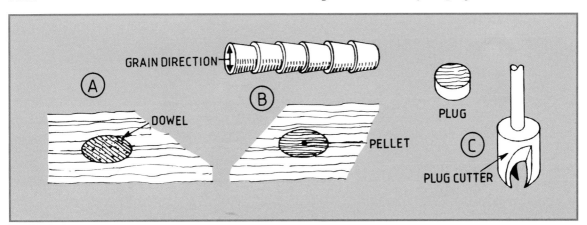

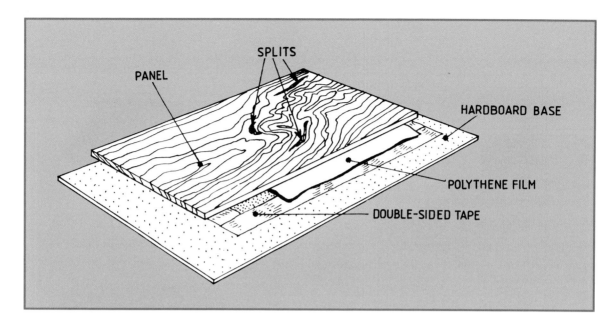

Fig 4:2 Split resulting from wild or dense grain

were (and still are) left loose and never glued into the grooves or rebates that held them.

One kind of split (Fig 4:2) is due to the use of wood of a wild grain, or figure in which the timber is denser than in the remainder. As a result, the two areas shrink at different rates and splits develop round the perimeter of the denser wood.

Dealing with this fault can be made easier and neater if before starting you lay a sheet of polythene on the back of the panel to cover the area being dealt with, and back this up with a piece of hardboard stuck down with double-sided adhesive tape. This will give you a firm foundation on which to work and any surplus glue will not stick to the polythene.

Usually the job can be done without the need to dismantle the frame and panel. The first step is to clean out any accumulated dirt and polish from the splits with a sharp pointed knife. What needs to be done next depends on the size of the splits. If they are large enough, you may be able to glue in slivers of a matching hardwood, even if it means enlarging the splits slightly to accommodate them. Also bear in mind that it may be advisable to insert them with the end grain showing if it matches the figure better. It does not matter if the filling pieces stand proud of the face of the panel because when the

glue has set you can trim them back flush. Any smaller holes and cracks can be filled with a paste composed of sawdust and glue rubbed in with the finger and glasspapered smooth.

Next, we come to the split that runs along the grain from top to bottom of the panel, dividing it in two. Again, this is caused by shrinkage, but frequently a contributory factor is that some excess glue has escaped on to the panel from the joints of the frame while they were being glued up, and this has prevented it from moving. Another possibility is that someone in the past has nailed the panel to the frame in a misguided effort to stop it shrinking, and the nails will have to be extracted. Begin by running the point of a sharp knife round the outer edges of the panel to remove any glue, and also to clean off any accumulated dust and polish. Then do the same along the edges of the split. If the parts of the panel are free, you may be able to close the split by levering them together with a sharp chisel dug into the back of the panel. The edges of the split will have to be glued before they finally meet.

If this method is unsuccessful, more drastic measures are called for and one of them is shown in Fig 4:3(A). In principle, two pairs of blocks are attached to the back of the panel, one pair near the top and the other near the bottom, and they are then cramped together to close the split. The question is how best to attach them. There are

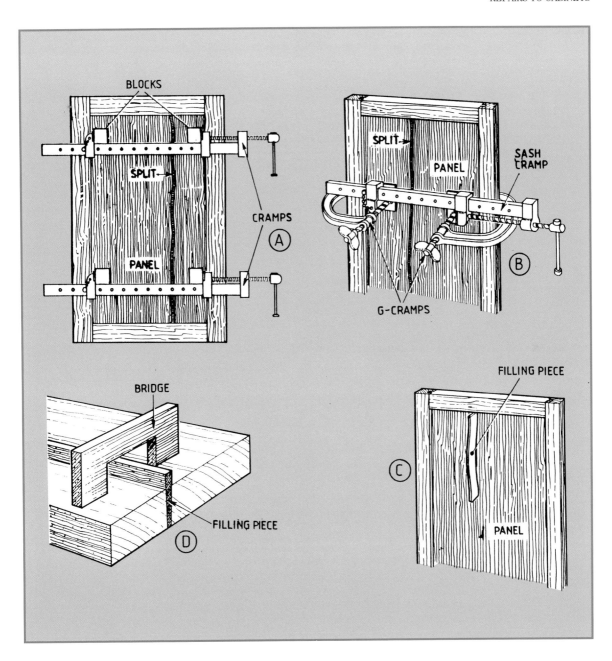

Fig 4:3 Methods of repairing split panels. (A) by means of blocks cramped together; (B) solely by means of cramps; (C) using a filling piece (an 'eke'); (D) a 'bridge' ensures that parts are flush

three ways of doing this.

One is to stick them on with double-sided adhesive tape, which has a surprisingly strong bond. Another way is to glue them on temporarily with Scotch glue, having interposed a piece of newspaper between them and the wood. The glue and paper can be swabbed off afterwards with a cloth wrung out in hot water, drying the parts immediately. Should the back of the panel be polished, however, this method cannot be used because the glue will not adhere to it.

The third way is to screw the blocks on to the

back of the panel temporarily. This is very effective if the panel is thick enough to hold the screws strongly without their points penetrating right through.

Probably the best method is shown in Fig 4:3(B), because you will need neither glue nor screws, the whole job being done with cramps. You will need two G-cramps, the throats of which must be deep enough to span the widths of the stiles, and a sash cramp. As you can see, the G-cramps have cramping blocks to avoid damaging the panel. The sash cramp is laid across so that its cramping shoes bear on the screws of the G-cramps and pull them inwards to close the split.

Fig 4:4 Dealing with a door frame which is 'in winding'

There is another kind of split as shown in Fig 4:3(C), which has developed from a natural shake in the timber. Unlike the other splits just described, its lips are not parallel, but tapered, and consequently the methods suggested above cannot be used. The remedy is to close the gap with an 'eke', which is a strip of wood let in as a filling piece. You will have to clean the gap, and there is no reason why you should not open it out a little with a fine saw so that the eke can be glued in more effectively. It will help, too, if you make it slightly tapered in section so that it tends to wedge itself in. Once the glue has set, it can be trimmed off flush.

Fig 4:3(D) shows a small device called a 'bridge' that is very useful in this kind of work, and you can make it yourself. Use it by placing one foot on each

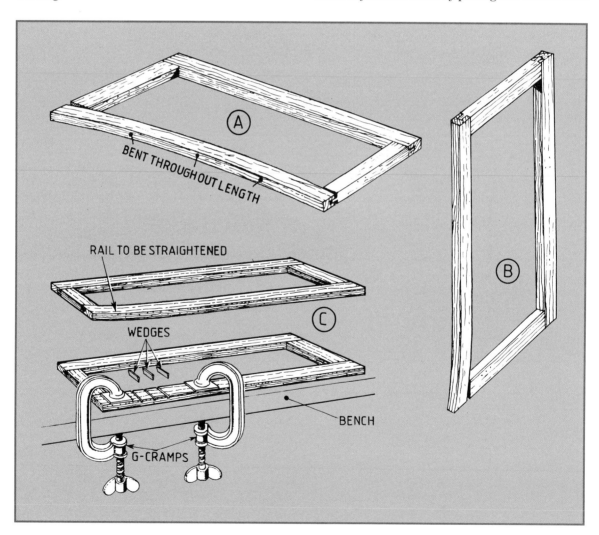

side of the split while you are gluing it up, to ensure that both pieces are in the same plane.

PANELLED DOORS

These are troublesome because they tend to go into winding easily. Sometimes it affects the whole frame, or it may be confined to one small area; see Fig 4:4(A) and (B) respectively.

In the case of (A) you have to decide whether any corrective measures are worthwhile, because if the bend is really pronounced it may be better to make a new stile altogether. If the bend appears to be reasonably tractable and is on the back of the door so that it curves inwards, you can try the method shown in Fig 4:4(C).

Here, the door is cramped down firmly on to a bench or a length of stout timber so that the bent part is straightened, and you are working on the

Fig 4:5 Correcting a bend on the face side of a door

back of the door. Make a series of sawcuts across it to a depth of just under half the thickness and tap small hardwood wedges into them. It's a matter of experiment as to how many sawcuts and wedges are needed, and how far the wedges need to be driven in. Once this has been decided, the wedges can be glued in, tapped home, and trimmed off flush when the glue has set.

In the reverse case, where the bend is on the face side of the door, a different treatment is called for, and is illustrated in Fig 4:5(A) and (B). The main thing here is to reduce the signs of any treatment having been necessary.

The easier method is shown at (A) and success depends on your being able to sandwich the bend between two pieces of strong timber and to cramp it up so that it is held straight. You can then make two sawcuts, as shown, on a circular-saw bench. Make sure (1) that each sawcut runs alongside the mortise (or the tenon, as the case may be); (2) that each sawcut penetrates almost to the full depth of the stile or rail, leaving, say, about $\frac{5}{16}$in

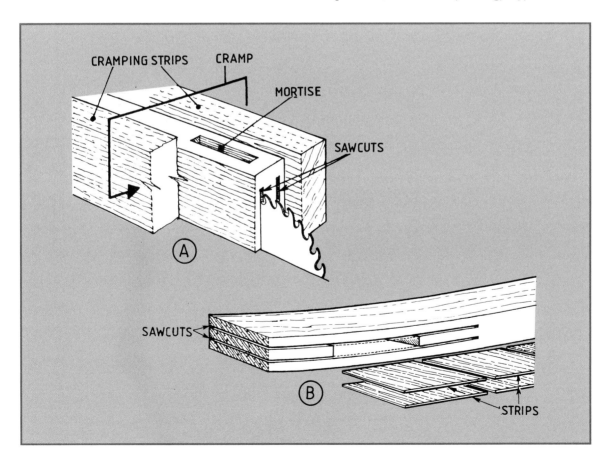

(8mm) unsawn; and (3) that the sawcuts extend an inch (25mm) or two (50mm) beyond the length of the bend.

Next, uncramp the assembly and glue thin strips of hardwood into the sawcuts. The strips should be the same thickness as the widths of the cuts – probably just over 1/16in (2mm) – depending on the set of the saw being used. After you have inserted the strips, cramp the assembly together again, and do any trimming that is necessary when the glue has set.

The procedure shown at (B) has to be adopted when the bend is too difficult to straighten out. The principle is the same as described above, namely, that strips of hardwood are glued into sawcuts. In this case the only feasible way to make the sawcuts is on a bandsaw because this will enable you to follow the bend exactly. You could possibly use a bowsaw, but it would be a tricky operation.

JOINTS OUT OF TRUE

A mortise and tenon joint out of true at one or more of the corners can also cause a door frame to twist. If this is the case, the offending joint or joints will have to be dismantled, and the tenon and the mortise examined. You should be able to see if the tenons are square to the rail or stile quite easily by

eye. You can test the mortises for truth by dropping a length of dowel down them and sighting along them as in Fig 4:6.

Correcting the faults usually involves the paring of shavings away from one side or the other of the mortise, or gluing pieces of veneer to the tenon to pack it out so that eventually the joint can be fitted and glued up square. Test for this by laying the door on a perfectly flat sheet of plywood or chipboard.

You may find, however, that the tenon has to be remade and this is where that handy device, the loose tenon, comes into its own. As you can see from Fig 4:7, the job is straightforward and consists of sawing off the old tenon, drilling and chopping out a mortise in its place, and fashioning a separate slip of wood that can be glued in as an extra-long 'loose tenon' for both mortises.

Fig 4:7 Using a loose tenon

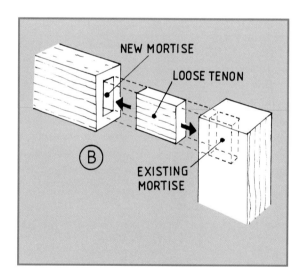

Remember that with any mortise and tenon joint an empty space of about 1/16in (2mm) or so must be left for the glue to collect at the bottom of the mortise, otherwise most of the glue will spurt out when you cramp up and the result will be a glueless joint.

FIELDED PANELS

These include several designs as shown in Fig 4:8, including one in which the fielding is worked on both the front and the back of the panel.

Fig 4:6 Testing mortises for truth using dowels or pencils – the effect has been exaggerated to make the method clearer

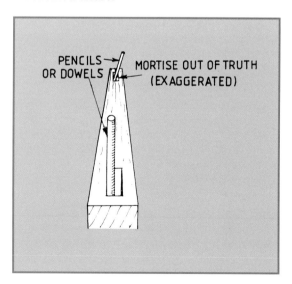

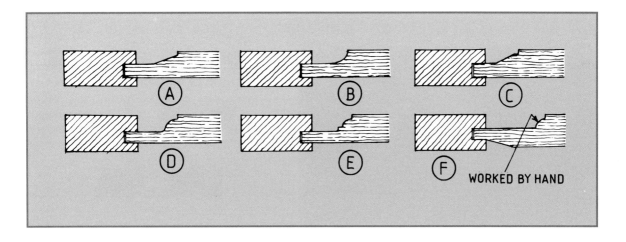

Fig 4:8 Sections of fielded panels

In the old days a special fielding plane, or a badger plane, was used for the job. A cutting gauge was run round the edges of the panel to mark the extreme width of the fielding, and then the small right-angled quirk was planed, followed by the planing of the fielding. The crossgrained areas were planed first so that, when the edges were dealt with, any splitting out was automatically removed. Today, however, the job can be done quickly and easily with a powered router fitted with a panel-raising cutter of the required size.

CARCASE DOORS: PLANK TYPE

These are the kind of doors found on old country-made furniture (often called 'vernacular') such as dressers, corner cupboards, and the like. Such doors are made up of several strips or planks arranged side by side, and usually joined together with rubbed or tongued-and-grooved joints, and strengthened by battens screwed at the back.

The most common fault is that the strips become 'cupped', as shown in Fig 4:9(A), and there is a valuable lesson to be learned from this. When

Fig 4:9 Correcting warping, etc, on planked doors

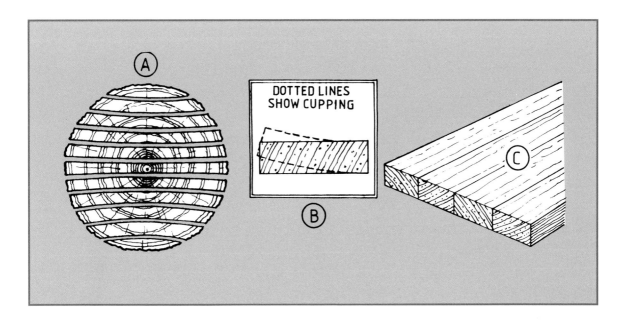

the end grain of a strip appears as shown in the inset drawing in Fig 4:9(B), it will have a tendency to shrink and curve. This effect is called 'cupping' and is very difficult to deal with. If the strips are being arranged side by side they should have the directions of their annual rings alternating as in Fig 4:9(C).

Returning to our cupped plank door, there is one treatment you could try before giving up hope and making a new door. First, remove the door and take off any battens, and then wet the hollow sides thoroughly. While they are still wet, apply heat to the other (bowed) sides with a hair drier, or place the door over a radiator to heat them. The latter method can only be used, however, if all the hollows are on one side and all the bows on the reverse. Otherwise the door will have to be dismantled and the strips dealt with separately.

Once the wetting-and-heating process has restored flatness, you can greatly reduce the tendency of the strips to cup again by cutting slots on the (formerly) bowed sides as shown in Fig 4:10. The slots should penetrate to within about ¼in (6mm) of the full thickness and should be spaced about ⅞in (22mm) apart. They should not run out at either end of the strips and for this reason it is better to use a portable powered saw rather than a circular-saw bench. Finally, the battens can be refixed.

RUBBED JOINT

If you have to make a new door you could joint the strips together with tongued-and-grooved joints, but they have the disadvantage of being visible on both the top and bottom edges.

A rubbed joint is easier, neater, and just as strong if it is made properly, and it was widely used in the old days. With the advent of modern synthetic adhesives it has fallen into disuse, which is a pity, the more so as it can be made equally well with either Scotch glue or most synthetic resin adhesives (except casein).

The first step with either kind of joint is to arrange the strips with their heart sides alternating, as already explained. For rubbed joints, the two meeting edges must be perfectly true and square to each other along their whole lengths. These used to be planed with a long plane called a 'jointer'. There is no reason why you should not do the same but if you have (like most woodworkers) a powered router, it will do the job to perfection if a little care is taken in setting up.

Fig 4:11 shows a recommended method where the two strips to be joined are held down on a baseboard, the gap between them being an inch

Fig 4:10 Slotting the strips to prevent cupping from recurring

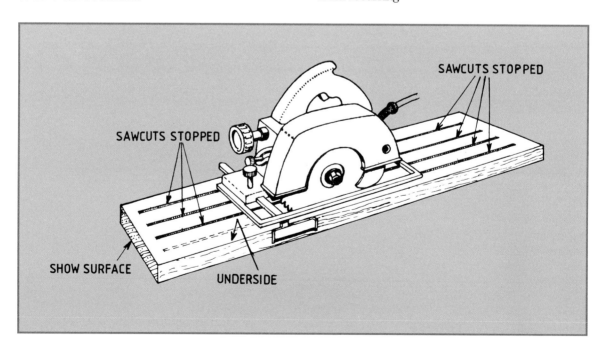

SAWCUTS STOPPED

SAWCUTS STOPPED

SHOW SURFACE

UNDERSIDE

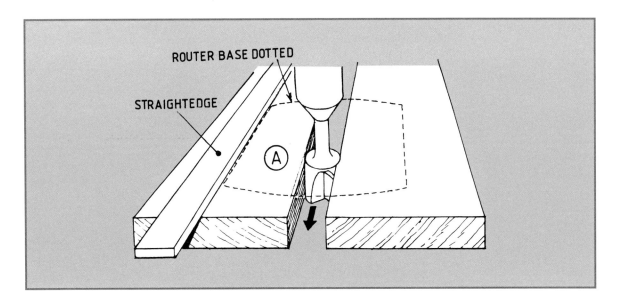

Fig 4:11 Using a power router and a straightedge to ensure exact matching before jointing

(25mm) or so wide so that it is slightly wider than the cutter itself. A straightedge can be fastened to one strip with double-sided tape; to ensure accuracy, both passes of the router must be guided by the straightedge without moving the latter. The router must pass along the work in the opposite direction to the rotation of the cutter – hence the need for two passes. The adjustable side fences on the router will need to be adjusted between passes. If you would rather cramp the straightedge to the strip instead of sticking it down, you can dispense with the side fences and run the router's sole plate along the straightedge.

Next, put one strip in a bench vice with the edge to be glued uppermost and hold the mating edge of the other strip alongside it. Apply glue to both edges simultaneously. Turn the strip you are holding upright so that the glued edges meet, and rub them along each other two or three times, pressing down at the same time and finishing the last rubbing so that the ends are flush.

Wipe off the surplus glue and lay the assembly on its side against some bearers, allowing the glue to set before attempting to joint on another strip. If you are using Scotch glue, it is a good plan to have a helper who can direct hot air from a hair drier on to the glue throughout the operation so that it does

not chill, and the strips should have been thoroughly warmed before starting.

BARRED AND GLAZED DOORS

Repairing and making these calls for delicate and painstaking work, but the end result is a door to be proud of and one that will be surprisingly strong.

Dismantling such doors was described in the preceding chapter. In almost every instance the repairs will involve making new moulded bars to supply deficiencies, or in bad cases, making up an entirely new door.

Fig 4:12(A) shows several patterns of moulded glazing bars of the kinds used on antique pieces. If matching replacements are needed, it's very unlikely that any stock design will suit, and they will have to be made by hand.

This means using a scratch stock of the kind described in Chapter 2, with a cutter ground and filed to the appropriate profile. The old-time craftsmen scratched along the edge of a piece of straightgrained timber, and when the job was finished they separated the moulding by sawing it off. The beauty of this method was that it could be adapted to scratch curved mouldings by first sawing the edge of the wood to the required curve, bearing in mind the direction of the grain, and then working the scratch stock along the edge.

If a completely new door has to be made, you can adapt the method for use with a powered router. Fig 4:12(B) shows the set-up, which

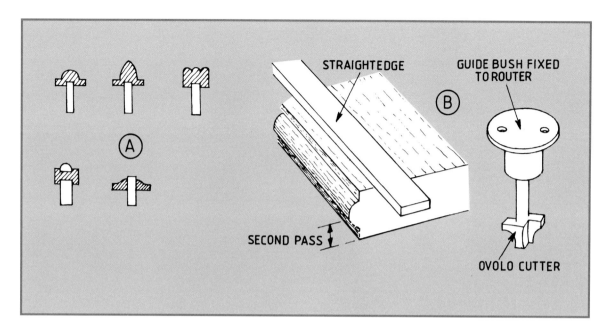

includes a shaped template that guides the router through a guide bush screwed to its sole plate. The cutter to use is an ovolo beading of the appropriate size. You will need to make two passes for each length of moulding because the router cutter can only complete half of the ovolo in each pass. Once the moulding is finished, saw it off with a powered jigsaw or a padsaw.

In the case of a new door, however, there are one or two preliminaries before you can machine the mouldings. Assuming that you have made and assembled the door frame, the first step is to cut a piece of plywood or hardboard and fit it exactly into the rebates on the door frame. Mark on it the precise points where the barred mouldings meet the frame and draw in the design, allowing for the thickness of the mouldings. Finally mark in the mitred joints, remembering that mitres always bisect the angle at which the mouldings meet. Once you have assembled the bars into the lattice pattern and checked everything, dismantle them and apply a small dab of glue to the mitred joints only and allow it to set. Then remove the board and turn the whole assembly over so that you can insert the flat stiffening bars at the back, checking them into the frame by ⅛in (3mm) or so. The last job before glazing is to glue on (with glue size) strips of thin canvas or linen into the joint intersections to strengthen them.

Modern glass is perfectly consistent in its

Fig 4:12 (A) designs of glazing bars; (B) using a powered router to create a replacement moulding

thickness, so panes can be fixed and held by small beadings that are pinned, but not glued, in place. The thickness of antique glass could and did vary, however, to the extent that the only way in which it could be held and at the same time accommodate the varying thicknesses was by bedding it in putty. No glazing sprigs, which are tiny headless spikes, were used to assist in holding the glass and, as a result, the putty had to be very strong and hard.

This was made up by using ordinary linseed oil putty of the kind employed by glaziers for wooden window frames, with an admixture of gold size. The method was to knead a handful of the putty in the usual manner and then to make a depression in it with the thumb. This was filled with gold size and the putty was re-kneaded until it was evenly distributed.

TAMBOUR DOORS

The commonest trouble with these is that the canvas backing perishes and needs to be replaced. Sometimes it also allows one or more of the strips to become slightly misaligned so that the whole door becomes jammed.

The remedy is to repair or, preferably, replace

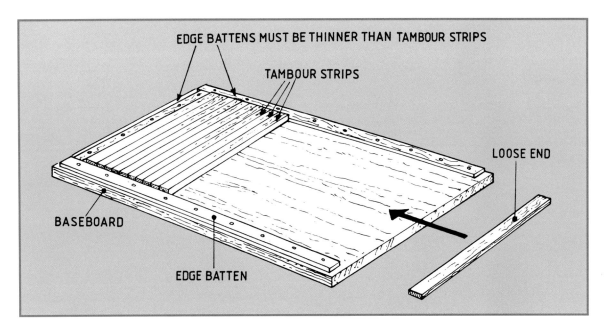

EDGE BATTENS MUST BE THINNER THAN TAMBOUR STRIPS

TAMBOUR STRIPS

LOOSE END

BASEBOARD

EDGE BATTEN

Fig 4:13 Showing the set-up for assembling tambours prior to gluing on the backing. A packing piece can be used to raise the tambours to the correct height

the canvas backing. This is glued on with Scotch glue so it can be easily removed by damping it with a rag wrung out in hot water.

Fig 4:13 shows a tray that you can make up to hold the strips in the proper manner prior to gluing on the new canvas. The edge battens must be precisely parallel, and the fixed end nailed on so that it is exactly at right angles. Note that the tambour strips must be numbered so that they are placed in the tray in their original sequence. Once they have been arranged, the loose end is pushed tightly against them (but not so tightly that any strips are forced upwards) and cramped down. You can then lay the canvas with Scotch glue if you are working on an antique piece, but if it is for your own use you can substitute any non-tensile material (cotton duck is a good one) for the canvas and stick the strips down with a modern impact adhesive. Then cover the assembly with a piece of plastic film and lay a thick board over it so that the whole thing can be cramped up while the glue sets.

PROBLEMS WITH HINGES

These occur with doors of all ages and are by no

means confined to antique furniture, because often it is the incorrect positioning of the hinge that puts it under strain and leads to eventual failure.

Fig 4:14 shows three typical examples. At (A) the heads of the screws have not been driven fully home and the fact that they protrude even slightly means that the hinge flaps cannot close fully. This state of affairs often results from someone in the past having used larger screws than the screw holes could accept in a misguided attempt to tighten a loose hinge. There are two ways to correct this. One is to remove the screws and enlarge the countersinkings on the hinge with a rose countersink bit, so that the original screws can be replaced. The other is to remove the screws and insert two or three slivers of wood moistened with PVA adhesive, then substituting smaller screws for the oversize ones.

The drawing at (B) shows how recesses that are too deep can strain a hinge until the flaps are bent. The remedy here is to use a new hinge, unless you can flatten the flaps of the old one, and pack out the recesses with strips of veneer to bring them to the right depth before screwing it on.

At (C) the hinge pin is too far in – it should stand just proud of the edge for the door to open fully. You will have to remove the hinge and reposition it, and this involves more work than appears at first sight. Old screw holes have to be plugged before you can drill new ones, and

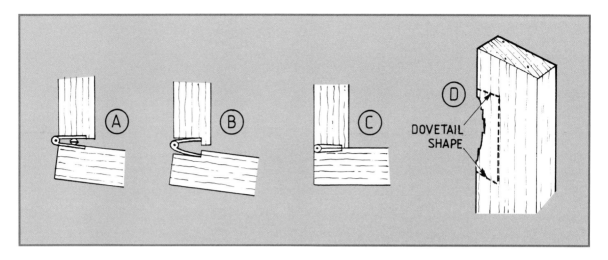

Fig 4:14 Problems with hinges

although lengths of dowel glued in would be perfectly good plugs, it is often difficult to make clean new holes which may be only ¹⁄₁₆in (2mm) away from the old ones. In these circumstances it is often quicker and more effective to cut away a portion of the edge and insert and glue in a new piece, as illustrated in Fig 4:14(D). Note that the edges are slightly undercut for added strength. You will find that this makes a much better fixing for the screws.

This leads on to the problem of hinge recesses that are split along the grain as a result of the continual swinging of the door, particularly if it is a heavy one, Fig 4:15(A). An epoxy resin adhesive can solve this problem. Once the adhesive and the hardener have been thoroughly mixed according to the manufacturer's instructions, it can be poked and pressed into the splits and the screw holes. Any excess should be wiped off immediately with a rag dipped in methylated spirit.

Next, coat the screws with wax or petroleum jelly, put them through the holes in the hinge flap, and screw them up. Follow this by cramping up as shown in Fig 4:15(B), using protective cramping

Fig 4:15 Dealing with damaged hinge recesses

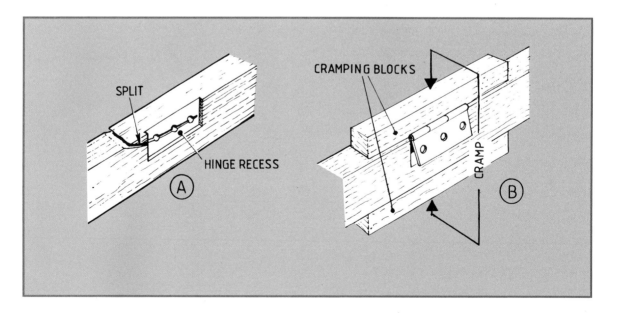

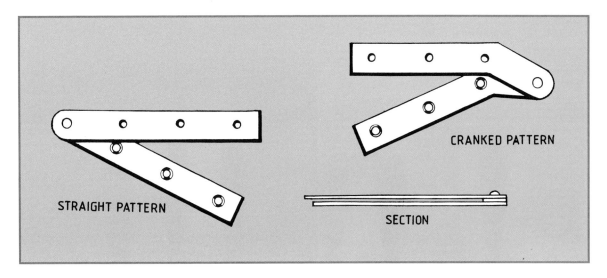

Fig 4:16 Centre hinges

blocks, and allow the epoxy resin to cure. How long this takes depends on the kind you have chosen – one type cures in five to ten minutes, which is much too fast for most of us – so the slower curing one is preferable. As the process depends to a large extent on the surrounding temperature and happens more quickly when it is 22°C (70°F) or more, you can speed things up with a hair drier or by standing the job near to a radiator.

CENTRE HINGES (Fig 4:16)
These are used to support heavy doors such as those of wardrobes, especially when the doors have large mirrors attached to them.

The commonest faults are (a) screws that have worked loose, and (b) worn pivots. In the case of (a) replacing the loose screws with longer ones should suffice, but if for some reason this cannot be done, use epoxy resin adhesive in the screw holes as described above, smear wax on the screw threads, and replace them. Worn pivots (b) can be made as new by removing the door and placing a small washer over the pivot to act as a bearing surface. This is only necessary on the bottom

Fig 4:17 Two methods of hanging doors

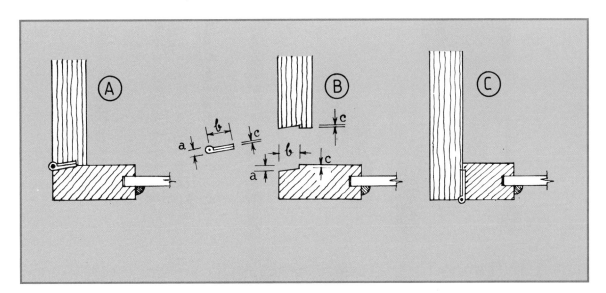

hinges because they are the ones that take the weight. Be careful when dismantling a piece of furniture fitted with centre hinges because (for instance) removing a top could allow the whole door to fall outwards with possibly dire results.

HINGEING AND HANGING A DOOR

There are two principal types of doors you may have to deal with. The first is the door that closes over the ends of the carcase, see Fig 4:17(A). The second is the one that closes between the ends, as at (C).

Taking (A) first, note that the knuckle of the hinge is completely recessed into the door and that the hinge flaps are screwed on at a slight angle. This angle is determined by taking measurements off the hinge itself as shown at (B).

The drawing (C) shows the more conventional arrangement, and here it is simply a matter of recessing in each of the hinge flaps to an equal amount on the edges of the door and the carcase.

There is no hard-and-fast rule about where the hinges should be located. As a general guide, they are usually positioned a distance equal to their own length from the top and bottom. Thus a 2in (51mm) hinge would be fixed 2in (51mm)

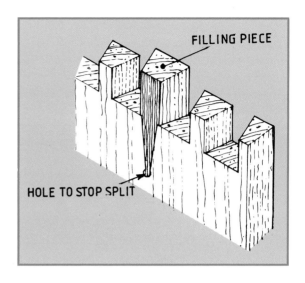

Fig 4:19 Showing how a replacement dovetail can be spliced and glued in; note the small hole to prevent further splitting.

downwards from the top and the same distance upwards from the bottom.

When hanging a door, you will normally find it best to screw the hinge to the door first, using the loose flap as a template for the recess on the carcase. To make sure of correct clearance, paste or temporarily fix a strip of thin card with adhesive tape to the bottom edge of the door, removing it when the door has finally been hung.

DOVETAILED JOINTS

These can work loose if the glue has perished and, if they do, the first and obvious remedy is to re-glue them, which will involve removing any old loose glue and replacing it.

If there is very little glue left and there are gaps in the joint, you could try making sawcuts with a gent's or a dovetail saw at 45° angles and gluing small wafers of matching veneer into them as illustrated in Fig 4:18. These two types of saw are the best to use because their teeth have no set on them and, as a result, make only a narrow cut.

In the case of a dovetail that has broken off, the best plan is to cut a notch as in Fig 4:19 and glue in a filling piece; this should be slightly larger than its final shape so that you can saw and trim it to size once the glue has set.

Fig 4:18 How wafers of veneer can be used to pack out a loose joint; they are eventually trimmed flush.

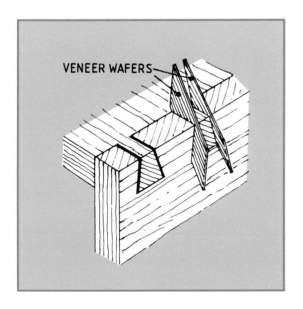

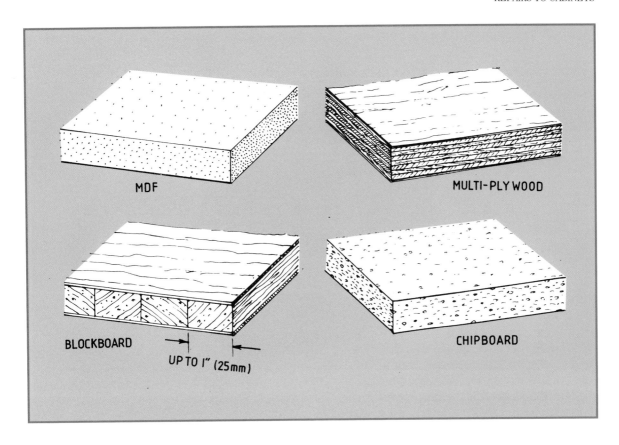

Fig 4:20 The internal composition of modern manmade boards

MODERN CABINETS

These are invariably constructed from one or other of the manmade boards such as MDF (medium density fibreboard), plywood, blockboard, or chipboard. The last-named is often faced on one or both sides with a plastic melamine laminate, and sections showing the internal composition of each are illustrated in Fig 4:20.

All four are virtually free from any tendencies to shrink or swell, and the commonest trouble is that screws do not hold well in most of them if they are positioned close to the edges of panels. Chipboard is particularly bad in this respect, and hinges and stays are likely to pull out their fixing screws under comparatively little stress. MDF is the exception because it will take and hold screws as well as, and often better than, most hardwoods.

There are several ways to get over this incapacity to hold screws, and probably the simplest is to re-fix the screws in their original holes, first filling each hole with an epoxy resin adhesive such as Araldite. Allow the adhesive to sink in for a few minutes and then top it up. Smear some petroleum jelly or rub some candle wax over the threads of the screws and insert them, driving them completely home but leaving the final tightening until the adhesive has set. How long this takes depends on the type you have used, and the recommended setting ('curing') time will be found in the manufacturer's instructions.

Another way, shown in Fig 4:21(A), is to glue in a short length of dowel or a small block of hardwood with epoxy resin adhesive, and drive the screws into this.

Finally, if you have been using ordinary wood screws, try using one of the styles of screws recommended for chipboard as shown in Fig 4:21. The one at (B) has a slotted, countersunk head and is threaded throughout its length. (C) is a 'Supajoina' screw developed for chipboard, and has a Pozidriv cruciform head and a thread specifically

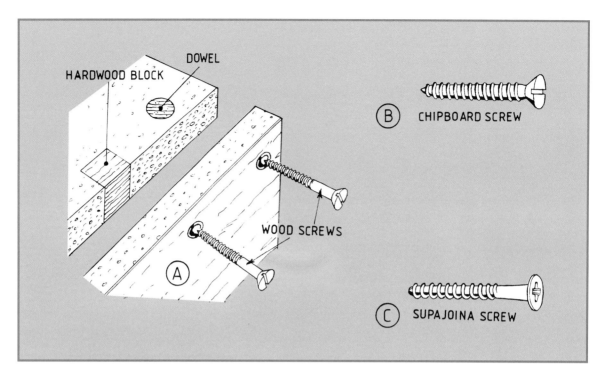

Fig 4:21 Making fastenings in manmade boards   Fig 4:22 Typical designs of lippings

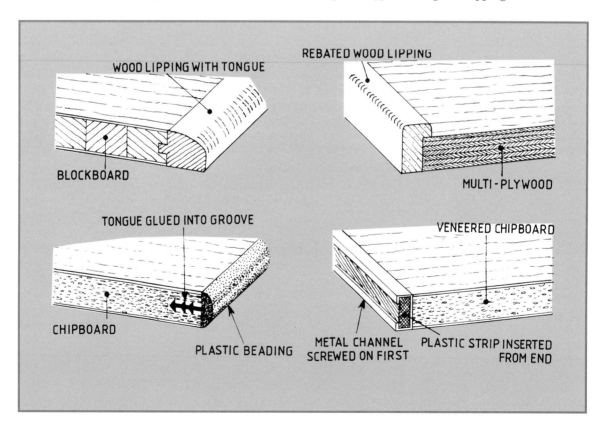

designed for the job. The same methods can be employed for plywood and blockboard.

JOINTING MANMADE BOARDS

Of the four kinds mentioned above, MDF board is the only one that can be dovetailed, tongued-and-grooved, and jointed in all other ways like solid timber. It is also possible to mould or shape its edges. In fact, it is so versatile that it has supplanted solid timber wherever large flat panels are needed.

The others – plywood, blockboard, and chipboard – can only be joined with simple butt or rebated joints, and their edges cannot be moulded. It is therefore usual to hide them under some form of lipping which can be wooden, metal, or plastic, and various designs are shown in Fig 4:22.

In order to make jointing the boards easier and to strengthen the joints, hardware manufacturers have developed a wide variety of mechanical devices that are collectively known as 'KD' (knock-down) fittings. Fig 4:23 shows three typical examples. The 'Bloc Joint' shown at (A) is used for joining panels at right angles. (B) is a screw socket, and a 10mm diameter hole is drilled to the required depth, the socket is inserted into it and driven home with a screwdriver located in its slot. A screw can then be tightened down into it. (C) is a panel-butting connector that requires the drilling of a 35mm diameter hole centred at 35mm from the edge of each panel. A 15mm wide slot is cut to join the two holes and the fitting is inserted into it and tightened up, thus pulling the panels together. These fittings have been selected from a wide range available from Woodfit Ltd (see List of Suppliers).

Fig 4:23 Range of KD fittings for jointing manmade boards

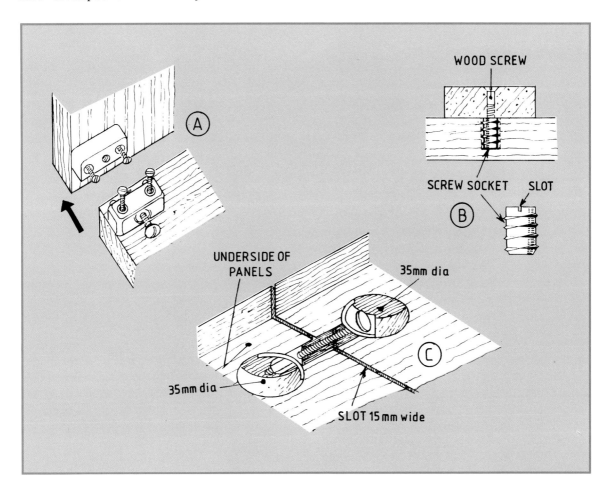

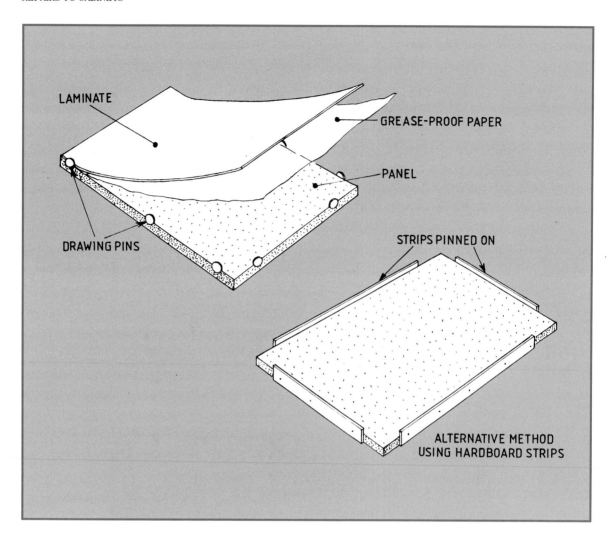

LAMINATE

GREASE-PROOF PAPER

PANEL

DRAWING PINS

STRIPS PINNED ON

ALTERNATIVE METHOD
USING HARDBOARD STRIPS

CUTTING MELAMINE-FACED BOARDS

The melamine facing on chipboard can easily splinter when you saw it unless you observe the golden rule that the direction of the saw teeth must enter the face you intend to have as the show surface. This means that if you are sawing by hand, or with a portable power saw, a circular saw, or a circular-saw table, the show surface must be uppermost. On the other hand, if you are using a jig-saw then the show surface must be downwards, because the saw blade cuts on the upward stroke. If you have to do a lot of sawing on the saw bench, it is worth investing in TCT (tungsten carbide tipped) saws because the melamine, plus the adhesive in the chipboard, play havoc with ordinary high speed steel blades. By the same token, you need TC cutters if you are routing it.

Fig 4:24 Interleaving method for laying a laminate

REPAIRING DAMAGED CHIPBOARD

As the boards are simply particles of timber glued together under compression, a piece of chipboard does not split like wood. Because it has no grain, it snaps across, usually quite cleanly.

Such a break can sometimes be repaired by butting the broken pieces together, aligning them carefully and then introducing epoxy resin adhesive into the split. Let the first application sink in, and then introduce some more, finally cramping the pieces together tightly. Any excess adhesive can be wiped away, while it is still liquid, with a piece of rag moistened with methylated spirit. Or you can wait until the adhesive assumes a cheese-like consistency and then cut it away cleanly with a sharp knife or a chisel. Don't forget that you can mix in powder pigments to colour it, and this is particularly useful if the piece you are repairing is melamine-faced and you want to match the colour so that the join shows as little as possible.

RESURFACING MELAMINE-FACED CHIPBOARD

If the existing surface is looking scuffed and tired, you can easily lay another laminate on top.

The first step is to clean the old surface, being particularly careful to get rid of all traces of grease because grease will very effectively stop the adhesive from sticking. Next, key the surface by scoring it with the teeth of an old hacksaw blade, and it will then be ready for coating with a contact adhesive such as Evostik. The new piece of laminate will need coating on the underside.

There are two problems that may arise when laying the new laminate. The first is making sure that it is lined up properly; the second, controlling the grabbing effect of the adhesive. The first can be overcome by pressing in large-headed drawing pins round the edges so that parts of the heads protrude and act as guides. For the second, use the interleaving method, where a piece of greaseproof paper placed between the coated surfaces is gradually withdrawn as the laminate is pressed down. Fig 4:24 shows both procedures.

USING HARDBOARD

This is also a man-made board, its principal use being for cabinet backs and infill panels, where little structural strength is needed. There are three grades: standard, medium, and oil-tempered (sometimes called 'super' grade). The first two are the ones you are most likely to meet because the tempered grade is for exterior use.

When cutting hardboard, use a fine-toothed saw and, as with plastic-faced boards, keep the smooth side uppermost to avoid splintering. If you are using the hardboard in a normal dry domestic situation there is no need to 'condition' it, but if it is likely to be situated in damp or moist surroundings such as a kitchen or bathroom, it would be as well to do so to prevent its buckling.

Conditioning hardboards involves lightly scrubbing the mesh (the reverse) sides with clean cold water and then stacking the boards back-to-back for 48 hours to dry out. If you are dealing with a single board, cover the wetted surface with a sheet of polythene to prevent its drying out too quickly. Fixing should be done with specially designed diamond-headed pins spaced about 6in (150mm) apart and at least 2in (50mm) in from all edges. If you use screws, choose round-headed ones and set them into screw cups, because countersunk-headed screws can soon pull through.

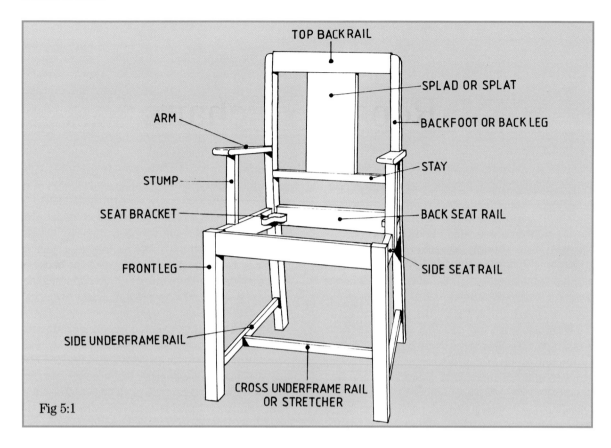

TOP BACK RAIL

SPLAD OR SPLAT

ARM

BACKFOOT OR BACK LEG

STUMP

STAY

SEAT BRACKET

BACK SEAT RAIL

FRONT LEG

SIDE SEAT RAIL

SIDE UNDERFRAME RAIL

CROSS UNDERFRAME RAIL
OR STRETCHER

Fig 5:1

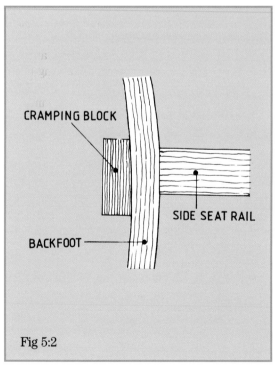

CRAMPING BLOCK

SIDE SEAT RAIL

BACKFOOT

Fig 5:2

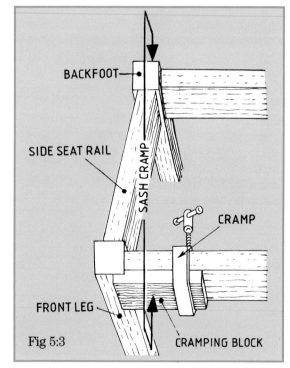

BACKFOOT

SIDE SEAT RAIL

SASH CRAMP

CRAMP

FRONT LEG

CRAMPING BLOCK

Fig 5:3

5 Repairs to chairs

Before dealing with the various repairs you are likely to encounter, it would be as well to describe the names of the different parts of a typical chair, and they are illustrated in Fig 5:1

REPAIRING BACKFOOT JOINTS

As mentioned in Chapter 3, the joints that cause most trouble are the ones where the side and back seat rails meet the backfoot. If you have been successful in separating the parts, and the tenons, dowels, and the mortises are all intact, the work involved is straightforward. Everything will need cleaning up and all old glue will have to be removed. It will then be a matter of re-gluing the joints and cramping them up.

It is this last job – cramping up – that may be difficult if the backfoot is curved just where you want to place the cramp. To get over this, you may have to make a cramping block with a slightly curved face, as in Fig 5:2

The situation may be further complicated by the side seat rails being fixed at an angle to form a seat that tapers from back to front. Unless you arrange a cramping block as shown in the view in Fig 5:3, any cramping force may distort the seat frame and weaken the joints all round. As you can see, the cramping block can be attached to the front seat rail with either a G-cramp or a thumbscrew.

Fig 5:1 Names of the component parts of a typical chair

Fig 5:2 Showing cramping block shaped to the curve of the backfoot

Fig 5:3 Arrangement for applying a sash cramp squarely across a seat frame

There is still another direction in which to cramp, namely the joint between the back seat rail and the backfoot, but as this is a square joint, a sash cramp can be positioned to span the backfeet and then tightened up. All of this presupposes that you possess at least one, or preferably two, sash cramps, otherwise you will have to use tourniquets or band cramps as shown in Chapter 2.

Staying with this joint, let us imagine that you have been presented with the worst state of affairs, which is that you have had to saw through the joint between the side seat rail and the backfoot, and the one between the back seat rail and the backfoot. This has resulted from the use of a modern synthetic adhesive that could not be dissolved or removed.

Before work can begin, you will have to ensure that the remainder of the chair frame is held firmly in place, because removing the rails and the backfoot will only lead to more weakening of the same kind at the other joints. Usually the best way to hold the frame together firmly is by pinning thin strips of wood temporarily on to the underside of the seat frame, arranging them crosswise.

Having done this, tidy up the areas which have been sawn through. You can begin re-jointing by chopping the old tenon out of the mortise on the backfoot to make a new one, and working a matching mortise on the end of the seat rail. There are a couple of points to watch for here. First, the end of the seat rail may have been cut at a slight angle to match the curve on the backfoot, and this angle must be retained. Second, before the joints are finally glued and cramped up, you may need to glue in some tiny pieces of veneer to compensate for the wood that was lost when sawing through them. The new tenon on the side seat rail needs to be a loose tenon that is equal in length to the

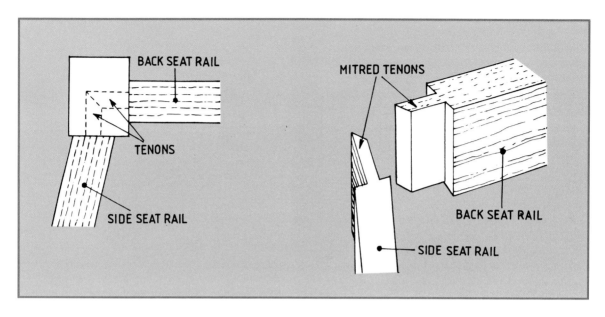

Fig 5:4 Mitred tenons inside a backfoot joint

combined depths of the two mortises, minus a total of about ³⁄₁₆in (5mm) to allow for glue spaces at each end. Remember that the part that enters the mortise on the backfoot must be long enough to allow the dowels on the back seat rail to penetrate and lock it.

Once the glue has set on this joint you can turn your attention to the one between the backfoot and the back seat rail. This is normally dowelled on modern chairs and should present no problems because you can drill out the old dowels and glue in new ones.

In the case of antique chairs, however, you may come across another variation of the joint as shown in Fig 5:4, where both the side and the back seat rails are tenoned into the backfoot; the ends of the tenons are usually mitred so that they meet inside the joint. Its main disadvantage is that a lot of wood is taken away at the very point where the backfoot is most vulnerable, and even if the joint is well re-glued with Scotch glue, it is still suspect. Modern synthetic adhesives, however, are frequently stronger than the wood they are applied to, and using one of them on this type of joint should give plenty of strength.

Fig 5:5 Repairing a balloon-back chair

REPAIRING SHAPED PARTS

Such repairs can only be dealt with generally because there are so many different shapes on so many different chairs that each one needs to be taken on its own merits. The one factor that is common to all such repairs is that cramps must be used very carefully because all too frequently they

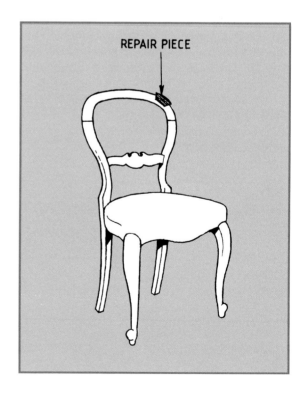

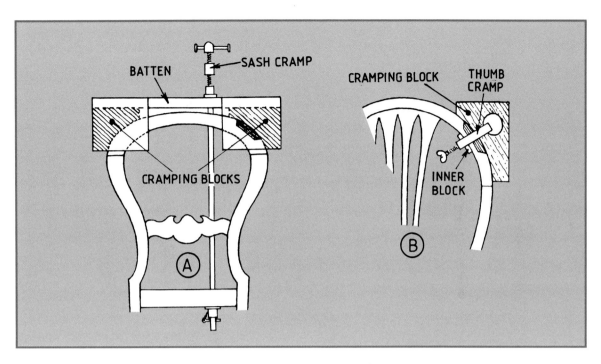

Fig 5:6 Cramping methods for the repair

have to be applied to shapes. If this is done carelessly, the whole frame may be distorted.

Balloon-back chairs like the design shown in Fig 5:5 were particular favourites with the Victorians and were made in great numbers. Let us assume that this design has been damaged at the corner of the back; that a new replacement piece has been glued and dowelled in; and that it has been roughly worked to shape. Final shaping and glasspapering will be done once the piece is glued firmly in place and the glue has set. The problem is how to apply cramping pressure to such an awkward shape.

Fig 5:6 shows two methods, (A) and (B). The bridging box at (A) is best used when the part to be cramped is shaped in two planes and when it is reasonably substantial. That at (B) is for lighter pieces – note the hole in the cramping block for the arm of the thumbscrew. This is an idea that can often get you out of trouble. All such cramping blocks need to be lined with some soft material

Fig 5:7 Cramping methods for repairs to a shield-back chair

such as a piece of felt or thin plastic foam sheet to avoid marking a polished finish.

The corner of the shield-back chair in Fig 5:7 is a more delicate proposition, and probably the best way to hold the repaired parts together while the glue sets is first to cover them with thin plastic film

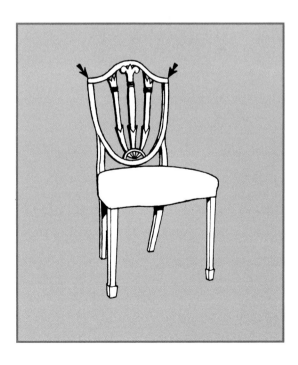

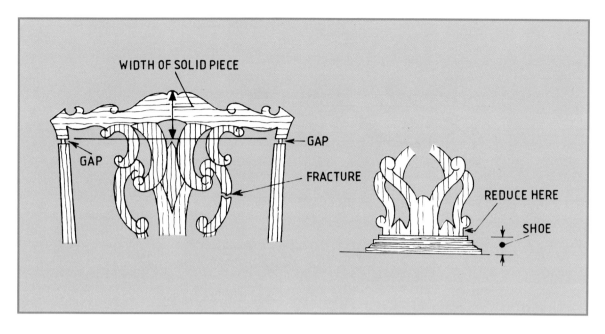

WIDTH OF SOLID PIECE

GAP

GAP

FRACTURE

REDUCE HERE

SHOE

Fig 5:8 Re-fixing a top or crest rail

and then bind them tightly with adhesive tape followed by strong twine.

Alternatively, you could adapt either of the methods suggested for the balloon-back chair, but the cramping strength of a sash cramp could easily buckle the entire back.

These chairs and others like them have their shaped top rails sawn from a single piece of wood, which can be as much as 8in (203mm) or 9in (228mm) wide, and the grain runs across horizontally. As we know only too well, timber shrinks across its width and sometimes a situation like that in Fig 5:8 is the result. Here, there are gaps at each side where the top rail has shrunk away from the backfeet and, although the gaps could be filled with pieces of veneer glued in, it would not be a good repair because sooner or later the veneer would be likely to flake or chip away.

There is a relatively straightforward solution, however, and that is to take off the top rail completely by tapping it upwards from beneath. This should enable you to take the splad out. It is good practice never to glue a splad at top or bottom so that any shrinkage across the grain can take place without splitting it. If you then carefully chisel or file away an amount of wood from the bottom of the splad so that the top rail is brought down by the width of the gaps you will have made

an almost unnoticeable repair. Go round the gaps and the bottom of the splad with a sharp pointed knife first to remove any accumulated dirt or wax which could stop the joints closing properly or prevent the glue from adhering to the wood.

REPAIRING BACK SPLADS

There are two golden rules to observe when these have to be repaired. First, make sure the splad is adequately supported all the time you are working on it; secondly, plan the shape of the repair so that the edges present as much area as possible for gluing.

To explain the latter point more fully, look at Fig 5:9 You will see that although the narrow member of the splad has broken across the face, the wood has been cut away so that the gap to be filled has slanting sides. These offer far more gluing area and consequently more strength than if the cuts had been made at right angles. Also, as the grain of the eke (or repair piece) can be arranged to run in roughly the same direction as the grain of the splad, the repair will be stronger and less noticeable.

Wherever possible it is worthwhile reinforcing the joint of the repair with some kind of dowelling. Often the wood is not thick enough for even the smallest size of proprietary dowel to be used. In this case, wooden toothpicks or even matchsticks cut off to length are better than nothing.

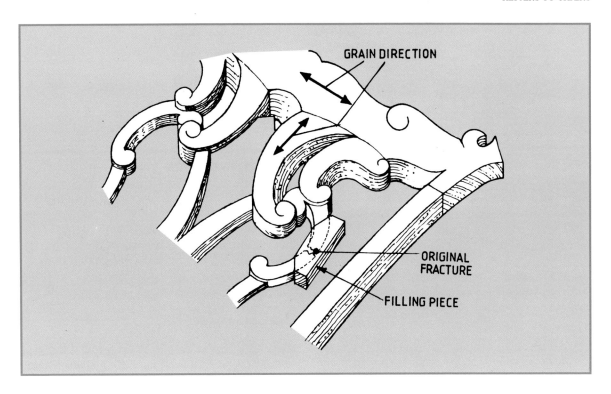

Fig 5:9 Repairing a back splad

Fig 5:10 Using a 'sprung' tenon joint

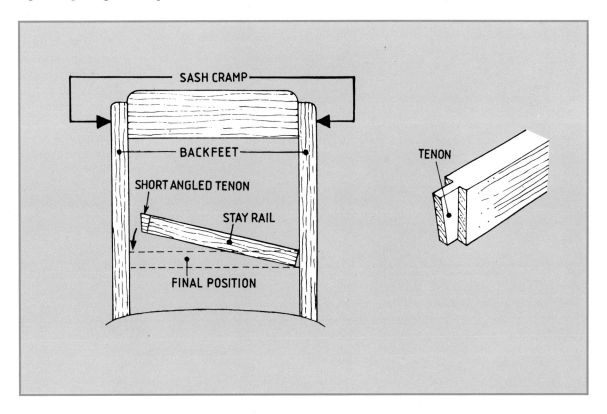

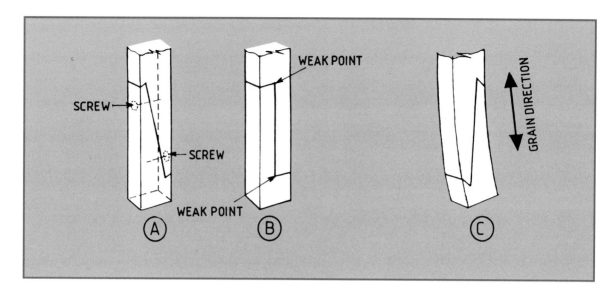

Fig 5:11 Details of the plain spliced joint   Fig 5:12 How to make a V-shaped splice

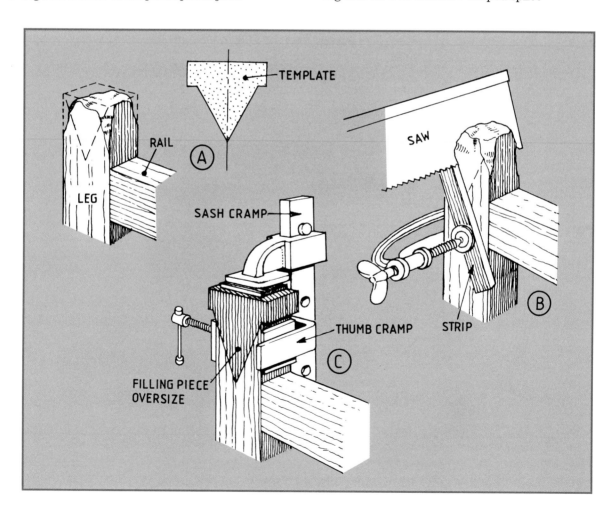

SPRUNG TENON JOINT

This is rather an unorthodox joint that can be useful where a new rail has to be inserted without dismantling the frame, but it should only be used for rails that are not subjected to undue stress. A typical example is the stay rail or slat in a chair back, as shown in Fig 5:10. As you can see, the end of the tenon is cut off at a slight angle. There has to be enough 'give' in the wood to enable you to spring the tenon into the mortise. For safety's sake, fix a sash cramp over the top of the back to avoid breaking the joints there.

SPLICING

This is the kind of repair that is often needed, either when a piece has been completely broken off, or where the end of a part (usually a leg) has been badly worn away. The methods described can be applied equally well to tables as well as chairs.

Fig 5:11 shows the recommended way to make a typical joint at (A). Here, the long face of the joint is slanting at an angle that follows the direction of the grain as much as possible (see C), and the hooked ends are kept small. This gives a large area to be glued, and reduces the likelihood of the joints breaking at the points shown in (B). The best plan is to glue and cramp on a slightly oversize repair piece. When the glue has set, it can be trimmed to fit and screws driven in as illustrated. Their heads should be well countersunk and plugged or pelleted.

On antique pieces, the toes of the legs can be badly rubbed away where they have been dragged backwards and forwards across a rough floor. In such cases, they may need tipping with new toes and, although the method just described may be appropriate, it may be better to splice them on with V-joints. Fig 5:12 illustrates a typical example. The main problem is to ensure that the two V-shapes (one on the leg, the other on the repair piece) coincide exactly. To achieve this, cut a template from a piece of hardboard or plywood. It should be slightly wider than either the leg or the repair piece. The V-shape should be marked out and cut exactly along the centre line as at (A).

Hold the template firmly against the leg and mark round it. If necessary, you can cramp a strip of scrapwood to the leg so that it lines up with one side of the notch and guides the saw (see B). The strip can then be moved to the other side and the sawcut repeated. Then use the template to mark out the repair piece, making sure the grain matches that on the leg as much as possible, and saw it out. If the two parts do not match exactly, always make any corrections to the repair piece and never to the notch on the leg. Once they do fit sweetly, fit a thumb or G-cramp temporarily to the leg, as shown in (C), to prevent any chance of its splitting when the repair piece is glued in and cramped up.

Fig 5:13 Repairing damaged toes on shaped legs

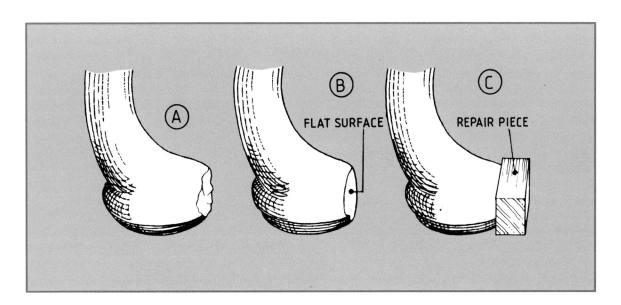

SHAPED LEGS

These comprise cabriole and Queen Anne legs, and also the claw legs of tripod tables. Making cabriole legs is described in Chapter 13.

A common repair job with both cabriole and Queen Anne legs is to make good a chipped toe as at (A), Fig 5:13. The remedy is to cut back the chipped part so that you have a flat surface in sound wood to which you can glue a block as shown at (B). The block is made deliberately oversize so that you can saw, chisel, and rasp it to the correct shape. This design is called a 'club foot' and was turned on the lathe so that rounding off the block to be circular should not present a problem.

Ear pieces are frequently loose or missing altogether on cabriole legs. Before dealing with either eventuality, check that the joint between the seat rail and the leg square is in good order. If not, scrape out the old glue and remake the joint, cramping it up until the glue has set.

Usually the easiest way to replace a missing ear piece is to glue in an oversize block and, once the glue has set, work it to the final shape with chisels and rasps. If you can insert a couple of screws with their heads well countersunk and plugged as at (A), Fig 5:14, it will be a good insurance against future trouble.

When the shaft of the leg has snapped (B), it is almost always because of some fault in the grain and, although a couple of dowels glued in may be strong enough, the result is by no means certain. There is another method you can try, as illustrated at (C). Here, an oversize strip of matching hardwood is let in at the back of the leg and rounded and shaped once the glue has set.

The tricky part is working the slot for the strip. If you have a steady hand and an iron nerve you could rout it with a powered router used freehand. Failing this, you will have to drill a series of holes that almost touch each other and make them into a slot with a mortise chisel. You can make a depth gauge for the drill with two strips of Sellotape, each

Fig 5:14 Dealing with damage to an ear piece, and the leg shaft

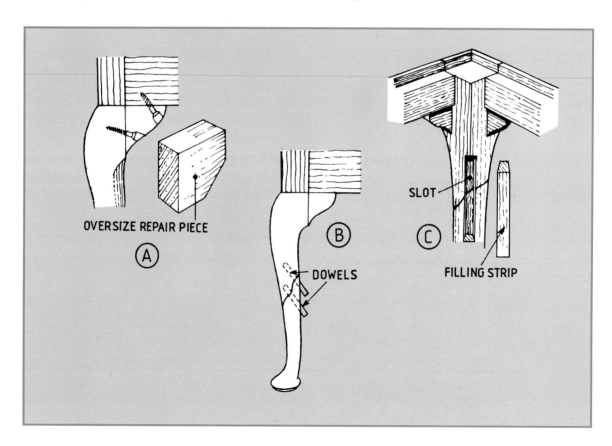

OVERSIZE REPAIR PIECE

(A)

(B)

DOWELS

(C)

SLOT

FILLING STRIP

about 1in (25mm) long and stuck either side of the drill to form 'wings' – quick to apply and easily removable!

TRIPOD TABLE CLAW LEGS

The design of these elegantly shaped legs is inherently unstable, and any damage usually occurs at one of two points – where the leg is jointed to the base of the pillar, or at the 'ankle', which is the thinnest and weakest part of the leg. Both are illustrated in Fig 5:15.

Fig 5:15 Locations of likely damage to claw legs

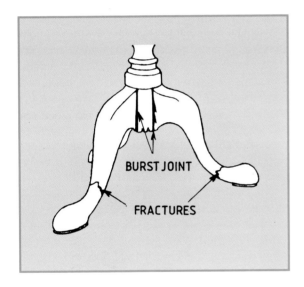

On many tables you will find that metal strengthening plates have been screwed to the lower ends of the pillars and the undersides of the legs, as shown in Chapter 3, Fig 9. The fact that a table is fitted with one does not necessarily mean that it has been repaired at some time, because the plate could well have been fitted when it was first made. In any case, if any tripod table you are working on does not have such a plate, it would be well worthwhile making one up and fitting it.

This involves making a cardboard template, bearing in mind that the arms of the plate should extend as far as possible on the undersides of the legs without looking unsightly. You can use a hacksaw, files, and a drill for the holes, to make it from 1.5mm thick mild steel plate.

The slot dovetail and its housing in the bottom of the pillar are, or should be, tapered so that each leg is introduced at the bottom of the housing and tapped upwards until it is home. This does make dismantling relatively easy because, after having been steamed, the joint should be loose enough for the leg to be knocked out downwards. Before you do this, however, make sure there are no screws that have been driven in to make a repair at some time in the past.

From Fig 5:16 you can see that mending a burst joint at the base of the pillar is a matter of introducing glue into any cracks and splits, with possibly a few dowels judiciously located to strengthen the whole thing. Unless you are repairing the table from the point of view of conservation, when you must use Scotch glue, the job is one that calls for a really strong adhesive such as epoxy resin.

Fig 5:16 Repairing a burst joint on a tripod table

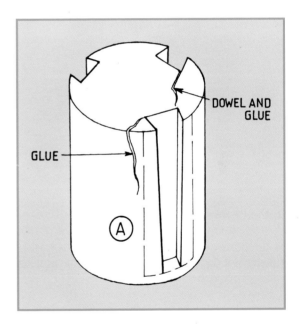

The next problem is how to apply cramps to close the splits effectively. If you have removed only one leg, the other two are bound to get in the way and prevent any kind of tourniquet being applied. In these circumstances the best plan would be to dismantle the two remaining legs. This leaves the base of the pillar around which you can apply a tourniquet type of cramp or, better still, a couple of hose clips – first protecting the polished surface with a piece of felt or something similar.

Once the glue has set, the next step is to glue the legs back in and cramp the joints up. There seems to be only one way to cramp them satisfactorily and that is to make up a 'shoe' as shown in Fig 5:17 on which you can position a couple of sash cramps. Again, line the shoe and the cramping block to avoid marking the polish.

Fig 5:17 How to apply cramps to a specially made shoe on a claw leg

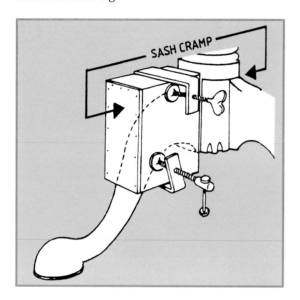

On cheaper tripod tables, the legs are sometimes dowelled on, or fixed with dowel screws. Neither method is very strong, and you will have to choose between straightforward replacement of the dowels or the dowel screws, or doing the job properly by cutting slot dovetail joints. It all depends on what value you attach to the table.

Breakages on the narrowest part of the leg can be very troublesome to repair. It may be possible to glue the broken parts together with a dowel to reinforce the joint, but it is not likely to be successful because this part of the leg is subjected to great strain. Even if the direction of the grain is chosen with the greatest care, there is bound to be one part where it is shortgrained enough for it to break comparatively easily.

One solution is to employ the same technique as was recommended in Fig 5:14 (C), namely, to glue

a strip of hardwood into a slot cut in the underside of the leg. Machining the slot with a powered router would involve using a slotting tool with a special arbor, and the whole set-up would probably be too unwieldy to use for such a delicate piece of work. In any case, it would almost certainly be quicker to drill a series of holes almost touching each other and then cut out and join them up with a mortise chisel to create the slot. Remember to use a depth gauge on the drill so that the holes are all the same depth. The hardwood strip can protrude beyond the leg surface and can be trimmed and shaped flush when the glue has set.

TURNED LEGS

Repairing a decoratively turned leg as shown in Fig 5:18 can be surprisingly easy, and the procedure is shown in three stages. At (A) the broken parts are shown re-glued together; (B) shows how a sawcut is made to separate the leg into two parts at a convenient point in the pattern of the turning; (C) shows how a dowel is glued into both pieces so that they can be re-glued together. The important requisite here is that both holes for the dowel must coincide, and the best way to ensure this is to use the centre finder described in Chapter 2.

This kind of repair can only be carried out where the two parts of the broken leg can be brought together and joined neatly. If, however, there are small chips or pieces missing, you will have to adopt a slightly different method. This is to cut out the offending part altogether between the two nearest turned members, and then to turn up a replacement piece on the lathe and glue and dowel it in position.

Fig 5:19 illustrates a turned and tapered leg that has split at an angle as shown at (A). Very often this is the result of faulty grain. At (B) you can see one possible remedy. The two parts can be glued together and held in place while the glue sets by binding the joint tightly with masking tape (to avoid marking the polish), followed by a further binding with strong twine. Once the glue has set, you can try boring a long hole (as shown by the dotted lines) and gluing in a length of dowel. Do this before removing the binding, and make sure that the hole extends a good distance into the upper portion.

Sometimes the damage is so far up the leg that you will not have a bit long enough to bore the

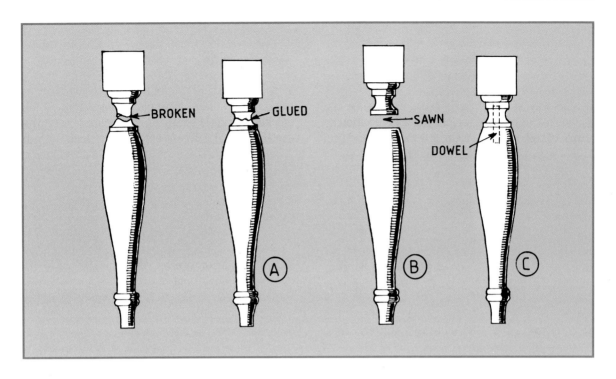

Fig 5:18 Repairing a broken turned leg

Fig 5:19 Dealing with a split turned leg

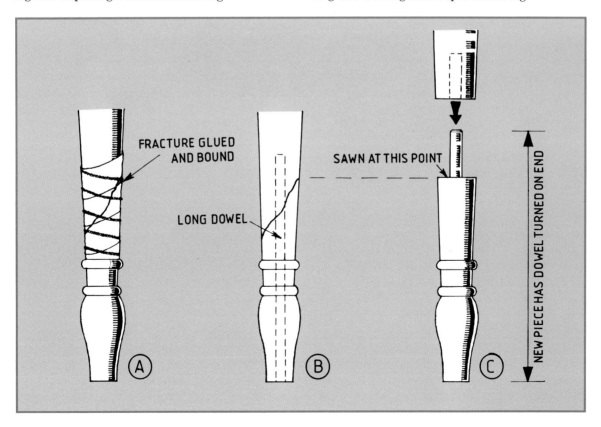

hole. If this is the case, try the method at (C), where the leg is sawn square across just above the break and a replacement piece with a pin on the end is turned up on the lathe; the parts are then glued together. Sometimes you may be lucky enough to have a decorative feature of the turning in just the right position above the break, and by cutting across the leg at that point the replacement piece will be unobtrusive if not unnoticeable.

WINDSOR CHAIRS

The seats of these chairs were, and often still are, sawn from one piece of solid elm. This wood was chosen because it is one of the few trees that consistently yields planks of the necessary width. In other respects the wood is one of the most difficult to deal with because not only do the growing trees contain huge amounts of water, which makes seasoning them a nightmare, but the grain is frequently wild and hard to work. As a result, some manufacturers have gratefully taken advantage of the improvements in modern adhesives to produce laminated seats that are usually made from beech, and these rarely give trouble.

SPLIT SEATS

A common problem with solid elm seats is the opening up of splits along the grain, and it is quite possible for these virtually to divide the seat in half. The cure is first to scrape away any accumulated dust or polish, and then cramp the parts tightly together with sash cramps but without glue at this juncture. Next, cut some dovetail keys (also known as 'butterfly' keys) shaped as shown in Fig 5:20. They are made from hardwood and are about ³⁄₁₆in (5mm) thinner than the wood into which they are to be inserted. As you will be working on the underside of the seat, they will not be seen from above. It's quite possible that two or three will be needed. Lay them in suitable positions to bridge the crack, and mark round them with a pencil. As they may not be identical, it is a good idea to number the keys to correspond with their individual positions. The bulk of the waste for the recesses can be removed by drilling, and the edges cut with a sharp mortise chisel.

Fig 5:20 Using dovetail keys on a split Windsor chair seat

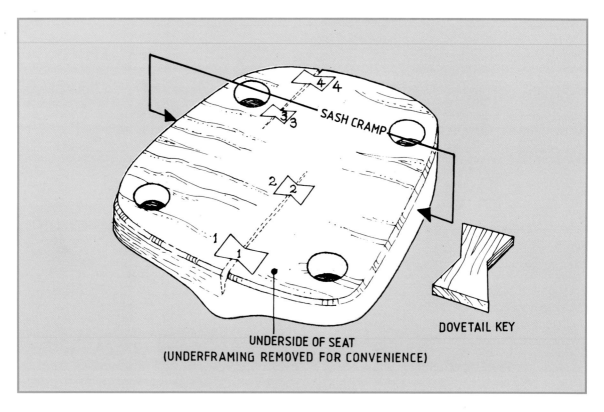

SASH CRAMP

DOVETAIL KEY

UNDERSIDE OF SEAT
(UNDERFRAMING REMOVED FOR CONVENIENCE)

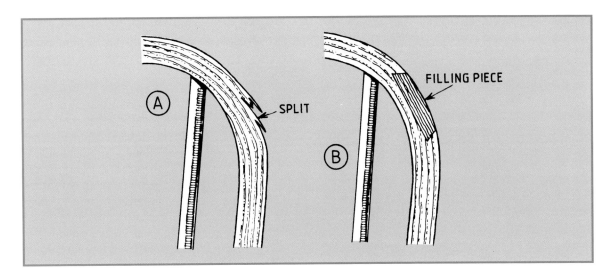

Fig 5:21 Repairing a split bow on a Windsor chair

Now remove the sash cramps and apply glue to the lips of the split and also to the recesses for the keys. Cramp up again, tap in the keys, wipe away any surplus glue, and leave the joint to set. This should make a sound repair.

SPLITS IN THE BACK BOW

Let us consider the split that has developed in the back bow as in Fig 5:21(A), probably as a result of some fault in the wood which was put under pressure while being bent. The obvious remedy is to splice a new piece in and this should make an effective repair provided its grain direction matches as closely as possible that of the bow itself. Make the new piece slightly oversize and glue it in. The best way to hold it in position is to bind it tightly with masking tape, followed by another binding with strong twine. Once the glue has set, it can be spokeshaved to shape, and two screws driven in, with their heads well countersunk and pelleted.

MAKING A NEW BOW FOR A WINDSOR CHAIR BACK

This is a major operation, and not one to be undertaken lightly because, in addition to the actual work involved, some special equipment will have to be built. The equipment and methods used for steaming and bending bows and other curved parts are described fully in Appendix D. At this juncture there are a few relevant points to bear in mind.

1 The toughest, easiest, and the traditional wood to use is ash. It should be as 'green' as possible, which means that the less seasoned it is, the better.

2 The ash should not have been kiln dried. If it has, avoid it, because it will tend to be brittle. Try a timber merchant who sells home-grown timber because he is likely to have ash branches in his yard that would be ideal.

3 Be sure to draw a template of the old back bow on to a sheet of hardboard or plywood before you separate it from the chair, because you will find that as the ends of the bow leave the seat they will spring outwards and make it difficult to plot the shape accurately.

4 Be sure to mark on the template both the centres for the sticks where they fit in the back, and the angles at which they splay, because these are vital statistics.

5 The template can also be used to determine the shape of the former round which the new bow will have to be bent.

6 The same bending technique can be applied to curved parts on other chairs, a good example being the curved back rails in ladder-back chairs.

PREPARING AND FITTING THE NEW BOW

Assuming that the bow for the back has been bent satisfactorily, you now have to assemble it into the seat of the chair. If it is a straightforward replacement, it will simply be a matter of preparing the new bow to match the old one. This means dealing with its ends, and also drilling new holes for the sticks in the back. You can obtain the drilling angles by referring to the template mentioned above, or by cramping the new bow on top of the old one so that they coincide all round. Drill one hole at a time by inserting one of the back sticks into one of the holes in the old bow and using it as a guide to drill the new one.

It is a more complicated job to prepare a new bow. First, you will have to fashion its ends to fit the mortises which are already on the seat. If, however, the seat is also new then there are several ways to fit the bow securely. In the trade, it came down to a matter of time, and therefore price, as to which one was employed.

Three methods are shown in Fig 5:22. At (A) the edges of the bow are simply rounded off and the ends are tapered slightly with a rasp so that they wedge into the mortises when they are glued and knocked into the seat. A neater way is to shape a rounded and shouldered pin on each end as shown at (B). If you want maximum strength, you can cut the mortise to penetrate right through the seat and then glue and wedge the ends from the underside. A foxed-and-wedged tenon (C) is neater and just as strong. Note the tiny ⅛in (3mm) hole drilled at the end of the split for the wedge – this helps to prevent the split from developing any further

when the wedge is forced home. The back bow is fitted at an angle of about 105° to the seat, but one or two degrees either way will not spoil the appearance.

To obtain the angles for drilling the holes for the sticks, try this procedure. First, drill a hole in the centre of the underside of the bow – the holes should be the same diameter as the sticks – and use a depth gauge on the drill to make sure it does not penetrate the bow. Next drill another hole in the centre of the back of the seat, using a sliding bevel set to 105° as a guide. If the end of the stick needs glasspapering slightly before it will enter the hole, do it now.

Now fit the bow and the central stick into the seat temporarily, and judge (by eye) the most pleasing arrangement for the splay of the other sticks, making sure the arrangement is symmetrical. You can then hold each stick in position while you mark the centres for it at top and bottom. When the holes have been drilled, the whole assembly can be glued and knocked together.

Most Windsor chairs have five sticks in the back but there is nothing sacrosanct about it and four, or even seven, are not unusual.

Fig 5:22 Different ways to fit a new bow to a Windsor chair

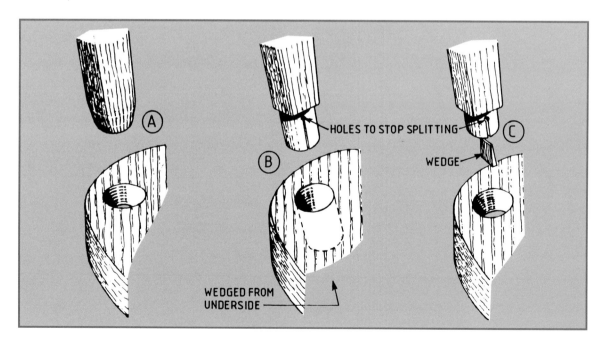

6 Repairs to tables, drawers, and drawer framing

TABLES

REPAIRS TO WARPED TOPS

One of the commonest problems with a planked top (that is, one made up of pieces laid side by side) has been discussed in Chapter 4, namely 'cupping', and the methods used to cure it were suggested.

A different solution is needed, however, when a top made from one solid piece has become hollow as in Fig 6:1. If the table is not particularly valuable and is going to be put to humble uses in your kitchen, you can try the remedy shown in Fig 6:2.

This illustrates how once the table top has been removed from the frame, it can be sawn lengthwise into strips about 3in (76mm) or 4in (102mm) wide, which should effectively remove any tension in the wood. You can then rub-joint the strips back together, pinning and gluing on thin strips of matching wood to the longer edges to compensate for the wood, and consequently the width, lost in the sawcuts. The method does have the disadvantage that the repairs are all too obvious both on the top and on the ends, but the top could be covered with a sheet of plastic laminate, and the edges lipped.

A more complicated development of this method is shown at Fig 6:3, and because all work is done on the underside, the top will show no signs of the repair. The idea is that the stress in the timber is relieved by cutting the longitudinal grooves, and the strips that are glued into them keep the top flat. The grooves should be cut to a depth of about two-thirds of the thickness and spaced about 1in (25mm) apart.

Fig 6:1 How a solid table top can become hollow

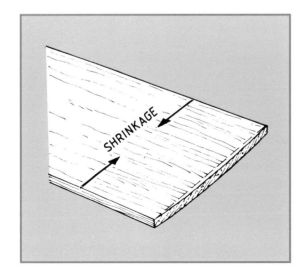

Fig 6:2 One way of dealing with a hollow top

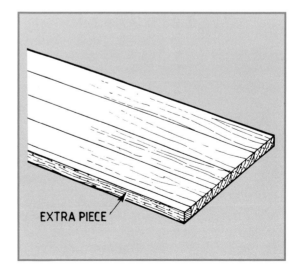

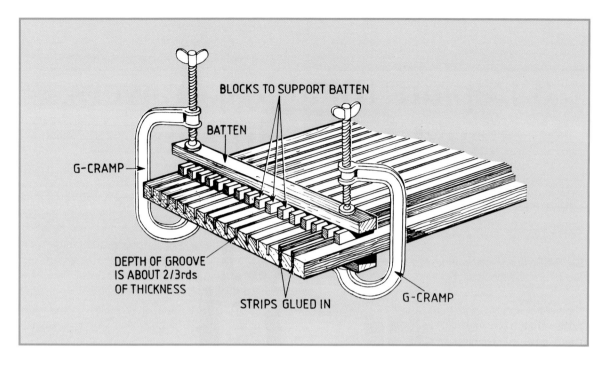

Fig 6:3 Grooving the underside of a hollow top to relieve stress

If the top is a manageable size, you can cut the grooves with a portable circular saw guided by a straightedge cramped from end to end, moving it across by an inch (25mm) after every pass. In the illustration the saw cuts run right out at each end, which means that you will have to apply lippings to hide them. The sawcuts need not run out, however, because you can mark the straightedge at each end to remind you to stop the saw an inch (25mm) or so from the ends. This will involve deepening and squaring up the ends of each groove with a craft knife or chisel afterwards, because the saw blade will leave them curved.

Alternatively, you could use a powered router, which would do a superlatively neat job and the grooves could be routed to within, say, ¼in (6mm) from each end. Again, the straightedge could be used as a guide. The only snag (and there is always one!) would be that at least three passes would be needed for each groove. This is because the depth of cut with a cutter of ¼in (6mm) diameter or less should not be more than its diameter (a ³⁄₁₆in (5mm) cutter should only cut ³⁄₁₆in (5mm) deep at one pass). Assuming that you would be working on

a table top ¾in (19mm) thick, three passes would make a groove ⁹⁄₁₆in (14mm) deep, which is about right. The recommended cutter would be a one-flute with bottom cut, ³⁄₁₆in (5mm) diameter with a ¾in (19mm) length of flute, preferably TC (tungsten carbide).

Although you can use hardwood strips, they are better cut from plywood, which is inherently more stable. Each strip must be in one full length piece and slightly wider than the depth of the groove so that you can plane them flush later. The method of cramping is slightly complicated because the cramping batten has to apply its pressure to the spaces between the strips themselves, which are glued into position and planed flush once the glue has set.

There is yet another way of pulling the top flat, as shown in Fig 6:4, and that is by laying a sheet of veneer on the underside. Any polish or wax must be cleaned off first, followed by planing and keying the surface by scratching it with the teeth of an old hacksaw blade so that the glue will adhere well. Use an inexpensive backing-quality veneer such as gaboon or obeche, and Scotch glue. The veneer must be laid with a veneering hammer (see Chapter 9), and the more the hammer is used across the grain, and the more moisture and heat employed, the more will be the subsequent 'pull' as

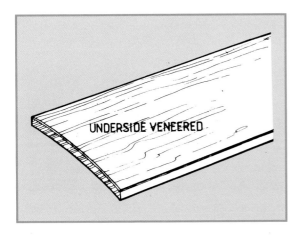

Fig 6:4 Laying a sheet of veneer to pull a top flat

the veneer and the glue dry out. Using Scotch glue rather than a synthetic adhesive will ensure that there is plenty of moisture.

You can choose between laying the veneer in one piece, or as strips. The second choice is usually better. If, for example, you lay 3in (76mm) wide strips of veneer with 3in (76mm) gaps between them, you can lay extra strips in the gaps if the first ones are not effective enough.

Finally, there is a method which can sometimes be adopted if the table has no framing rails that

Fig 6:5 Using battens to force a top to become flat

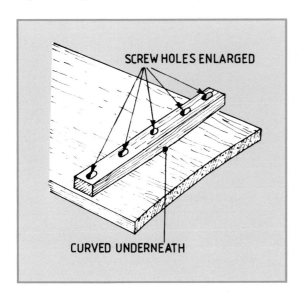

might get in the way, and that is to screw on a batten across the underside, see Fig 6:5. It helps if the face of the batten that meets the underside is given a very slight curvature opposite to that of the top because this will exert a stronger force to pull it straight. The screw holes should be slightly enlarged as shown to allow for any movement of the timber that might otherwise cause splits.

SPLIT TOPS

Several ways to repair splits in panels have already been described in Chapter 4, and they apply equally well to many splits in table tops.

Fig 6:6 (A) Dealing with an end split by inserting a filling piece, plus (B) a dovetail key to prevent further splitting.

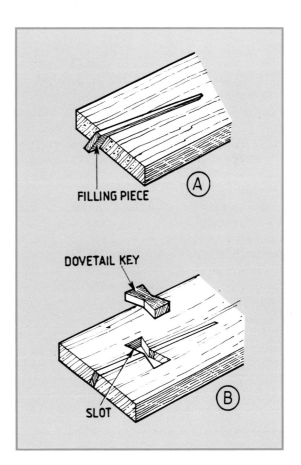

There is, however, one awkward kind of split as shown in Fig 6:6 (A), which follows the angle of the annual rings. The best way to deal with this is first to clean out any dust, wax, etc, and then cut the split to a regular tapered shape, using a saw tilted at the appropriate angle. You can then glue and tap in the filling piece, which should be oversize so that it can be planed back flush when the glue has set. The natural tendency of one of the lips of the split will be to slide upwards. This can be prevented by thumb-cramping two 'bridges' together around the joint.

If you still have doubts about the strength of the repair, a dovetail key sunk in across it as shown in (B) should dispel them. It is better to use an adhesive other than PVA, which has a tendency to creep, even after it has set.

PATCHES AND HOLLOWS

Patches can be used to replace unsightly knots, scars, or blemishes in general, and although they are usually diamond-shaped, there are occasions when the grain configuration calls for a curved patch. Usually a patch need not be much thicker than ¼in (6mm) or so, but its grain has to be chosen very carefully, not only from the point of view of colour but also so that the light will be reflected from it as it is from the remainder of the table top. To help you to decide, try brushing a coat of shellac on to each of the prospective samples because this will give them a simulated 'polished' appearance. The patch should be slightly lighter in colour because you can always darken it far more easily than you can bleach it.

Make a template out of thin card and lay it over the blemish, and mark the grain direction on it. You can then transfer it to the wood you are using for the patch, adjusting it and marking round it to give the best effect. When you have decided this, tape the template to the wood with double-sided adhesive tape and saw it out. Use a file or glasspaper to undercut the edges slightly as in Fig 6:7. It is also a good plan to scratch a few small grooves on the underside because they will act as reservoirs for the glue, most of which would otherwise be squeezed out when the patch is pushed home. Don't forget to make the patch thicker than the depth of the recess so that it can be planed flush when the glue has set.

Marking the recess from the template and

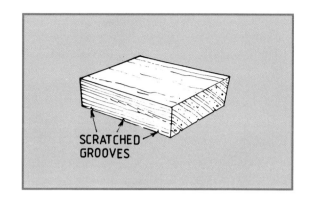

Fig 6:7 Using a patch cut to a template to mask a blemish

cutting it out is straightforward enough because it is unlikely to be larger than, say, one inch (25mm) square. A patch bigger than this would be too obtrusive. If the top is polished (as it probably will be), lay strips of masking tape round the marks. Not only will they protect the polish but will also act as guides when you drill and chisel out the waste. There is a definite procedure for the latter, the first step being to incise the marks with a craft knife. Next, using a drill with a depth gauge, or a power router, remove the bulk of the waste from

Fig 6:8 Chopping out round a pre-bored (or routed) hole

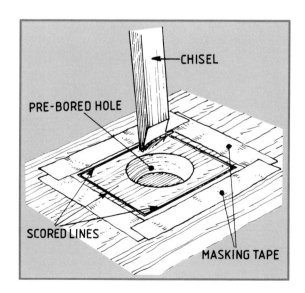

the centre. Don't work too close to the marks at this juncture, but leave about ⅛in (3mm) of margin all round. Removing this marginal waste with a sharp chisel is shown in Fig 6:8. Note that the chisel is held at a slight angle from the vertical, and that the blade is tilted so that you start at the corners by cutting across the grain first. This avoids the likelihood of subsequent chisel cuts along the grain running beyond the marks – an unsightly fault that can also occur when you are cutting hinge recesses.

RAISING HOLLOWS OR DENTS

The adoption of this remedy depends upon (a) whether the surface is polished or not, and (b) whether it is veneered or solid. In either case, you would be well advised to leave well alone and accept the fault, because either the polish or the veneer, or possibly both, would be seriously affected. The polish would almost certainly be marked, and the glue beneath the veneer could be

liquefied, allowing the veneer to lift.

If the timber is in the white (a technical term for any wood in its unpolished state), the method is as follows. Cut a few slits along the grain with a craft knife and fill the hollow or dent with a puddle of water. Allow it a quarter of an hour or so to sink into the grain. The slits will help it to do so and will close up during the treatment. Then soak a small piece of rag in water and lay it in the hollow. Press down lightly on the rag with the point of an electric iron set at a medium heat until the water steams and raises the grain to fill the hollow. That finishes the job.

DROP-LEAF TABLES

It sometimes happens with this type of table that the top shrinks across the grain and thus becomes narrower. As a result, the flaps can no longer hang vertically but are pushed outwards slightly by the underframe, as shown on the sofa table in Fig 6:9.

Unscrewing the rule-joint hinges and removing the leaves is the first step, followed by taking off the top. You now have to examine the top to ascertain whether it is solid or veneered. We shall be dealing with both kinds, so let us assume that in

Fig 6:9 A fault that can develop with a drop-leaf table

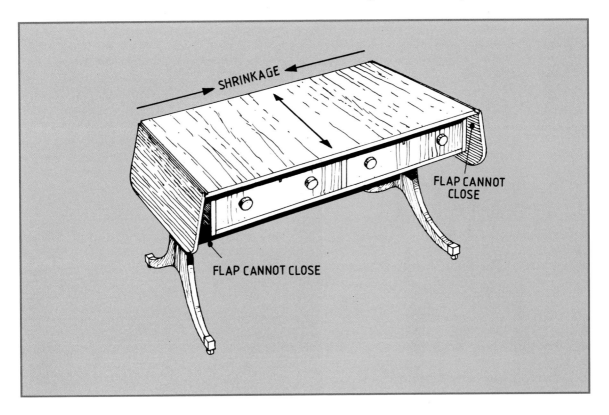

the first case it is solid.

This means that the grain will run parallel to the shorter side, across the top. This must be so because it would be difficult to work the rule joints on end grain. If the grain and figure are not too flamboyant and distinctive, the easiest solution is to saw across the top at the centre so that you separate it into two halves. You can then glue in a filling strip.

This strip is unlikely to be greater than an inch (25mm) in width, so it would be a good plan to strengthen the joint with ³⁄₁₆in (5mm) diameter dowels, which could penetrate right through the strip. If possible, it would also help to screw and glue a batten on the underside of the top as a further reinforcement.

There remains, however, the second case where the top has been veneered, and inserting a filling strip would obviously spoil its appearance. Your choice here is between making the repair as unobtrusive as possible, and leaving things as they are.

It may be possible to scrape or plane away some wood from the end frames so that the leaves can hang vertically, but this can only be effective in mild cases. The alternative is to cut away the rule joint at each end of the top to a width of say, 1½in (38mm), and fit replacement strips that will bring the top to the required size. The strips will need rule joints worked on them first so that you can check that they fit those on the leaves. The strips

can then be dowelled and glued in place. The wood for the strips should be chosen to match the veneer as far as possible.

REPAIRS TO JOINTS

The three joints most frequently used on flap or drop-leaf tables are the rule joint, the knuckle joint, and the finger joint – the last named being found mainly on antique pieces.

The rule joint is the one most generally employed to hinge the leaf of a drop-leaf table, and the faults that usually develop are that the joint binds, and opens and closes with difficulty; and damage occurs to the hinge because of misuse.

Binding that occurs even when the hinge is in good order and correctly positioned is usually due to dampness that has swollen the wood on the meeting edges. The best and usually the most effective remedy is to unscrew the leaf and leave it and the table in a warm, dry atmosphere for as long as possible. It sometimes helps if you glasspaper the convex edge lightly, holding the glasspaper on a wooden rubber shaped exactly to the reverse of the profile. This will remove any polish that prevents the moisture from escaping.

If the old hinges need replacing, you must position the new ones precisely to make the joint work properly. Fig 6:10 shows how it must be done. There are several points to bear in mind. (1) The countersinking of the holes is on the opposite side to the knuckle. (2) The rounded convex shape of the table top edge supports the weight of the leaf when it is in the raised position, instead of the hinges doing so. (3) The hinge flaps have to be

Fig 6:10 Fitting a new rule joint hinge

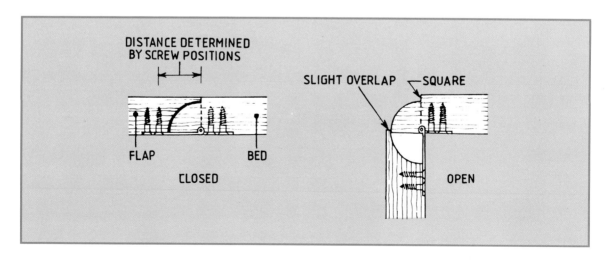

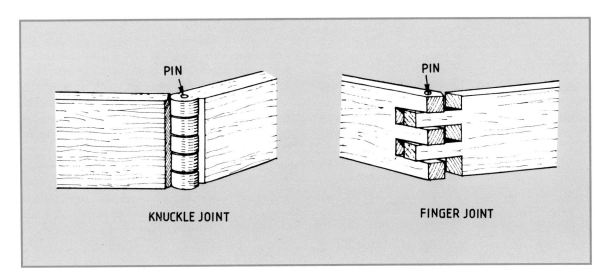

KNUCKLE JOINT

FINGER JOINT

recessed carefully into the wood with the larger flap screwed to the leaf. (4) Most importantly, the centre of the hinge knuckle must be precisely located vertically below the square member as shown, otherwise the joint may bind. (5) When the leaf is lowered, the tip of the concave edge just overlaps the bottom of the round section, so avoiding an unsightly gap. (6) The best way to screw on the hinges is to turn the table upside down on a flat surface and fit the leaf up to the edge, because this will guarantee that the two parts are in the same plane.

You may be lucky enough to find that the screw holes on the new hinge match those on the old one, or as nearly as makes little difference. If necessary, you can use the epoxy resin adhesive plugging method already described to fix them. If the old holes are differently spaced or have become too large, you will almost certainly find it advisable to chop out the old recess, glue in a new filling piece, and carry on from that point when you will be able to position the hinge exactly.

Both knuckle and finger joints swing laterally to provide support for their flaps, and the trouble that usually arises is that they become sloppy and do not hold the flaps at a truly horizontal level. From Fig 6:11 you will see that both hinges pivot round a metal pin, which can be, and often is, a large nail cut off to length. Over the years, the holes wear away and become too large.

The simplest solution is to remove the pin, enlarge the holes, and insert a new pin with a slightly larger diameter, but this is more easily said

Fig 6:11 Dealing with a loose knuckle or finger joint

than done. First, the old pin must be punched out of the holes. This is straightforward enough, but the difficulty arises when it comes to drilling out the holes for the new pin and ensuring that they are truly vertical.

If you are careful and take your time, it can be done by eye. But a vertical drill stand will help considerably because its base can be cramped to the bench and the drilling arm swung over so that a power drill in it is centred over the holes. You will have to lay the table upside down on the bench and cramp it down so that it will not move while drilling is taking place. The fly rail (as the leaf support is called) should also be cramped flat against the table frame.

There is another possible cause of the sloppiness, which is that the bearing surfaces of the knuckles or fingers have worn, and slackness is the result. Some kind of bushing is required, and small slips of veneer can be glued on to the bearing surfaces. These can be trimmed and glasspapered to shape after the glue has set, until the required sliding fit is obtained. There is no need to apply the treatment to both parts but only to the fly rail. By holding it in the vice and chiselling away a shaving or two from each face, sufficient space will be created to insert the slips. In bad cases, using a fine-toothed gent's saw instead of chiselling will be quicker and more effective.

DRAWERS

REPAIRS TO DRAWER BOTTOMS AND SIDES

Drawer bottoms are particularly liable to be damaged from (1) the contents being forced in too tightly; (2) the contents being too heavy; and (3) the underside being rubbed and worn by the drawer stops. In modern pieces the bottoms are usually made from plywood or hardboard and it is quicker and cheaper to replace the entire bottom than to repair it.

In the first two instances, if the bottom is made up from two pieces, they probably no longer meet at the joint (see Fig 6:12). On the other hand, if the bottom is in one piece, then probably it will have split. To correct both faults, you will have to remove the drawer bottom. This should be easy, because the only fixing is by means of nails or screws driven up through it into the drawer back. Remove these, and you should be able to withdraw the bottom from its groove.

If the pieces that make up the bottom are intact

Fig 6:12 After a period of use, the two parts of a drawer bottom no longer meet

but have bent so that the joint is broken, the repair will mean remaking it as in Fig 6:13. Because the pieces are thin, they can only be re-glued while they lie on a flat surface, and the first job is to clean off any old glue. Then lay a few sheets of newspaper on a flat bench or table top, glue the edges, and place a heavy weight on one of them to keep it flat. Hold the other piece flat and rub the edges together sideways. You may need a weight on this as well, so it's a good idea to keep several house bricks handy! Let the glue set, and clean off any adhering newspaper with a damp cloth. A narrow strip of canvas glued along the joint afterwards will help to prevent the joints opening again.

A drawer bottom with a small split in it which does not extend the full width can often be made good by gluing on a canvas strip to the underside. The lips of the split should be cleaned before dribbling some glue into it, and rubbing it in with your finger.

When the bottom has been worn by the drawer stops, look first at the lower edges of the drawer sides, because they have probably worn away with constant use and so allowed the drawer stops to rub on the bottom. Unfortunately the amount of wear is usually unevenly distributed along the edge, and this makes it difficult to mark a line to

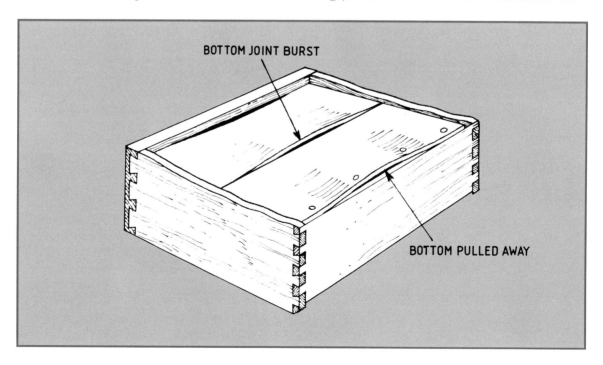

74

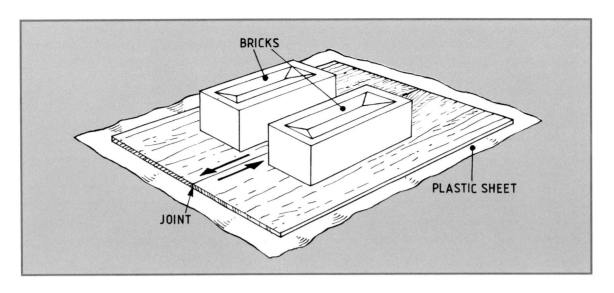

Fig 6:13 Remaking the joint

Fig 6:14 Repairing worn drawer sides

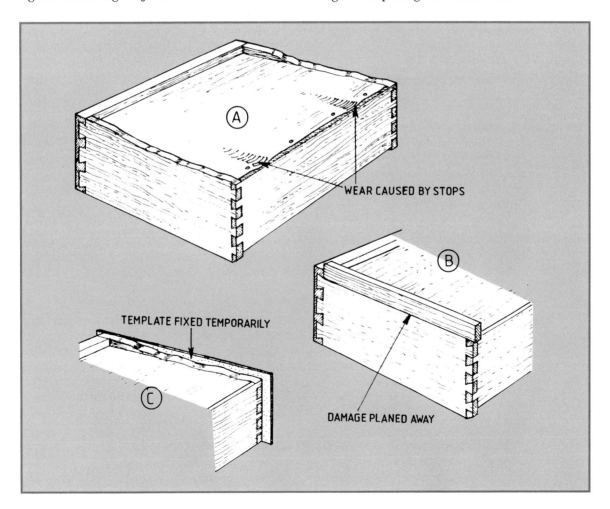

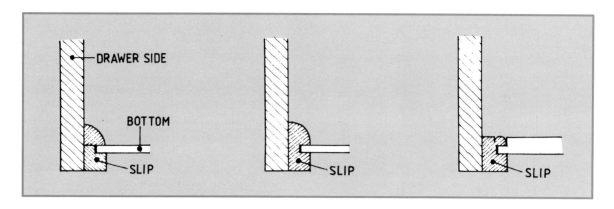

which you can plane the drawer side after a repair piece has been fixed to it.

Fig 6:14 shows how to overcome this. The drawing at (A) shows the effect of wear and tear. (B) shows how the worn part is chiselled and/or planed away and a repair piece glued in. A small bullnose plane is handy for this because the blade is set close to its front edge. (C) shows the drawer upside down with a hardboard or plywood template fixed to the side as a guide. Note that the repair piece is made deliberately oversize so that, once the glue has set, it can be planed level with the edge of the template. The latter can either be made the same size as an undamaged drawer side or, if both sides are worn, it can be measured against the aperture for the drawer, allowing 1/16in (2mm) or so for opening and closing. You can either pin the template temporarily to the drawer side or hold it by means of double-sided adhesive tape. Once you have planed the side to the correct size, you can remove the template, and tap a few pins into the joint to make it stronger, punching their heads well below the surface.

If the drawer side or sides are so badly damaged that the grooves in which the drawer bottom is fitted can no longer be used, you could first splice on a repair piece as just described and then support the bottom by means of drawer slips. A variety of these is shown in Fig 6:15. Choose the design that best suits your purpose, and glue and pin the slips in place. This practically doubles the bearing surface and avoids future trouble.

DRAWER FRAMING

Most commonly, the drawer sides wear an unsightly trench, caused by the constant opening and closing of the drawer, see Fig 6:16. First,

Fig 6:15 Sections of drawer slips

remove the runner. This is normally held in position in three places: by a tenon glued into a groove in the back of the front rail; with a tongue that fits (dry) into a groove on the carcase end; and finally by a screw through the back. If you remove this screw, a good tug will invariably loosen the glued joint at the front and the runner can then be prised away. This is almost always made of softwood, so fit a new one.

This leaves the trench in the front rail to be attended to. The difficulty here is to saw downwards, where the rail meets the end, without

Fig 6:16 How a drawer rail can be worn away

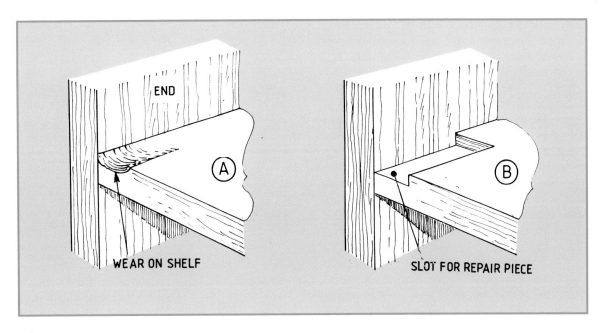

Fig 6:17 Using a filling piece to effect the repair

damaging the latter. As the depth to be sawn is likely to be small – probably no more than ¼in (6mm) – a padsaw with a handle that accepts not only padsaw blades but also hacksaw blades would be a suitable tool. It can be used with the blades either at 90 or 45° to the work. The same saw can also be used to make a slanting cut on the other side of the trench, and the waste can then be

chopped out. Finally, a filling piece can be prepared and glued in, and trimmed to size when the glue has set.

The same trouble can occur to a carcase where the front drawer rail and runners consist of a solid piece of wood running from front to back as in Fig 6:17. Here, the repair is complicated by the fact that the wear is usually concentrated at the front end and runs out towards the back, see (A), but the filling piece needs to be a rectangular block as shown at (B). You can cut out a slot with a padsaw, as already described, although an offset gent's saw will give a better result. This is shown is Fig 6:18 and has a cranked handle which can be bolted to

Fig 6:18 An offset 'gent's' saw

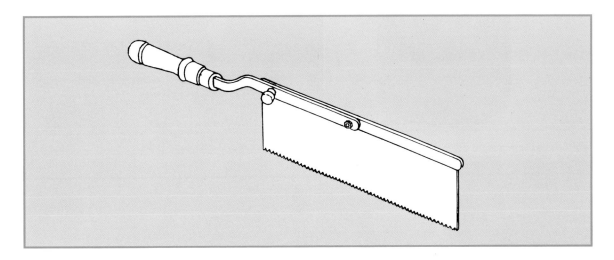

either side of the blade. It is, in fact, an old design that had disappeared but has recently been re-introduced. Gluing in a filling piece and trimming it to size when the glue has set, completes the job.

REMOVING WOODEN KNOBS

First of all, check to see if the knob unscrews; some have pins turned on their ends which are threaded. If not, chop the knob away as shown in Fig 6:19 because this avoids damage to the drawer front. The grain of the knobs runs from front to back, and a light blow on a chisel will remove the waste without the blade even touching the front. You can punch out the remainder of the pin from the inside of the drawer front.

OPENING A LOCKED DRAWER

This can be an irritating and time-consuming business. The trouble is usually caused by a broken lock, a missing key, or swollen wood.

Assuming that one or other of the first two eventualities applies, there are several ways to deal

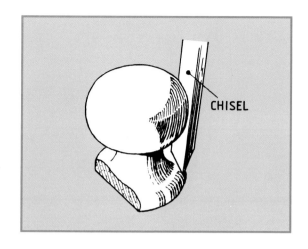

Fig 6:19 Removing a wooden knob handle on a drawer

with it, ranging from the simple to the drastic. Try tapping some small wooden wedges into the gap between the top edge of the drawer and the rail above. It may then be possible to slide a thin-bladed knife along the opening thus formed and push the bolt of the lock down, so freeing the

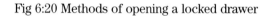
Fig 6:20 Methods of opening a locked drawer

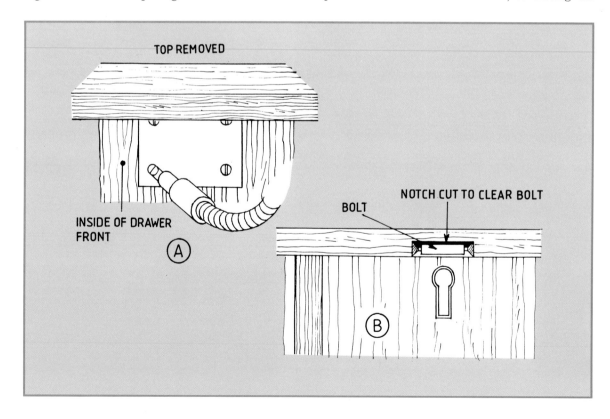

drawer. If the gap is wide enough, you could insert the padsaw-cum-hacksaw referred to above and saw through the bolt. Be careful not to force the wedges in so far that the rail breaks.

Much depends on whether the drawer is the top one or not. If it is, the treatment becomes more complicated. If you can remove the top, it may be possible to get at the screws on the lock with a flexible screwdriver; see Fig 6:20(A). Alternatively, if you can remove the back, do so. A little prising and levering with an old chisel or a screwdriver should loosen the fixing of the drawer bottom to its back and enable you to withdraw the bottom from its grooves. Take out the drawer below the locked one and, if there is no dustboard, you should be able to unscrew the offending lock with a long-handled or flexible screwdriver.

There are two 'last resort' methods. One is to remove the back and get a helper to push the drawer forward while you hammer a punch against the pin of the lock. Because the screws holding the lock are quite small, they will soon give way and the lock will fall off. A new lock will have to be fitted, which entails, at best, plugging the old screws and drilling new ones or, at worst, having to cut a recess and glue in a filling piece into which you can drill the new holes.

The other method, and the only one you can adopt if you cannot remove the back and dustboards get in the way, is to chop out a notch in the drawer rail as shown in Fig 6:20(B). This will free the bolt so that you can pull out the drawer. Again, a filling piece (as shown by the dotted lines) will need to be glued in, and a slot for the bolt cut in it.

If the wood has swollen in a damp atmosphere, the only remedy is to move the piece into a warm and dry location and leave it for as long as possible.

REPAIRING COCKED BEADS AND MOULDED DRAWER FRONTS

These are both dealt with in Chapter 8.

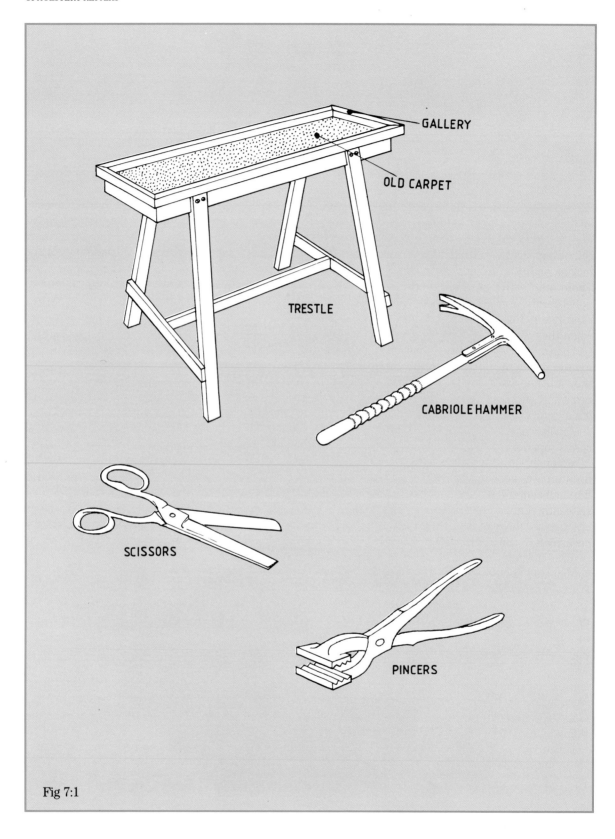

GALLERY

OLD CARPET

TRESTLE

CABRIOLE HAMMER

SCISSORS

PINCERS

Fig 7:1

7 Upholstery repairs

Upholstery is a separate trade from cabinet-making and chair-making, and a very ancient one. There are early references to 'upholders' (as upholsterers were called until the nineteenth century) in the middle of the fifteenth century when they were concerned mainly with beds and bed-hangings made in the most sumptuous materials for the aristocracy and the rich. Over the years, they became what we would call today interior designers and decorators; and they employed a variety of tradesmen, including cabinet-makers and chair-makers, to whom they considered themselves superior.

Although fixing some form of padding to seat furniture was known to have been employed in the fifteenth century, it was not until the middle of the sixteenth century that it was applied as common practice to the padded backs and seats of the backstools in use at that time.

All upholstery consisted solely of padding and stuffing materials until the 1830s. A Mr Samuel Pratt patented the first design of a coil spring in 1828, and the idea soon caught on. Although it was the first commercial application of coil springs to furniture, they had been used by a Mr Henry Marsh in 1739 in his design for a 'chamber horse'. This was a boxlike contraption which contained coil springs and had leather sides. By sitting on the wooden seat on the top and with his feet on a foot board, the occupant could imitate the motions of riding a horse. Whether this was an early exercise machine, or a device to accustom would-be riders to the movement of a horse, history does not say,

but such a design must have delighted the hearts of some eighteenth-century children.

The most marked historical change has been the introduction of a wide variety of springing during the last forty years, including the most versatile of them all, latex and plastic foam.

THE TOOLS

Fortunately, upholstering does not demand a large kit of tools and, if you indulge in DIY or woodworking, you will probably have many of them already. Fig 7:1 shows the ones you will need.

TRESTLES

Two are needed, and as you can see, each one should have a tray fixed to its top so that chair legs can be placed in it without the risk of the chair's toppling over or moving about too much.

HAMMER

Although you can use an ordinary hammer provided it is a small, light one, the upholsterer's 'cabriole' hammer is worth buying if you have a lot of upholstery work to do. However, if most of the work is on modern designs or is renovation rather than restoration, a stapling gun could be more useful.

SCISSORS

You will need two pairs, both of which should be of good quality and kept sharp. One pair with 6in (152mm) long blades for cutting fabrics and one pair 3in (76mm) long for cutting twine and thread should suffice.

Fig 7:1 Various tools for upholstering

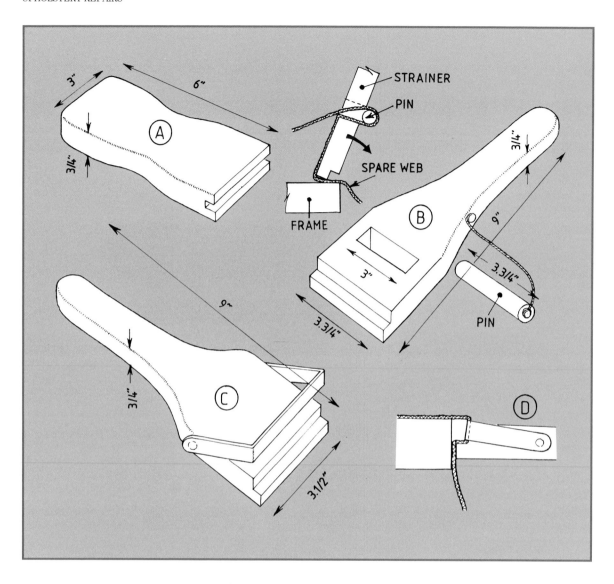

Fig 7:2 Three kinds of webbing strainer

WEBBING PINCERS

These have corrugated jaws, and are used to grip short ends of webs so that you can pull them taut. If the wood is polished, the webbing should be inserted under the lower jaw to form a pad that protects the wood.

WEBBING STRAINER

There are three patterns, any of which you could make for yourself in hardwood, although beech is probably best. All three are illustrated with suggested sizes: Fig 7:2.

The plain type shown at (A) has a groove cut across the end which fits over the edge of the frame with the webbing held round it. Raising or lowering the handle controls the degree of tautness.

A 'bat' type is shown at (B). To use it, make a loop in the webbing, push it through the slot, and then insert the pin into the loop.

The last, 'lever-type', strainer (C) uses a metal strap to grip the webbing as illustrated at (D).

RIPPING CHISEL

Although you can buy one, an old chisel or

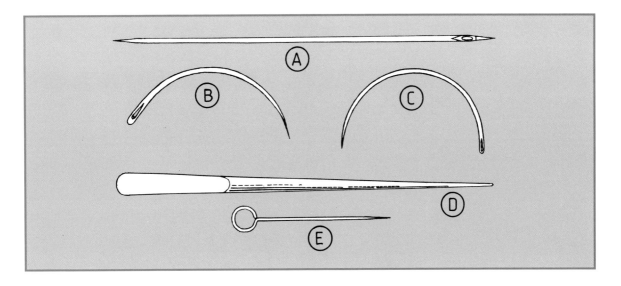

Fig 7:3 Needles, regulator, and skewers

screwdriver, or better still the nail and tack extractor described in Chapter 3, will all do the job satisfactorily.

There is a correct technique for using the tool, which is to locate its edge under the head of the tack and then give the handle a smart blow or two with a mallet. This should be enough to lift the tack. Always use the tool in the direction of the grain. At corners, hold it with the handle outside the frame so that you are striking inwards – this will lessen the risk of splitting the grain in both instances.

NEEDLES, REGULATOR, AND SKEWERS

Because of the thicknesses of the various stuffing materials, ordinary darning or sewing needles are far too small. The best general purpose straight needle is a 9in (228mm) or 10in (254mm) long mattress needle, Fig 7:3(A). There are also two curved needles that are useful, namely, the spring needle (B) used to sew springs to webbing and hessian, and the half-circular needle (C) for sewing in awkward places.

The regulator is a metal rod with a long point at one end and a round-cornered flat blade at the other (D), and is used to arrange and distribute stuffing materials such as hair or fibre evenly. For occasional use, there is no reason why you should not make one for yourself out of a piece of dowel

about 10in (254mm) long shaped as required; or you could even use a large knitting needle.

Skewers (E) are used for holding covering materials temporarily in place.

MATERIALS

WEBBING

This has hardly changed since the days of Queen Elizabeth I. Today it is available in 2in (51mm), 2⅛in (54mm), and 2¼in (58mm) widths. Some modern webbings are made from polypropylene, but the traditional kinds (in descending order of quality) comprise black and white twill weave of flax; black and white made from mixtures of jute, hemp, and cotton; and plain or striped brown made of jute. They are usually sold by the metre, or in 18yd rolls.

HESSIAN

This is made from jute and includes several qualities, the best being known as 'spring canvas' for covering over springs. There is also an open-weave kind called 'scrim', which is used to cover the first stuffing of hair or fibre. Use 10oz (283.5g) quality over seat springs, and 7oz (198.5g) on backs.

CALICO

This unbleached cotton cloth is used as a final cover under the actual decorative fabric as, for instance, tapestry or moquette.

CANVAS

This is plain open-weave cloth with twisted yarns, usually made from hemp. When dyed black it is used to cover the undersides of upholstered chairs. Also, of course, it is used for deck chairs and folding camp chairs and stools.

TRADITIONAL STUFFINGS

Really old upholstered furniture contained an amazing variety of stuffings, including horsehair, feathers, wood shavings, wool, dried seaweed, moss, and hay.

If you are restoring antique pieces for conservation, you will still need to use some of the old stuffings that have survived through the years. During the 1950s, latex and plastic foam fillings more or less ousted them from favour, but the following is a survey of those most commonly used in the old days.

HAIR STUFFING

Horsehair is the best, and it is often mixed with cow-tail and hog-hair, and sometimes has an admixture of vegetable fibre. The result is a stuffing that is perfectly suitable for upholstery work provided the hair is not too short and therefore lacking in resiliency.

There is no reason why you should not use secondhand hair; it will first need shaking and teasing to get rid of dust and lumps. As this is a dusty and dirty business, it's best to do it out of doors. The hair can then be washed and thoroughly dried by putting it into a pillow case with the end tied up, then into a washing machine, and finally into a spin drier.

COIR FIBRE

Also called coco-fibre or ginger fibre (from its colour), this comes from the husks of coconuts. Use the long fibres for best quality work, and the short ones for cheaper jobs.

ALGERIAN FIBRE

This consists of split leaves from a dwarf palm tree grown in Algeria. Some is dyed black, and some retains its green colour, the two being known as black and green fibre respectively. Of the two, the black is usually the more resilient, softer, and easier to shape.

FLOCK

Sometimes called black wool or linsey wool, flock consists of old rags washed, macerated, and carded. It must conform to strict health standards. It is a cheap alternative to the other stuffings and is notorious for the ease with which it forms lumps.

WADDING

Cotton wadding can be bought in various thicknesses in 12yd (9m) rolls from which you can cut your own sheets, or in 1lb (454g) packets, when it is called 'pound' wadding. Some kinds have a skin on one side and this should be laid face downwards, the soft side being uppermost. Wadding can be separated into layers, and is then used to fill in irregularities in the stuffing and to prevent the latter from working through the cover.

STUFFING PADS

Consisting of various kinds of stuffing woven on to hessian backings, these pads were introduced as a convenient and neat alternative to the long and often untidy process of building up loose fillings. They can be obtained as rolls, or in cut-off lengths.

TWINES, CORDS, PIPING, GIMP

Twines are made from flax or hemp, and there are different strengths and thicknesses for different jobs. Spring twine is a fairly thick twine used for stitching the springs to the webbing, while a finer variety (called stitching twine) is for stitching rolls and fine edges. Laid cord is a strong twine in which the yarns are laid together to resist any tendency to stretch, and it is employed for lashing the

Fig 7:4 Types of tacks, nails, pins, and buttons

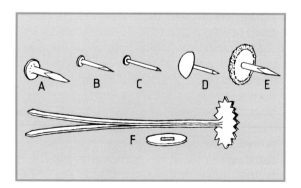

springs in position. In practice, spring twine and laid cord are interchangeable for most jobs.

Piping cord can be made from either cotton or compressed paper. It is sewn into a narrow strip of the cover fabric and sewn in to form a 'piped' seam, which is explained later in the chapter.

Gimp is a kind of decorative braid, usually about ½in (12mm) to ⅝in (16mm) wide, which is fastened round the edges of the job after the final cover has been put on. It hides any tack heads and greatly improves the appearance. It is fixed by means of gimp pins, although where it has to negotiate corners or awkward curves it can be stuck down with upholstery adhesive first before being pinned at strategic points. You can choose a pattern and colour to suit your work from the wide range available.

TACKS, PINS, NAILS, AND BUTTONS (Fig 7:4)

Machine-made tacks replaced hand-made ones about 1860. Blued, cut tacks are the ones used today, and two kinds are available. (A) These are the 'ordinary' tack, and the 'improved' tack, which is stouter and has a larger head. Use ⅜in (10mm) or ½in (12mm) fine tacks for covers, ⅜in (10mm) and ½in (12mm) improved tacks for fixing hessian, and ⅝in (16mm) improved for webbing.

Gimp pins are made in two types: cut, like tacks (B); and wire, like a small nail (C) – and in two sizes, ⅜in (10mm) and ½in (12mm). You can also buy coloured ones to match the colour of the gimp.

Round-headed nails (D) or as they are often called, dome-headed antique nails, have been used for centuries as final fixings for cover fabrics in general, and leather in particular. You can space-nail, close-nail, or cluster-nail them as shown in Fig 7:5. The last two styles were popular in the sixteenth and seventeenth centuries.

Buttons (E) can also be used for final fixing, and can be obtained with their heads covered either in fabric or PVC materials.

The traditional buttons used on Victorian-style upholstery not only created an appearance of opulent luxury but also fulfilled the more prosaic purpose of holding the underlying stuffings in place. Today, there is an alternative design (F) which resembles a giant paper-fastener with long prongs turned over a washer at the back and flattened down. It is particularly suitable for buttoning divan and bed headboards. Finally, there

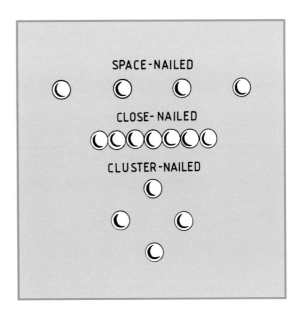

Fig 7:5 Patterns that can be used when fixing round-headed nails

are PVC-covered bandings in various colours which, in some cases, have fixing pins already inserted in them. They are used mainly for pieces upholstered in leather or simulated leather.

TRADITIONAL AND MODERN SPRINGING (Fig 7:6)

COIL SPRINGS (A)

These are the traditional double-cone springs that have been used for more than 150 years, and the design is such that even when under compression, the coils do not bind against each other but spring back easily. They were still in commercial use until the 1950s when they were superseded by cable and serpentine springs and foam cushions.

It follows that almost any restoration work means that you will need to employ them, and they are available in the following sizes and gauges: for backs, arms, and shallow seats – 4in (102mm) by 13 gauge, and 5in (127mm) by 10 and 12 gauge; for deep backs and seats – 6in (152mm) by 10 and 12 gauge, 7in (178mm) by 9 gauge, 8in (203mm) by 9 gauge, 9in (228mm) by 8 or 9 gauge; 10in (254mm) by 8 gauge. The thicker gauge (that is, the larger number) in each size can be used for

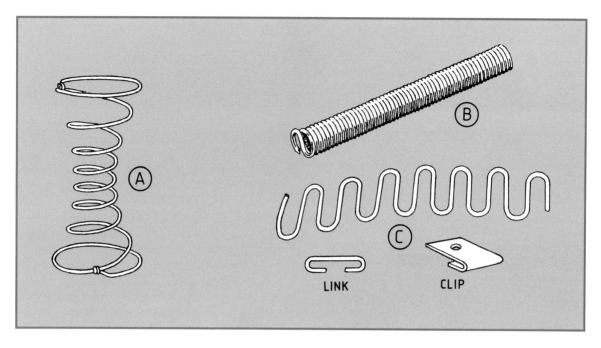

LINK   CLIP

Fig 7:6 Types of springing

seats. The thinner gauge is used for arms and backs.

Cone springs were a variation of the coil spring, being cone-shaped instead of double-cone, and were used mainly in spring units.

SPRING UNITS

These are only of historical interest because they are now unobtainable, having been displaced by foam cushioning. They were most popular from the 1930s to the 1950s. They consisted of a number of coil or cone springs riveted to a frame of metal laths, and covered with a fine mesh wire. The whole thing was nailed in place and the stuffing materials were laid over it.

CABLE SPRINGS (B)

Also called 'tension' springs, these are composed of sprung wire wound tightly in the form of a cable. They are available in ⅜in (10mm) (for backs) and ½in (12mm) (for seats) diameters, and frequently form the bases for foam cushions. When they were first introduced in the 1950s, they were supplied in the bare metal, but because this tended to mark the cushions, they are now usually covered with plastic sleeves.

SERPENTINE SPRINGING (C)

Also called 'No-sag', zigzag, or sinuous springing, this was introduced about twenty years ago, and is frequently used with foam cushions. It is made by first bending a length of wire into a serpentine-shaped strip and then forming it into a circle of large diameter. It is tempered while in this shape. The circle is then cut into segments of the required size, and when anchored at each end, each segment becomes an arc with permanent inbuilt resiliency. Two gauges of wire are used, namely 12 gauge for seats and a lighter 9 gauge for backs. Anchoring clips and connecting links can be supplied with the springs.

RESILIENT RUBBER WEBBING

This is a comparatively modern innovation and is an easy-to-fix and versatile form of springing. The webbing is supplied in ¾in (19mm), 1⅛in (28mm), 1½in (38mm), 2in (51mm) and 2¼in (58mm) widths. The first two are intended for backs and arms, the next two for seats, and the last for beds and divans. Fitting and fixing are dealt with later in this chapter.

FOAM CUSHIONS

These consist of latex or polyether foam. Latex cushioning is expensive and is employed more or less solely for specialist seating (as in aircraft), so we will concentrate on polyether foam, which is the one available for general use.

The first point to bear in mind is that any foam you buy should conform to the recent regulations on fire resistance and the emission of toxic fumes. Any foam cushioning that is fitted to second-hand furniture is most unlikely to do so and should be replaced.

One of the most important factors in choosing polyether foam is that it is supplied in different densities. The density of any particular grade is expressed as the weight of a cubic metre. As you are unlikely ever to get the chance to weigh such a large slab, it is more practical to divide the grades into seat densities and back densities. As you would expect, the heavier the density/weight, the more suitable it is for hard wear.

Next, we have to consider the best thickness to use. This depends to a large extent on the kind of support backing up the foam. On a solid wood base (as used on some divans, for example), a heavy seating grade will need to be 3½in (90mm) thick, or a lighter grade 4¾in (120mm). The same provisions apply to any support made of traditional webbing. If, however, you are using cable springs,

serpentine springs, or resilient rubber webbing, the thickness of the foam can be reduced to 3in (75mm) in the case of a heavy grade, and 4in (100mm) for lighter ones.

Chipfoam, which consists of offcut chips glued together, is widely available in both slab and sheet form and is graded in a similar fashion to ordinary foam.

WORKING METHOD

FIXING WEBBING
Start by laying the webbing across the seat rail, allowing about 2in (50mm) spare at the cut end as in Fig 7:7, and hammer in three tacks. Now cut the spare piece so that about only 1in (25mm) is left loose, and fold this over and put in two more tacks. Then carry on by straining the webbing, and repeating the fixing at the other end.

FIXING RESILIENT RUBBER WEBBING
This can be tacked down with ⅝in (16mm) improved tacks as shown at (A), Fig 7:8, but the method has two disadvantages in that the holes may become enlarged because of continual flexing, and the heads of the tacks may mark or tear the fabric of the cushion placed over them.

Fig 7:7 Fixing upholsterers' webbing

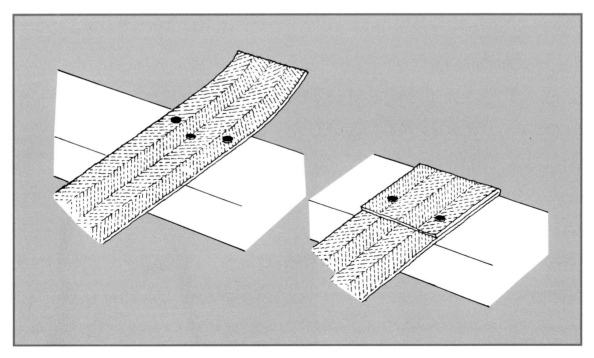

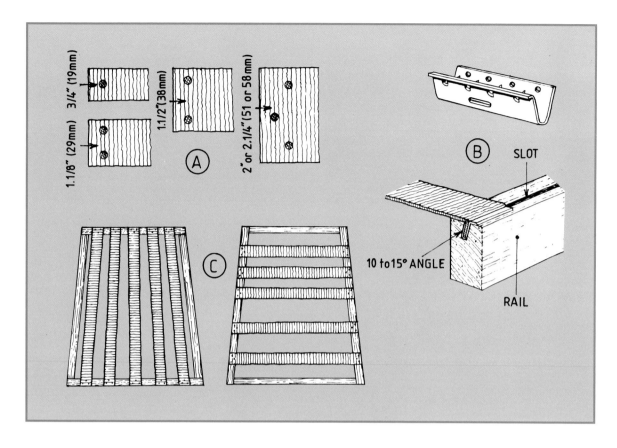

Fig 7:8 Fixing resilient rubber webbing

By far the better method is to use the clips shown at (B), which can be supplied with the webbing. They are then pressed on to the ends in an ordinary bench vice. The clips are inserted into the angled slots, which you can cut on a tilting saw bench or on a router-table. Note that the inner edge of the rail can be rounded off to prevent its chafing the webbing.

The spacing of the webs is governed by the fact that the gaps between them should generally not be more (or very little more) than the width of the webbing itself. At (C) you can see two suggested ways to web up a chair seat. Note that in the example where the webs run transversely they are closer together at the back than at the front because this is where most support is needed.

Tension should be applied to the webbing at the rate of 1in (25mm) or 1¼in (32mm) in every 10in (254mm). In other words, if you have to span a width of 20in (508mm), mark this length on to the webbing from one end with a pencil, and then make another pencil mark 17½in (445mm) or 18in (457mm) from the same end. Use the latter mark as the one to be fastened down.

FIXING COIL SPRINGS

When webs are tacked down they are interlaced (or 'checked' as it is called in the trade) and, if coil springs are used, one spring is fastened at each intersection so that the number of springs determines the number of webs. On small chairs with only three springs, the arrangement is shown at (A), Fig 7:9; and with five springs on a larger chair at (B). Both illustrations are views of the underside of the seat.

Using a spring needle and twine, sew each spring in place as shown in Fig 7:10(A) so that you achieve the result shown at (B). The knots you use are important. You should start with a slip knot, continue with half-hitches, and finish with a double hitch.

Having secured the springs to the webs, the next job is to lash them together at the top. Start by

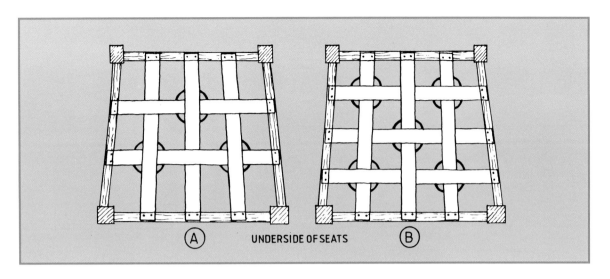

Fig 7:9 Arranging springs on a chair seat   Fig 7:10 Sewing springs in place

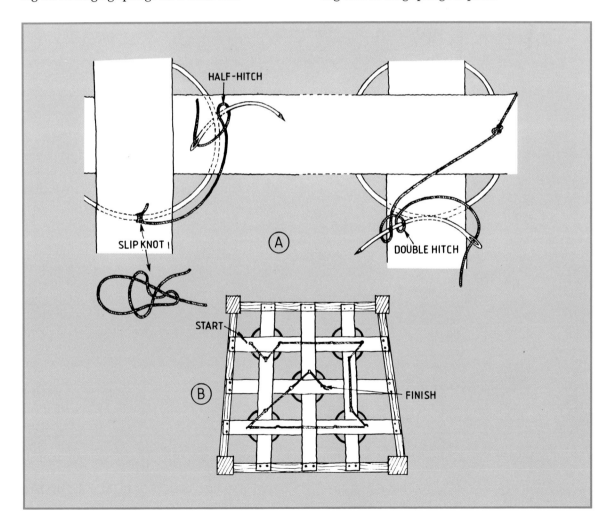

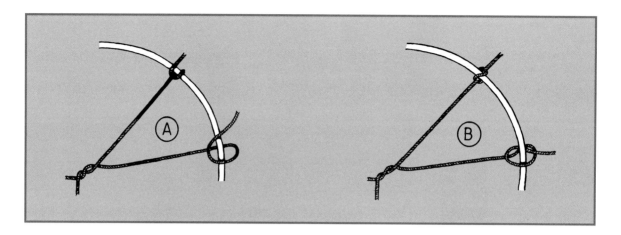

Fig 7:11 Knots you can use for fixing springs

tapping in two ⅝in (16mm) improved tacks, one at the centre of the front rail and the other at the centre of the back rail. Both tacks are situated on the upper edges of the rails and should not be driven completely home at this juncture.

Lay a length of laid cord over the springs from back to front, add about 12in (305mm) to 14in (355mm) working allowance, and cut it off. Tie a slip knot and loop it over the tack in the back rail. Pull it tight and hammer the tack down, then knot each spring as you work forward to the tack in the front rail, where you finish off with a double hitch and hammer the tack down. Use either of the knots

shown in Fig 7:11 for the springs; of the two, (B) is to be preferred because it is more secure. Do not press the springs down because the lashing is used to stop their moving sideways and not to compress them.

Repeat the complete procedure along the other rows of springs, and the final result should look like Fig 7:12. Note that the outer segments of the side springs are lashed down well to give a rounded effect. Finally, cut a piece of good quality hessian to size, lay it over the springs, and sew them to it in the same way as you sewed them to the webs.

Fig 7:12 How the seat should appear when springs are finally fixed

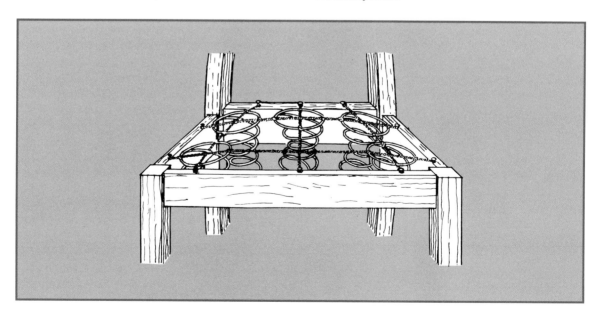

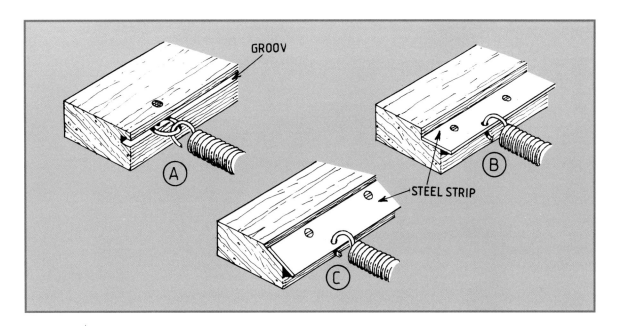

Fig 7:13 Fitting cable springs

FITTING CABLE SPRINGS

Fig 7:13 shows several ways of doing this. The illustrations are self-explanatory. The only points to note are that in (A) the rings through which the hooks are passed must be strong, otherwise the tension put upon the springs will pull them out of shape; and that the steel strips are normally supplied with the springs.

Seat springs are ½in (12mm) diameter and need a tension of 1in (25mm) in 1ft (305mm), while ⅜in (10mm) back springs need rather more, usually 1½in (38mm) to 2in (51mm). If the springs are not already covered with plastic sleeves, you can make a platform out of black canvas or any suitable material, as shown in Fig 7:14. It is simply a matter of sewing a sleeve on each side of the fabric to contain the outermost springs.

Don't be tempted to fix the hooks of the springs by means of clout nails or staples, because both methods can result in the marking or tearing of the cushions, and both look unprofessional.

FIXING SERPENTINE SPRINGS

These are easy to fix because no tensioning is needed, and the ends of each strip are simply pushed into clips nailed to opposite sides of the

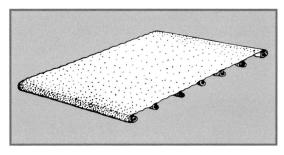

Fig 7:14 Fabric platform used on cable springs

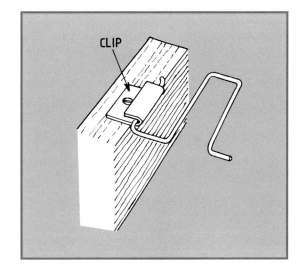

Fig 7:15 Fixing serpentine springs

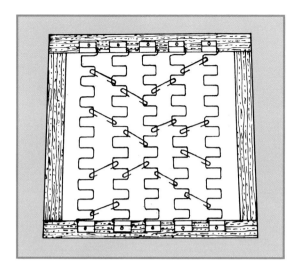

Fig 7:16 Positioning the links on serpentine springing

frame, Fig 7:15. The bent side of the clip needs to overhang the edge of the frame by about ⅛in (3mm). Usually four strips back to front are enough for an armchair seat (although a really large one could have five), and four strips for the back, running from top to bottom, using 12 gauge for the seat and 8½ or 9 gauge for the back.

Links are usually supplied with the springs and are positioned so that the whole thing becomes one assembly rather than individual springs. There are no hard-and-fast rules about where to put them, but Fig 7:16 shows an example.

Fig 7:17 (A) cutting a circular piece of foam to a template; (B) cutting a bevelled edge; (C) making a rounded edge; (D) making a 'bullnose' edge

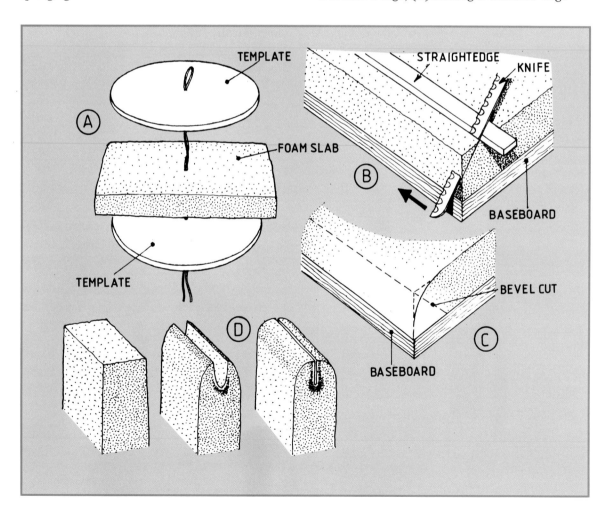

WORKING WITH PLASTIC FOAM

The first and most difficult job is to cut it. There are several ways of doing this. You could use scissors, a sharp, pointed cook's knife, or an electric carving knife. Cutting it with scissors often results in a ragged, uneven edge, because if the foam is 3in (75mm) or 4in (100mm) thick the only way to cut it is by compressing it. A cook's knife is better, but it must be sharp. Best of all is an electric carving knife, which makes the work a pleasure.

Cutting a circular piece involves making two identical circular templates from hardboard or thick cardboard, and sandwiching the foam between them. Secure the three components together with a piece of wire inserted through the centre as in Fig 7:17(A) and cut round the templates.

Fig 7:17(B) shows how to cut a bevelled edge. Place the foam exactly up to the edge of the bench, and use a straightedge as a guide. This type of cut is useful when you want to make a rounded surface as in (C), because after bevelling the edges you can glue and stick them down to the baseboard as shown.

Rounded bullnose edges are also easy to make; see (D). Simply apply adhesive to the edges, allow it to become tacky, then pinch the edges together.

The several ways of fixing cushions, either to each other or to a baseboard, are shown in Figs 7:18, 7:19 and 7:20. The simplest way to fix a cushion to a solid baseboard is to apply a 2in (51mm) wide band of adhesive all round the edges of both the foam and the base. Allow the adhesive to set (as recommended by the manufacturer), then press them together. You can also use wide adhesive tape; this can also hinge two pieces of foam together, or form a rounded edge. There are several proprietary adhesives on the market, two of the best known being Dunlop Thixofix, and Copydex.

There are a few points to remember when making cushions. Always cut the foam about ¼in (6mm) oversize all round because this will put the

Fig 7:18 The two pieces of foam are joined end to end by a strip of tape that acts as a hinge; another length of tape is stuck transversely across the top for strength

Fig 7:19 Here the rolled edge of the foam cushion is formed by attaching the tape to the top and pulling it down; the tape is then tacked to the baseboard

Fig 7:20 A simple and effective way to fix foam to a baseboard by means of tape and tacks

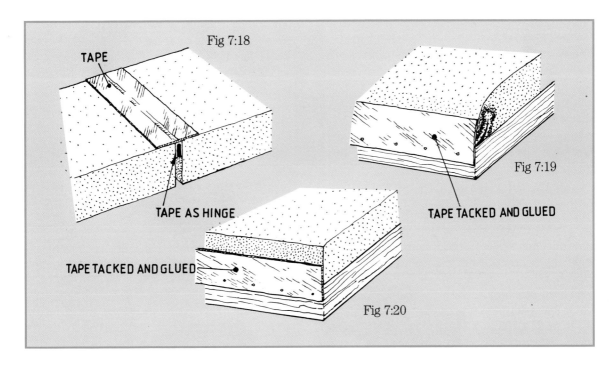

Fig 7:18

TAPE

TAPE AS HINGE

TAPE TACKED AND GLUED

Fig 7:19

TAPE TACKED AND GLUED

Fig 7:20

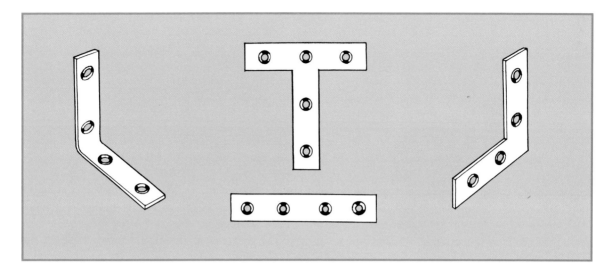

Fig 7:21 Chair repair plates

cushion under slight compression when it is inserted into the cover. The results will be slightly rounded surfaces that look attractive, and there is less likelihood of the cover's creeping out of shape.

Because of the tendency for the cover and the foam filling to move relatively to each other, it is best not to use piped seams on the cover because these will accentuate any irregularity. Also, heavy fabrics are not suitable for covering soft foam cushions because the outlines will be misshapen.

It may seem at first glance that modern methods of upholstery have been given undue prominence. The reason is that upholstered furniture, more than any other kind, can be brought up to date easily and be made as good as new. Auctions and sale rooms abound in armchairs and suites that simply need re-springing and re-covering to give them a new life.

REPAIRS AND RE-UPHOLSTERY

Because the frames of upholstered furniture are protected by the covers and the stuffing, it is very rare to come across one that cannot be repaired, especially as any repairs will almost certainly be hidden.

One of the best timbers for frame-making is birch, and many better-quality antique chairs were made of it. It has to be said, however, that some were constructed of totally unsuitable softwoods.

Today, birch of the necessary kind is so scarce and expensive that beech is widely used instead because it is closegrained, holds tacks well, and is easy to obtain.

Typical repairs involve the gluing and screwing on of wooden struts or corner blocks to strengthen the joints. Metal chair-repair plates can be bought for the same purpose; some are shown in Fig 7:21. A common problem is the wooden rail that has had so many tacks put into it over the years that its surface has become spongy and crumbly. If the job is one of pure restoration, which demands that no new wood should be introduced unless it is essential, you could treat the rail with Ronseal Wood Hardener. This will invisibly harden the surface. Otherwise it probably means splicing in a new piece of wood.

MAKING A NEW LOOSE SEAT

Loose seats have been in use since the late seventeenth century. If you need to make one, you can use any suitable hardwood such as beech, ash, oak, or sweet chestnut. Its construction is more carpentry than chair-making, because the corners are simply halved joints, glued and screwed together; see Fig 7:22(A).

Its size depends whether it fits into rebates cut in the seat rails (as is the case of most antique chairs), or on to braces fixed across the corners of the seat frame. Both methods are illustrated in Fig 7:22(B) and (C). Whichever pattern is needed, the outer edges have to be well bevelled off so that the top of the seat is level with the tops of the rails.

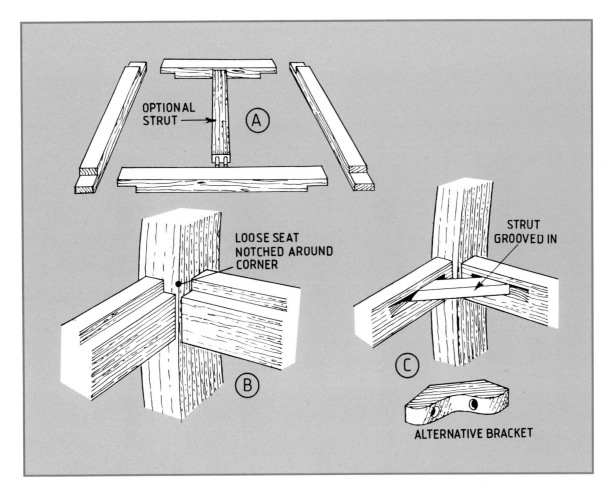

OPTIONAL
STRUT

Ⓐ

LOOSE SEAT
NOTCHED AROUND
CORNER

Ⓑ

STRUT
GROOVED IN

Ⓒ

ALTERNATIVE BRACKET

Fig 7:22 Stages in making a new loose seat

The loose seat itself, before being upholstered, should be about ⅛in (3mm) smaller all round than the frame to allow for the thickness of the cover. If you should make a mistake and the seat is too loose, you can always tack a double or treble thickness of webbing to the edges to pack them out.

STRIPPING OFF THE OLD COVER

This should always be done most carefully because it will be an invaluable guide when you have to calculate the yardage of the replacement cover and it forms a perfect template for cutting out a new one.

You will probably find pieces of lining fabric, hessian, or some similar material sewn to the cover. This is an acceptable practice in upholstery. Such pieces are called 'flys', and they are used to economise on an expensive cover in places where it is not seen.

Creases and faded areas on the old cover will help you to judge how to arrange the pattern on the new one. If the cover you have chosen has a large 'medallion' style of pattern which is centred, say, round a bunch of flowers, then this motif should appear in the centre of the back and of the seat. If the cover is striped, the stripes must be centred on the seat and back, and those on the arms must match each other.

Materials with a 'pile' finish, such as velvets and moquettes, require special consideration because the direction of the pile must be the same on the seat, the back, and the arms. If the pile on one piece is opposed to that on another, they will appear a different shade. It is a good idea, therefore, to use tailor's chalk to mark arrows on the back of the cover to indicate the direction of the pile.

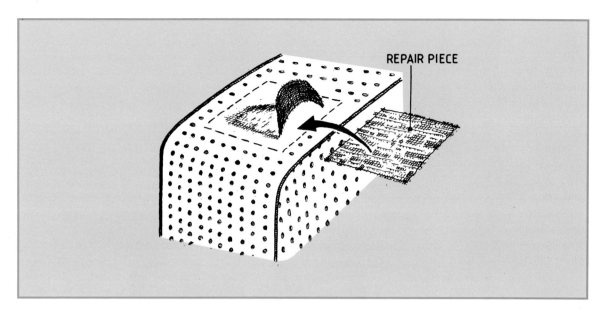

Fig 7:23 How to repair a tear in a cover

Fig 7:24 How to make neat corners on stuffover seats

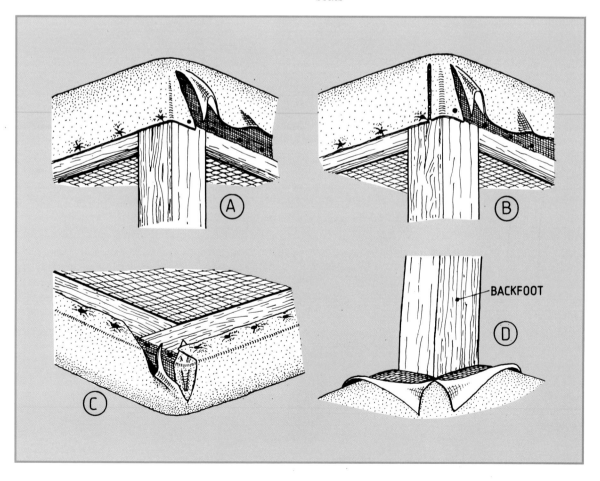

REPAIRING A TEAR IN THE COVER (Fig 7:23)

This should be repaired as soon as possible otherwise the fabric round it will stretch and become misshapen. You will need a base on to which you can stick the torn part of the cover. This can be a piece of canvas, calico, or even an offcut of covering material, as long as its colour does not show through.

Whatever material you employ, cut a patch about an inch (25mm) larger all round than the area of the tear, and coat one side of it and the underside of the tear with a thin layer of upholstery adhesive. Push it carefully through the tear, adhesive-side uppermost, and arrange it with your fingers until it is flat and taut; then hold it in place with a few skewers. Allow the adhesive to get tacky, then gently press the flap of the tear on to the patch, and allow the job to dry.

TREATMENT OF CORNERS

The main aim when dealing with corners is to make sure that the upper ends of the pleat or pleats are kept below the top surface, otherwise the corner will look amateurish and unsightly. Fig 7:24(A) shows a single pleat used on a square corner; (B) a double pleat on a rounded corner; (C) how the corner of a loose seat is finished; and (D) how the cover is cut at the corner round a backfoot.

TYPES OF STITCHES

The illustrations in Fig 7:25 show the various types commonly used in upholstery work. The descriptions are as follows.

Bridle ties are long loops of twine sewn into hessian so that handfuls of hair or similar stuffing

Fig 7:25 Types of stitches

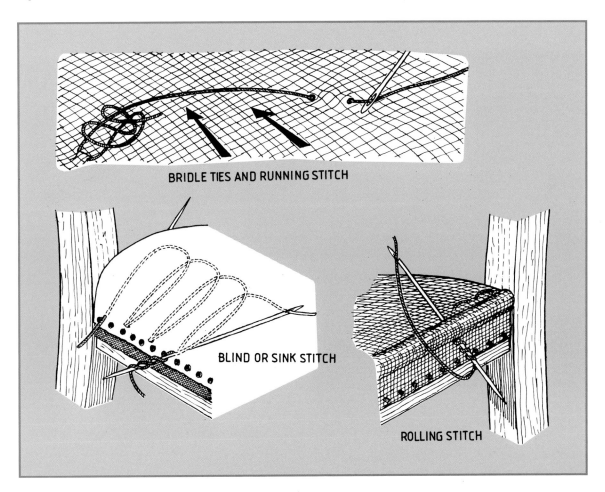

BRIDLE TIES AND RUNNING STITCH

BLIND OR SINK STITCH

ROLLING STITCH

can be pushed under them. As a guide, each loop should be just large enough for your fingers to slide beneath it. Begin by threading a mattress needle with twine and making a slip knot at any one corner of the frame, at least 3in (76mm) away from both edges. Continue all round the seat at the same distance away from the edges with a 'running through' stitch, which has the large loop above, and a small stitch below. When you arrive back at the slip knot, the twine can simply be tied off.

'Blind' or 'sink' stitching is used to stiffen the edges of the upholstery after the bridle ties have been made and covered with scrim. Thread a mattress needle with twine and start the first row of stitching as near to the seat frame as possible. Knot the twine to the scrim and, holding the needle with the threaded eye at the bottom, push it up and through the scrim. Try to hold the needle at such an angle that it emerges between 2in (51mm), and 3in (76mm) away from the edge.

Pull the needle through until the eye reaches the scrim (do not let the whole needle emerge), then swing it sideways to scoop in as much filling as possible. Continue by pushing the needle downwards so that it emerges about an inch (25mm) or so from the original point of entry. To complete the stitch, loop the twine three or four times round the needle so that when it is pushed in for the next stitch the loops will form twisted turns and prevent the stitch from loosening. The first

row of stitches is carried round the edge of the seat frame, followed by a second row (and possibly a third) higher up, until the edge is firm and well shaped, using the regulator to push the stuffing well forward. You will need only two rows of stitching between the backfeet of the chair and three rows on the other three sides of the seat to make a neat, firm edge.

The rolling stitching is put in when you have completed the blind stitching described above. Its purpose is to make a well-defined hard edge to the front and sides of a chair seat. In the case of a stool, it is carried right round. It follows that the roll should be as neat and even as possible, so it is a good plan to mark a line with tailor's chalk about 1½in (38mm) in from the edge round the top, and another one the same distance down round the sides.

Thread the needle and hold it in the same way as you did for blind stitching. Insert the needle about 1¼in (32mm) away from the backfoot and on the chalked line at the side, and push it upwards at an angle of 45° until it emerges through the chalked line on the top. Push the needle in again about 1in (25mm) back towards the backfoot so that it comes out on the chalk line at the side. Tie a slip knot in the thread and pull it tight. Take the needle forward again along the top line about 1in (25mm) and push it down. When it emerges, make three turns round it with the twine and push it up again. Repeat the process all round, making the stitches about 1in (25mm) long, and tying the final stitch off in a knot.

Fig 7:26 Making piping

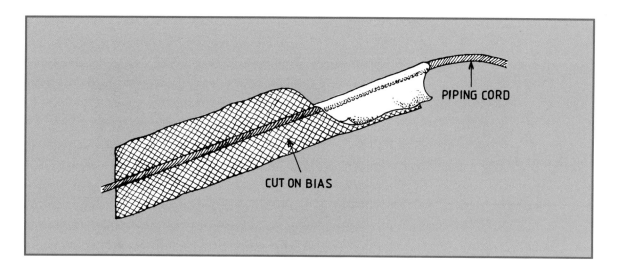

PIPING CORD

CUT ON BIAS

MAKING PIPING CORD

Piping is made from strips of cover about 1¼in (6mm) wide which are cut on the bias as shown in Fig 7:26. The strips are folded in half lengthwise with piping cord inserted in the fold and sewn in. The finished piping is then sewn into the seams on the cover. Before you decide to use piping, remember that it uses a lot of material, so save all offcuts and join them together if necessary.

REPLACING BUTTONS

If only one or two buttons are missing you will probably have to renew them all, because although buttons are available in many colours it is unlikely that you will be able to get ones to match precisely.

To stitch a button in place, you will need a mattress needle and a length of twine. How much you will need depends on the thickness of the upholstery, but three times the thickness is a good working rule. Thread one end through the eye of the needle, leaving a loose end about 3in (76mm) long; then push the needle right through and out at the back. Return it through to the front about ¼in (6mm) from the original hole and unthread it. Pull the two ends of the twine tightly and cut them both to the same length, about 6in (150mm). Thread the button on to one of the ends and tie a slip-knot, Fig 7:27, pulling it very tight, then secure it with a half-hitch knot. Cut both ends off to about 1in (25mm) long, wind them round the shank of the button, and push them into the cover.

RE-UPHOLSTERING VARIOUS SEATS

LOOSE SEAT

Lay the frame on the bench with the underside uppermost and its front edge farthest from you.

Tack on the front to back webs, doubling the ends over at the front and fixing them with five tacks. Strain each web and tack it down at the back with three tacks, leaving about a 2in (50mm) long loose end which will eventually be tacked down over the hessian cover. Use ⅝in (16mm) improved tacks for all the webbing.

Now turn the frame through 90° and fix the side-to-side webs in just the same way, leaving one end of each web loose. You should now have a frame looking like Fig 7:28

Next, tack on the hessian with ⅜in (10mm) or ½in (12mm) improved tacks. Start with one tack in the centre of the front rail, stretch the hessian taut and tack it down at the centre of the back rail with another tack. Go back to the front rail and turn the edge of the hessian over by about ¾in (19mm) and tack it down from the centre outwards, tacking each side alternately. Next, turn the edge of the hessian over at the back and tack this down similarly, with the loose ends of the webs laid over the hessian and tacked down; see Fig 7:29. Space all tacks at about 1¾in (45mm) centres and try to keep the weave of the hessian parallel to the seat frame.

Fig 7:27 Fixing a button

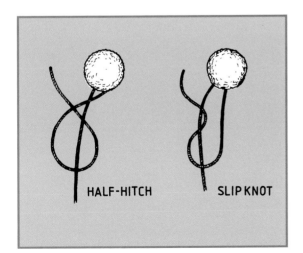

Fig 7:28 Webbing a loose seat

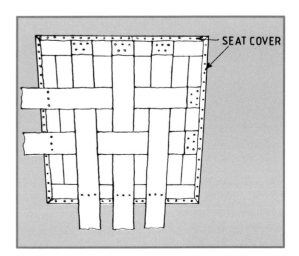

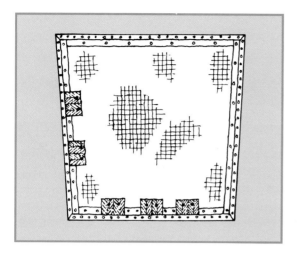

Fig 7:29 Tacking on the hessian

Make a series of bridle ties with twine threaded through a spring needle, about 3in (76mm) in from the edges all round, and push handfuls of stuffing (hair or fibre) under each loop. Repeat the operation with another set of bridle ties about 3in (76mm) inwards from the first and push stuffing under these loops as well. Keep all the stuffing on the top of the seat and don't let it fall down at the edges, or the finished seat will be too big for the frame. Aim at giving the stuffing a nicely rounded, flat-domed shape with no lumpy patches.

The next step is to cover the seat with calico. Measure across the seat with a flexible tape, from front to back and side to side, allowing for the calico to turn over the bottom edge about 1in (25mm) so that it can be tacked off on the underside of the frame. Lay the calico on the seat, arranging the overhang equally all round, and temporarily hold it in place with part-driven tacks in the edges – they are removed later. Start with a tack at the centre of each edge and work outwards along each edge at about 3in (75mm) intervals, smoothing the calico as you go. It should not be under tension, but just taut enough not to ruck up under the final cover. When you are satisfied, take out the temporary tacks from each side in rotation, and turn the calico over the edge, tacking it down on the underside. The corners should be dealt with as already described.

Finally, fit and tack down the upholstery cover in exactly the same way as the calico. Bear in mind the various requirements for arranging the pattern/pile already mentioned, and don't forget that if you are re-upholstering a set of chairs and not just one, the patterns must match on all of them. A piece of black canvas tacked to the underside of the frame hides the 'works' and gives a neat finish.

PINCUSHION SEAT

This is an upholstered seat where all the work is done on the frame of the chair itself because there is no loose seat. An example is shown in Fig 7:30. The procedure is the same as for a loose seat, but use fine tacks throughout because there is usually only a narrow margin round the frame into which you can put them, and too many large tacks will split the wood. The outer raw edges of the calico and the cover have to be turned under before being tacked down. This kind of upholstery needs gimp to be fastened all round to hide the tack heads, or use a banding with simulated leather.

Fig 7:30 A 'pincushion' seat

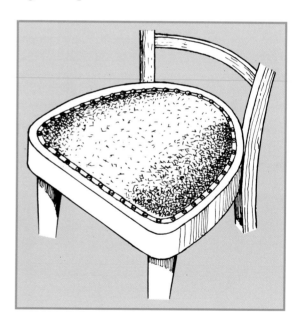

SPRUNG SEATS

The method of making these is virtually the same for both dining chairs and easy chairs, and most of the techniques involved have already been described.

Start by webbing up and stitching on the

springs, then lash them to each other and to the frame. Next, put on the hessian .cover and sew each spring to it; then make the bridle ties and fill them with the stuffing. Cover the whole assembly with hessian or scrim, tacked in place.

You are now ready to sew in the first stuffing. The stitches are made with a long needle threaded with twine. They have to be positioned between the springs so that the twine will not become entangled in the coils. Tie the first stitch with a slip-knot and, working from the top, stitch round the seat until you achieve the result shown in Fig 7:31

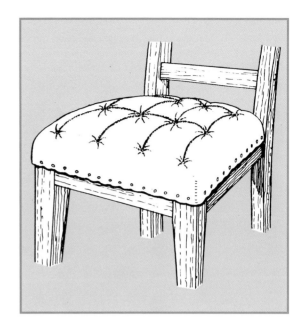

Fig 7:31 Stages in upholstering a sprung seat

Fig 7:32 Cutaway drawing of a stuffover easy chair

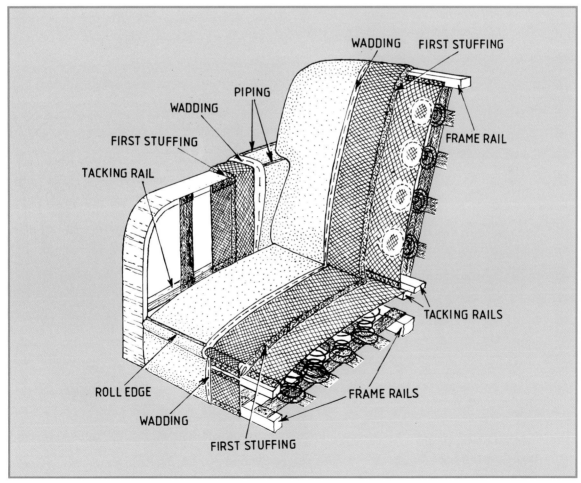

Continue with blind stitching, followed by rolling stitching, both of which have already been described, and you will be ready for the second stuffing. This is needed because all the stitching will have tended to make the surface flat instead of the nicely rounded dome shape it should be. To bring this about you will have to stitch some more bridle ties into the central area and introduce as fine a stuffing as you can under the loops, arranging it carefully to avoid lumpiness.

Covering the seat with calico is the next step, and this is simply fixed with tacks. Continue by covering it with a layer of wadding over which you can cut, fit, and tack the final upholstery cover. If necessary, use gimp to cover the heads of the tacks.

Fig 7:32 shows a cutaway view of the method applied to an easy chair.

SERPENTINE SPRINGING

Although this is most frequently used as a base for loose cushions, if you are using it on a seat, it should be regarded as a substitute for coil springs. Cover it with hessian and proceed as above.

8 Repairing mouldings and beadings

Doubtless you have often admired the sure and confident way in which the old-time craftsmen designed, made, and applied mouldings and beadings to their furniture, particularly the designs made in the eighteenth and early nineteenth centuries. Their methods were not based on what looked right or appeared pretty, but on definite and geometrically calculated proportions and shapes derived from the classical orders of architecture – Tuscan, Doric, Ionic, Corinthian, and Composite.

In his book *The Gentleman and Cabinet Maker's Director* (3rd edition, 1762), Thomas Chippendale shows drawings of these orders, plus the mouldings that derive from them with full

Fig 8:1 **Roman-style designs of moulding sections**

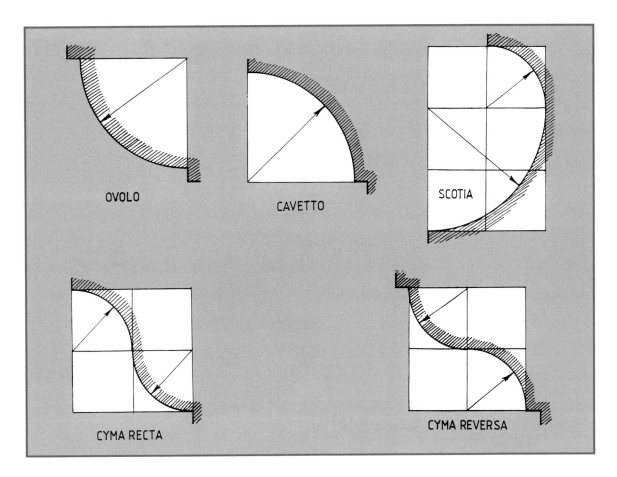

OVOLO

CAVETTO

SCOTIA

CYMA RECTA

CYMA REVERSA

details of how to calculate the sizes and shapes of the various members and profiles. It is impossible to describe them all here because there is a large number scattered throughout his book, but the following is a survey of the principal designs most commonly met with today as well as in antiquity. A reprint of the book is available from Constable & Co Ltd, 10 Orange Street, London.

MOULDING DESIGNS

The five principal designs are the ovolo, the scotia, the cavetto, and the two recta and reversa cymas, also called 'ogees'. Each of the designs can be plotted in either the Roman style, which is based on squares, or the Grecian, which is based on ellipses. Fig 8:1 shows the Roman patterns, and the drawings are self-explanatory. Fig 8:2 shows the corresponding Grecian patterns, which need some explanation.

The cavetto (design A) is contained in a rectangle ABCD, and both the longer and shorter sides are divided into four parts respectively, although you can use any convenient number of divisions. The base line AD is extended to E so that AD and DE are equal, and reference lines are drawn from E through each of the points of division on CD. Similarly, reference lines are drawn from A to the points on BC. Where the reference lines intersect gives you a series of plotting points which you can join up to create the profile. The scotia (design B) and the two cymas (C and D) are all plotted in a similar fashion.

There are several additional mouldings that are not, strictly speaking, of classical origin but which nevertheless are widely used. These are shown in

Fig 8:2 Grecian-style designs of moulding sections

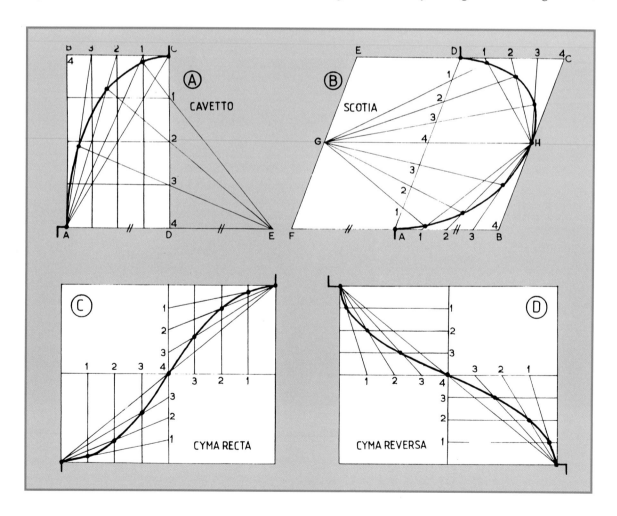

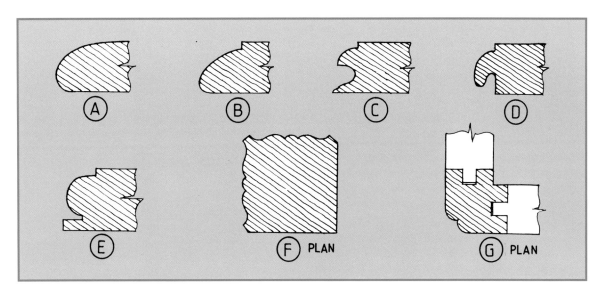

Fig 8:3 Sections of some commonly used
mouldings

Fig 8:3. (A) is a bullnose, (B) a thumb, (C) a bird's
beak, (D) a 'treacle', and (E) a torus moulding. The
toad's back moulding (F) was sometimes used on
chair legs, and the staff bead moulding (G) can be
worked on the vertical edge where two pieces
meet at right angles. This was favoured for
finishing the corners of plinths or bracket feet
because its design helped to disguise any faults in
the joints.

Mouldings can be subdivided into three groups:
(A) stuck, also called 'struck', mouldings that are
worked on the edge of a solid piece or a panel;
(B) bolection mouldings, which are moulded
separately and rebated on to the job – they are
more likely to be met with in carpentry than
cabinet-making; and (C) the composite patterns in
which the mouldings are built up by gluing
together small mouldings to make larger ones, or
where there are moulded facings backed by pieces
of softwood. All three groups are shown in Fig 8:4.

If you are restoring an antique piece, you may be
interested in the illustrations of designs of
mouldings used in the different furniture periods
which are included in Chapter 13.

BEADS (BEADINGS)

In classical terms a bead is a small semicircular
moulding worked on the solid, and is also known as
an 'astragal', Fig 8:5(A). Variations include the
bead and flush (B) and the bead and quirk (C).
Also illustrated are some standard commercial
patterns, such as the quadrant (D); the half round
(E); the cushion corner (F); the half astragal (G);
and the hockey stick (H).

The cocked bead (I) is a small bead which can

Fig 8:4 Types of mouldings

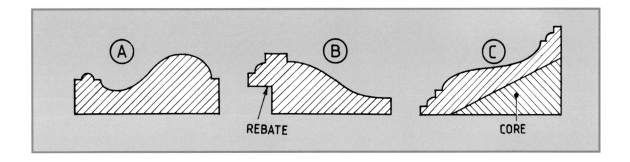

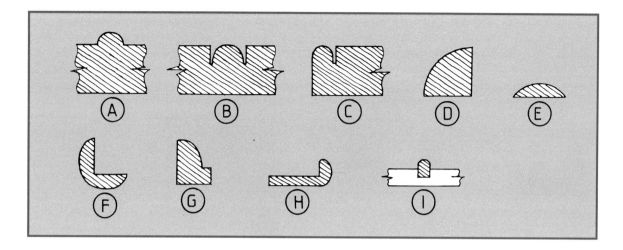

Fig 8:5 Sections of typical beadings

either be grooved into a panel or pinned and glued round, for example, a drawer front. It was widely used in the old days, and is still very popular.

MAKING MOULDINGS AND BEADINGS

The industrial method is to shape them on a spindle moulder or a four- or six-cutter machine, but this is for large-scale production and does not concern us.

A portable router mounted upside down in one of the proprietary router tables (or one you have made for yourself as mentioned in Chapter 2) is very handy for short runs of mouldings that do not exceed ¾in (19mm) in thickness, but anything larger than this would tend to be too much for it to cope with. This leaves the alternatives of employing moulding planes, or scratch stocks.

If you intend to use a moulding plane, you are well catered for, because they are still made today. Probably the best one is the metal multi-plane, which is supplied with a kit of various cutters that will enable you to make not only mouldings but grooves and rebates as well. The old-time crafts-man would have used wooden moulding planes, a different one for each shape (there were eighteen hollows and rounds in a set). Such planes often turn up at auction sales and are worth buying. Remember that there are two distinct patterns – the French, which is held upright while working; and the English, which is held at an angle indicated by a line marked on the front end of the plane.

Before using one of the wooden planes you should bevel the edge to be moulded at the angle referred to above for an English plane, although a bevel to suit the moulding profile when using a French plane will also be helpful. As a result, the planes will run better and there will be much less waste to remove. Fig 8:6 shows how to use the

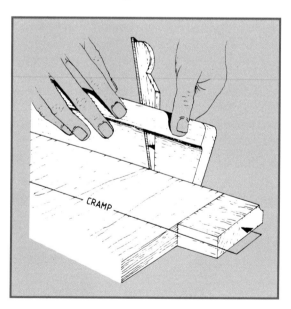

Fig 8:6 Here, a moulding plane is being used across the grain and a small block of scrapwood is cramped to the workpiece to prevent the grain from splitting

Fig 8:7 Stages in building up a composite moulding

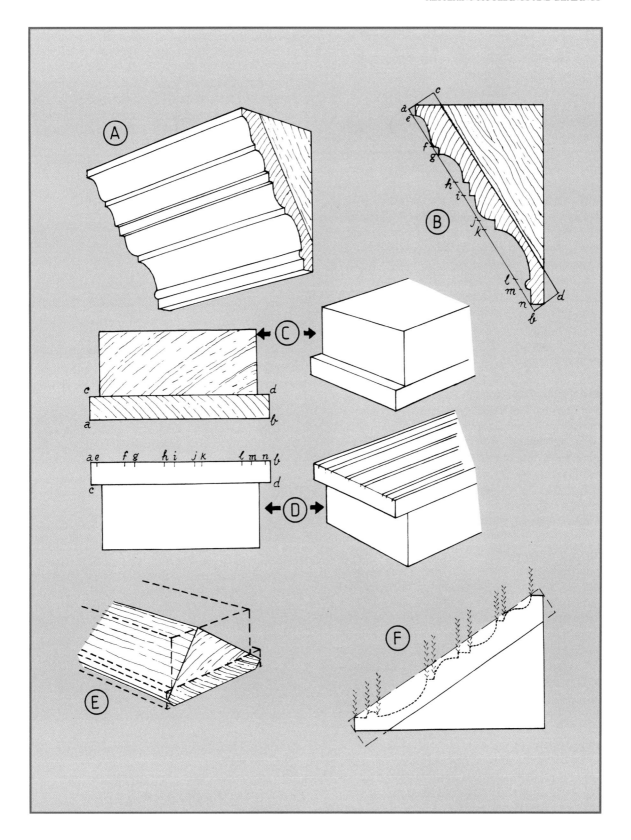

plane and how to cramp on a waste block to prevent splintering. Note that the plane is entered inwards from each end when working end grain, again to avoid splintering.

The scratch stock (see Chapter 2) can also be used to work mouldings, but it is best confined to hardwoods with a close grain and crisp texture. Good examples are birch, mahogany, and walnut. Timbers with an open, ribbed grain such as softwoods generally, and elm or oak, are best moulded with the plane.

COMPOSITE MOULDINGS (CORNICE OR BACKED-UP)

Heavy cornice mouldings must have been laborious to work by hand, because each 'member' (that is, each separate section of the shape) would have had to be planed before moving on to the next. Fig 8:7 illustrates the procedure as follows:

(A) The finished moulding in perspective.

(B) The moulding in profile with the reference lines from the various members projected and lettered. It would undoubtedly be a great help to make a template of the finished profile out of cardboard before starting the actual shaping.

(C) The mahogany facing is glued to the softwood backing.

(D) The reference lines are marked or gauged on to the facing.

(E) The backing piece sawn and planed to shape.

(F) The facing is rebated to correspond with the reference lines. The actual shapes are planed with the appropriate hollow and round moulding planes.

A built-up moulding with a softwood backing is illustrated in Fig 8:8 and should be self-explanatory.

Some cornice mouldings used a series of applied Gothic arches, or an applied dentil as a design motif. Making these is straightforward though arduous. The difficulty arises when gluing on the applied decoration and subsequently cleaning up and polishing it. If you brush the glue on to the back, there is bound to be quite a lot of glue exuding, and you will have to scrape it away – a thankless and laborious task.

The old-timers were nothing if not ingenious. Their method was first to polish the fascia, then lay the applied decoration on to it and mark round it. The decoration was then lifted off and the polish

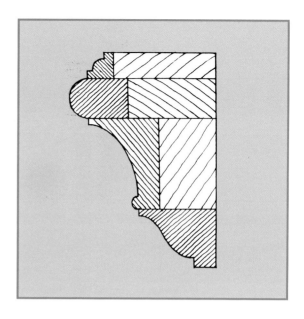

Fig 8:8 A typical built-up moulding with a softwood backing

scraped away from the area inside the marked outline. Next, they warmed a long, flat strip of metal and brushed a coating of glue on to it. The warm metal prevented the glue from chilling, which would have made it useless. Then the back of the decoration was laid on the glue and drawn backwards and off the metal so that it was covered with a thin, even coating of glue that was ideal for the job and did not need cleaning up.

PLOTTING AND CUTTING MITRED JOINTS ON CORNICES AND PEDIMENTS

Almost all cornices comprise a front piece and a return piece at each end, with a mitre joint at each corner. In all probability, the cornice moulding will be too big for you to hold in a mitre box while sawing, so the arrangement shown in Fig 8:9(A) can be adopted.

Here, a board is cramped in the bench vice with enough of its width standing up beyond the bench top for you to use a thumb cramp to hold the moulding while you saw the mitre. If you can get the moulding in the mitre box, make sure you hold it in the position shown at (B). This also applies if you use the bench vice method. If the moulding is held as at (C) your mitres will not meet.

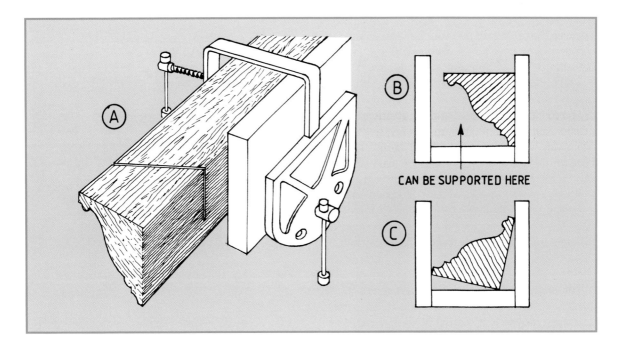

Fig 8:9 Mitring a cornice moulding

MITRING ARCHITECTURAL PEDIMENTS
These are often used on bookcases, cabinets, and clocks, and are basically similar in style to cornice mouldings. The front pieces, however, are 'raked' (that is, sloped at an angle to the horizontal), with

a return piece at each end. Fig 8:10(A) illustrates a typical arrangement.

You can find the angle at which to cut the mitre at the apex by bisecting the angle between the two

Fig 8:10 Mitring an architectural pediment moulding

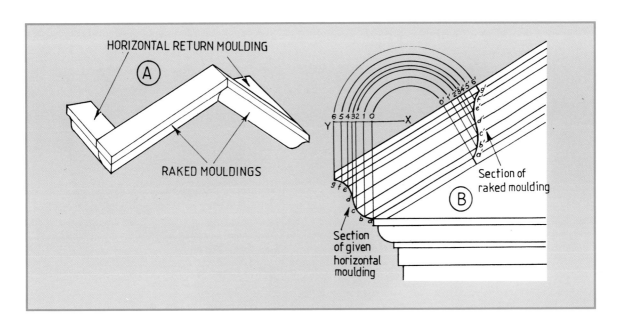

front pieces. But a difficulty arises at the corners because the profiles of the front mouldings and the return pieces have to be different if they are to coincide perfectly. The way to plot them is shown in Fig 8:10(B) but you will have to draw a full-size diagram to suit your own moulding.

The next thing you will need is an accurate profile of the raked moulding, and the easiest way to do this is to use a moulding profile gauge; see Chapter 1. This consists of many leaves (usually about 180) held in a clamp under slight tension so that when pressed against a moulding they take up a reversed configuration of its profile. If you don't possess one, try improvising with several packs of playing cards bound together with elastic bands. Athough not so easy to use, this does give quite good results.

Transfer the profile to the position shown, then mark several reference points along it. The more you use, the easier it will be to plot the curves. From each reference point extend verticals to the edge and mark them 0, 1, 2, 3, etc. From the same reference points, draw lines parallel to the edges of the raked moulding.

The point X can be at any convenient distance from (O), depending on the size of the moulding. From X, draw a horizontal line to the left. Now,

Fig 8:12 Typical damage to the corner of a solid table top

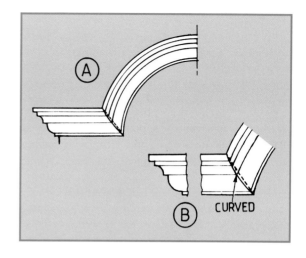

Fig 8:11 Mitring curved mouldings

with X as the centre for your compasses, draw a series of arcs from 0, 1, 2, 3, etc, so that they intersect the horizontal line at 0', 1', 2', 3', etc. Drop vertical lines from them. Their intersections with the parallel lines will give you plotting points from which you can draw the required profile freehand.

MITRED CURVED MOULDINGS

When a straight piece of moulding meets a curved piece and both have the same profile you can

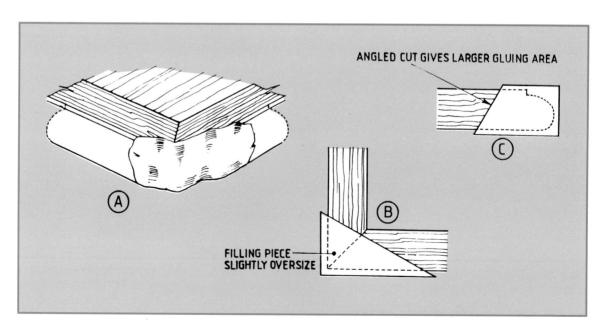

either alter the profile of one, which involves virtually remaking it, or use a curved mitre, which is far easier.

Fig 8:11 shows how the curved mitre is plotted. The first step is to draw the straight moulding full size, inserting as many reference points as may be convenient. Next draw the curved moulding, marking in the reference points to be identical with those on the straight moulding. The easiest way to do this is to lay a paper strip across the straight moulding and mark off the reference points on it. Then position it radially across the curve and transfer the reference points. These will enable you to draw in the curved lines. Where these intersect with the lines on the straight moulding will give you a series of points that can be joined up freehand to form the curve.

REPAIRING STUCK AND APPLIED MOULDINGS

As stuck mouldings are worked in the solid, the most common damage occurs on table tops where corners may be damaged and edges bruised.

Fig 8:12 shows typical damage to the corner of the solid top of a table, and because a repair piece will obviously be necessary, it should be chosen to

match as closely as possible. It should also be slightly oversize in all its dimensions, including the thickness: see Fig 8:12(B). You will need to plane off the damage and expose a smooth, fresh surface. If you can, plane the edge to an angle as at (C) because this will give a larger area for gluing.

Because the edges of both the top and the repair piece are angled, it may be difficult to cramp them together without the glued edges misaligning by sliding against each other. You can get over this by nailing two lengths of batten at right angles to each other, and using them as a cramping corner. You will also need to introduce a packing piece of cardboard or something similar under the top but remember to interpose a thin plastic sheet to prevent the packing from sticking to the work.

If you want a stronger job, the method illustrated in Fig 8:13 should be satisfactory. Cut away the damaged area as shown at (A), noting that on the longer edge the cut is made at a slanting angle of about 45° so that the gluing area is increased. Choose your repair piece to match as closely as possible, and shape it to fit, bearing in mind that it should be slightly oversize – say ³⁄₁₆in (5mm) on the edges and ⅛in (3mm) on the thickness. Next, drill a hole in the repair piece and glue in a short length of dowel. When the glue is dry, hold the repair piece against the work and mark a cross to indicate where the centre of the dowel touches it. Instead of using this mark as the

Fig 8:13 Making a strong job of the repair

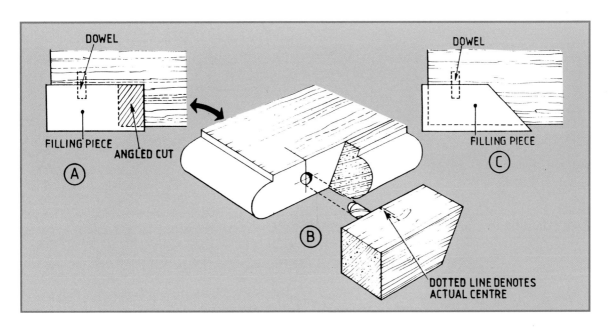

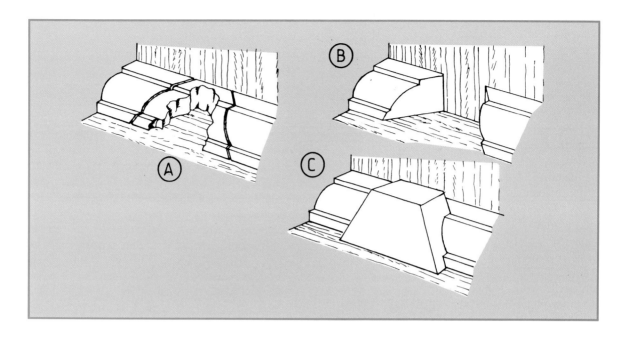

Fig 8:14 Repairing a damaged moulding   Fig 8:15 Repairing a crossgrained moulding

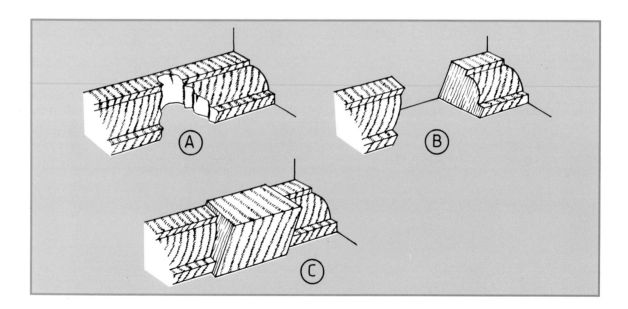

centre for the dowel, mark another centre about ⅓₂in (1mm) away from it, as in (B), and drill the actual hole there. This will have the effect of pulling the slanted faces tightly against each other. When the glue has been applied and allowed to set, the repair piece can be shaped and cleaned up.

There is a variation, shown at (C), which can be used if the edge is plain and square, and here the slanted angle is cut into the face and not the edge. This may be more effective should the damaged area extend more on to the face than the edge.

Damage can occur anywhere along the length of the edge and need not necessarily be confined to corners. Fig 8:14 illustrates the sequence of operations to deal with it. At (A), sawcuts have been made at either side of the damaged area, and the waste is chopped away to achieve the result shown at (B). The important point to note is that the sawcuts are again made at a slanting angle so that the repair piece (which is made oversize) is wedge-shaped as at (C). When it has been glued in and the glue has set, it can be trimmed and shaped to match the remainder of the moulding.

Usually, most damage to applied mouldings can be remedied by the same methods as are used for stuck mouldings. Differences arise when a length breaks off and needs re-fixing.

The golden rule when a moulding breaks is to replace the pieces and mend the break as soon as possible, otherwise pieces will be lost and the area will become dirty. In any case, the prerequisite to any repair work is to remove all accumulations of dirt, wax, etc, and to scrape or wipe away all traces of old glue – the latter by means of a cloth wrung out in hot water. You will often find that C-cramps cut from old upholstery springs can be linked together to form a very effective cramping device.

CROSSGRAINED MOULDINGS

These can either be worked in the solid as stuck mouldings, or as an applied moulding which is rebated into a solid groundwork and butted against a veneer.

Fig 8:15 shows an example of a crossgrained stuck moulding where the grain runs diagonally. This emphasises the point that the sawcuts must be slanting, as at (A) and (B), so that when the repair piece has been glued in and shaped, its grain direction matches the remainder (C).

A similar repairing method can be used when making good the damage to a crossgrained moulding. If the veneer has also been damaged, it will have to be patched (see Chapter 9) and laid over the affected part of the moulding.

Fig 8:16 Dealing with cocked beads

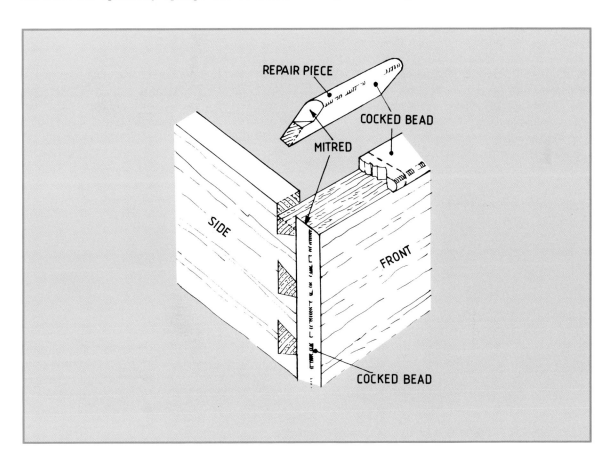

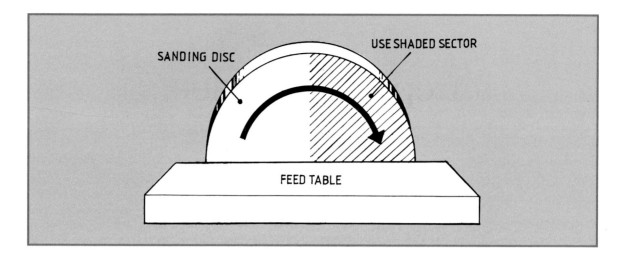

SANDING DISC

USE SHADED SECTOR

FEED TABLE

Fig 8:17 A cardboard facing has been temporarily fastened to the sanding disc to show the direction of rotation. Any work being sanded needs to be held against the shaded portion

REPAIRING COCKED BEADS

Where a cocked beading has simply been fixed into a groove or rebate and part of it has been damaged, the method of repair is obvious and simple. Cut away the faulty section (watch for hidden fixing pins), clean up the rebate, and glue and pin the replacement moulding.

In the case of some drawer fronts, however, the cocked beading is made to cover the full thickness of the drawer front along the top edge but is laid into a rebate on the other three edges (the two ends and the bottom), as shown in Fig 8:16. Note that the end of the upper beading has to be specially shaped, because the back is square while the front part is mitred. Because the pieces are small, it's best to use a chisel to make the cuts. The sizes are gauged from the job. Glue and pin on the new beading, and anchor it with two or three veneer pins.

TRIMMING MITRES

Fig 8:17 shows a method of trimming the ends of mitres, once they have been sawn in a mitre box, so that a hairline joint which is almost invisible can be achieved. You will need to make up a simple jig so that the mitred end can be held at exactly 45° against the face of a disc sander. The important point is that the mitred end should only be held against the one sector of the sanding disc that tends to pull it downwards as it rotates.

9 Repairs to veneers and bandings

Veneering has a long history and was used by the Ancient Egyptians, Greeks, and Romans. It disappeared (like many other arts and crafts) during the Dark Ages but had its own renaissance in Europe during the sixteenth century, and finally arrived in England in the seventeenth.

It must not be thought of as a cheap substitute for solid timber or as a means of covering slipshod work. Many timbers are unstable when used in the solid and can only be employed in the form of a veneer (burr veneers are a good example). Far from making a piece of furniture cheaper, it is more likely to add to the cost because it is not a cheap process. And in these days of conservation of trees, it is the most efficient and economic way to use them. Certainly it has been used to hide shoddy workmanship, but this is as much an abuse of a craft as hammering in nails where screws ought to be employed.

HISTORICAL METHODS OF PRODUCING VENEERS

If you are engaged in restoring antique furniture, you should know a brief history of how veneers were made at different periods, because their thicknesses are often crucial in dating a piece.

Veneering (and marquetry) were introduced into England from the Continent of Europe from 1660 onwards, when it was called 'faneering'. At that time, and until about 1820, all veneers were sawn by hand and, as a result, were much thicker than present-day ones because six or eight leaves were the most that could be sawn by hand from one inch (25mm).

In 1811, a circular saw for cutting veneers commercially was invented by John Barton, but it was several years before its use became widespread. Spear & Jackson exhibited a giant circular saw at the 1851 Great Exhibition and this, like Barton's saw, produced veneers from ⅟₃₂in (1mm) to ⅟₁₆in (2mm) thick, depending on the kind of timber. Veneers of the modern thickness of about 0.5mm were first introduced about 1900 onwards, and were created by the new processes of knife or rotary cutting.

TYPES OF VENEERS

Saw-cut veneers were originally produced as shown in Fig 9:1, and later by means of the circular saws described above. If you are continually restoring antique furniture, you will certainly know how often a small repair piece of saw-cut veneer is needed, particularly for bandings of one sort or another, and such veneers are no longer commercially obtainable.

It's usually possible to saw small pieces by hand

Fig 9:1 How saw-cut veneers were originally produced (from a drawing in *Le Menuisier Ébéniste*, by J. A. Roubo)

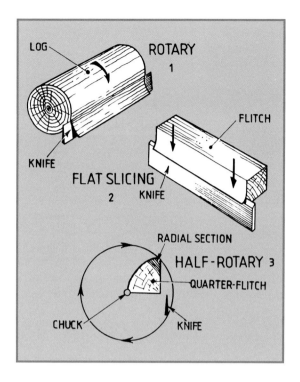

Fig 9:2 Three types of commercially produced veneers

with the fine-toothed tenon saw, but larger ones will need to be sawn on the circular-saw table. You will have to use a saw blade with the finest teeth. The best blade for the work is the 'planer' blade, which is sometimes called a 'novelty' saw. The fact that it is hollow-ground means that you can achieve finer and more accurate cuts than with other blades.

The three other types of veneers produced commercially are (1) rotary-cut; (2) knife-cut or flat-sliced; and (3) half-round. Fig 9:2 is a diagrammatic representation of the different methods.

Rotary-cut veneers are normally made from second-class timbers and are used mainly in the production of plywood. But there are two veneers – bird's-eye maple and birch – which are also cut by this method because it is best suited to their nature. As the diagram shows, the flitch (which has been softened by steam treatment) is mounted in a kind of huge lathe and rotated so that the knife peels off the veneer.

Knife-cutting is employed for producing decorative veneers. The log, or 'flitch', has a slice sawn off one side by a giant bandsaw, and this makes a base for the flitch to lie on. Again, it is steam-treated to soften it, and the knife traverses across it to shear off the leaves of the veneer.

Half-rounding is the best method to use for converting highly figured woods and burrs into veneers. The flitch is bolted to the stay log, which moves radially against the knife to produce the leaf.

The three special grain 'figures' are the burr, the curl, and the fiddleback, and Fig 9:3 shows how they result from different physical characteristics of the tree. Burrs are a small malformation of the tree and usually occur at its base, or where some damage has radically affected its growth, as in pollarding. They consist of a tightly packed mass of buds that have not developed because of lack of nourishment.

Curl figure comes from a crotch in the tree, either where the main trunk divides, or where a major limb branches out. Fiddleback figure is found in the African pseudo-mahoganies and sycamore, and results from cutting through layers of undulating grain.

Oyster shells are thin slices cut obliquely across branches of such trees as laburnum, walnut, olive, kingwood, yew, etc, and, as a result, are oval in shape. They were sometimes used in Queen Anne furniture when they were laid side by side with straight joints between them.

The veneer suppliers World of Wood, (address in List of Suppliers), quote the following sizes for different types:

Quartercut veneers Lengths up to 7ft or 8ft (2.13m or 2.44m) by an average of 8in (203mm) wide. Typical woods are sapele, African walnut, and afrormosia.

Crown-cut (flat-cut) veneers Lengths from 6ft to 8ft (1.82m to 2.44m); widths vary according to species from 9in to 20in (228mm to 508mm).

Centre bundles, which are half-width and cut from each side of the heart, are the same lengths but from only 5in to 8in (127mm to 203mm) wide.

Curl veneers From 12in to 36in (305mm to 915mm) long by 8in to 18in (203mm to 457mm) wide. Average size 24in by 12in (610mm by 305mm); most curl veneers are tapered.

Fancy butts are short ends which are, in a sense,

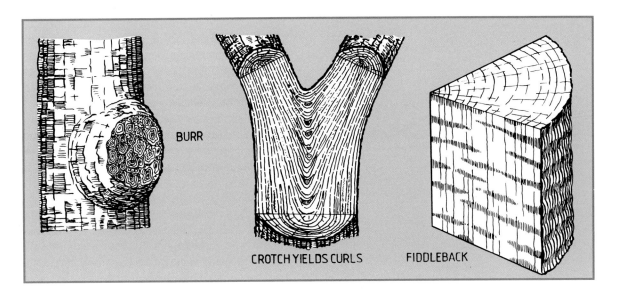

BURR

CROTCH YIELDS CURLS   FIDDLEBACK

Fig 9:3 Three characteristic grain figures

offcuts that are valuable because they have a fancy figure. Average size 18in by 10in (457mm by 254mm). Narrow exotics such as kingwood, Macassar ebony, and tulipwood produce only narrow leaves from 5ft to 8ft (1.52m to 2.44m) long by 3in to 6in (76mm to 152mm) wide.

Rotary cut and half-round veneers are 6ft to 8ft (1.82m to 2.44m) long, by widths from 12in to 24in (305mm to 610mm).

Burr veneers are completely individual and vary from 6in by 4in (152mm by 102mm) to 2ft or 3ft (610mm or 914mm) long, and from 12in to 18in (305mm to 557mm) wide.

STORING VENEERS

Leaves of veneer are tied in bundles of 24, 28, and so on by the supplier, always in units of four for matching purposes. Ideally, they should be stored in a dark, cool place which is fairly humid, because if they dry out they become brittle and crack. A cellar is a good place, but for those of us who don't have one, the cupboard under the stairs is an alternative, especially if you can place a jar with water in it near the veneer to keep the humidity at a reasonable level.

Some veneers which have wild, irregular grain will tend to start splitting at the ends if left lying around for a long time, and this can be prevented by sticking gummed brown paper tape over the ends. This can be removed easily by being dampened. Don't use adhesive plastic tape because you will almost certainly split the ends when removing it.

SEASONING OYSTERS

As the normal practice is for you to cut your own oysters rather than to buy them, you will have to season them yourself. The greatest problem is that when they have been sawn from the branch, the tensions that accompany normal growth are released and have to be controlled to avoid excess buckling and splitting. This is so likely to happen that you can expect 50 per cent wastage.

You can, however, minimise the risk by observing the following points. First, as far as the 'raw material' is concerned, don't use a log or branch that has been lying around for several years because the sapwood will probably have softened and become discoloured. By the same token, don't use one that is freshly cut, or it will buckle and become distorted beyond recognition. The ideal is a piece which has been cut for six to twelve months and has had the sawn ends coated with paraffin wax before being left to season in a cool, airy place.

Cutting the oysters is the next step. Normally they are about ⅛in (3mm) thick, and you should take great care to saw them all to a uniform thickness so that, when they have been laid, they

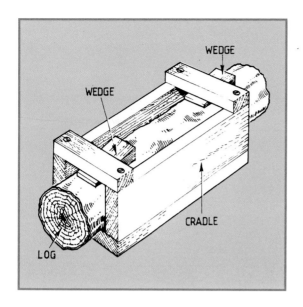

Fig 9:4 Illustrates a laburnum billet held in a cradle by wedges prior to sawing

are all perfectly flat without any one standing proud of the others. Whether you cut them on a bandsaw, a saw bench, or by hand depends on the size of the log. If you decide on the bandsaw, use the widest saw blade you have – preferably ¾in (19mm) wide, because it will cut truer and keep vibration to a minimum. A cradle as shown in Fig 9:4 will enable you to present the log to the saw safely, and the wedge-fixing means that you can easily expose another length for cutting. One more point – sweep away the sawdust after each cut or you may not get slices of uniform thickness.

Seasoning the oysters involves standing them upright in a box filled with sawdust which, being absorbent, acts as a kind of equaliser to create an equilibrium between the moisture in the oysters and that in the surrounding atmosphere. This can take several weeks or even months, because today's centrally heated rooms require the oysters to be drier than those used in the old days when houses were colder and damper.

Although this process will stabilise the moisture content, it will not prevent the oysters from buckling, as they certainly will. To flatten them, adopt the following procedure, which is also applicable to burr veneers that have become brittle and buckled.

Damp the oysters (or the burrs) slightly with a thin solution of glue size and water. Then sandwich them between, preferably, two sheets of thick cartridge paper or plain paper, but not blotting paper because it is too absorbent. Put the 'sandwich' between two pieces of chipboard and lay weights on top; then leave the arrangement for 24 hours to dry out. They can then be laid with Scotch glue; other adhesives would be incompatible with the glue size.

VENEERING TOOLS

To a large extent, the number of tools you buy depends on the depth of your pocket and whether you prefer proprietary tools that make the job easier, or tools you can make for yourself.

You will certainly need a straightedge and, although you can make one from wood, a steel one is much better because the edges do not become worn when used to guide trimming knives and saws.

One tool you will need to buy if you do a lot of veneering is a veneer saw (Fig 9:5A). This is double-edged: the teeth are very small and have no set. In use the saw is guided by a straightedge cramped across the veneer, and you will find it

Fig 9:5 Proprietary veneer saw and veneer hammer

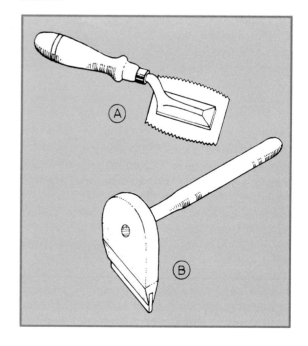

easy to cut three or four knife-cut veneers at a time if required. Alternatively, if you only do veneering occasionally, you can make do with a fine-toothed backsaw such as a dovetail or a gent's saw, again using a straightedge as a guide. Take care that the sharp point at the front end of the saw does not dig in and spoil the cut – the curved edges of the veneer saw are designed specifically to avoid this.

For certain kinds of veneering you will need a special hammer (Fig 9:5B). You can either buy one or make one from the details given in Fig 9:6. Because it is not used like a normal hammer, the blade can be a strip of brass, a piece of really hard wood, or even rigid, hard plastic. Whichever you decide on is glued into a groove or saw kerf made

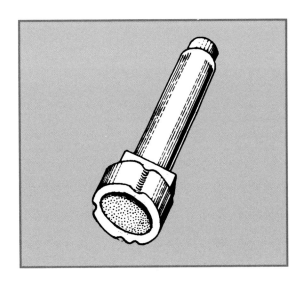

Fig 9:7 A proprietary veneer repairing punch

Fig 9:6 Details of a home-made veneer hammer

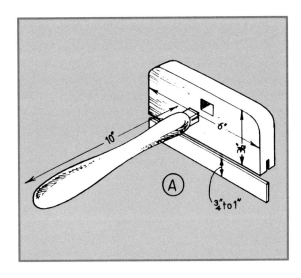

along the bottom edge of the stock.

Professional craftsmen use a toothing plane to remove any saw grooves from the back of sawcut veneer which might otherwise trap the glue, which would eventually shrink and cause ridges in the veneered surface. The most notable feature of the plane is that the back of the cutting iron has a series of V-grooves machined on it so that the actual cutting edge becomes a row of teeth. Also, the cutting iron is fixed almost vertically to make the teeth fully effective.

A 'toothing tool' can certainly be home-made from a strip of broken hacksaw blade. You can

either hold it in your fingers or jam it into a saw kerf cut in a block of wood. Scrape it across the surface of the groundwork (also referred to as the 'substrate') in all directions to make a network of tiny grooves that will form a key for the glue.

A useful (but rather expensive) device for repairing blemishes is the veneer punch shown in Fig 9:7. It is a dual-purpose tool because, by striking it with a hammer, you can remove an irregular patch of veneer that includes the blemish; and by positioning the punch on a piece of matching replacement veneer and striking it, you will cut out an identically shaped patch. The punches are fitted with spring ejectors to expel the repair patches easily, and are made in a range of sizes from ½in to 2½in (12mm to 64mm).

For cutting and trimming veneers, you will need some sharp, robust craft knives, and these are sold at all tool shops and DIY centres. There are three other cutting devices for those who intend to do a lot of veneering. The veneer-trimming chisel for removing surplus veneer from panel edges is fitted with a nylon guide block to stop its wandering along the grain; a cutter for trimming the edges of veneered panels works with and across the grain; and a combined joint and strip cutter will cut perfect joints with and across the grain. It will also cut inlay strips from ⅟₁₆in to ⁵⁄₁₆in wide (2mm to 8mm).

As well as craft knives for cutting veneers, you will also need a cutting gauge for making bandings. It is very similar to a marking gauge except that instead of a sharp-pointed pin, it is fitted with a slightly stouter pin with its end filed and sharpened to a chisel point. Note that it should be tilted slightly forward in use to avoid tearing the veneer.

Finally, you will find that a thermostatically controlled electric iron is invaluable, together with a damp cloth, for softening the Scotch glue when making repairs.

REPAIRS

BLISTERS AND DEFECTS

How you deal with a blister depends on its size, whether or not it has split, and what kind of finish has been used on the wood. This last point is important because if you have to use a damp cloth and a warm electric iron to remedy the trouble, and the finish is French polish, you may find yourself saddled with a complete repolishing job.

With an unbroken blister, the cause is usually that the glue underneath has perished. First, remove the finish round it (bearing in mind that you will have to make it good afterwards) either by gently scraping it if it is varnish, rubbing it with methylated spirit if it is French polish, or white spirit if it is wax. Next, cut a slit along the grain and

Fig 9:8 Cramping down the repair

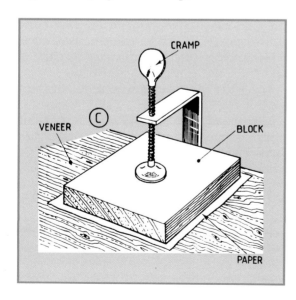

warm the blister and the surface under it with a damp cloth pressed down with the point of the electric iron. This should be set at 'cool'. If you can, clean out the old glue with a cotton bud or a piece of kitchen paper, but make sure that no strands are left that could cause small lumps under the new veneer.

Before you introduce fresh glue, wait until the veneer is dry and then press the lips down with your fingers, because quite often they overlap by a hairsbreadth, and they must be shaved away until they lie flat. Now you can insert the glue either with a sliver of veneer or on the point of a knife. Then press the lips down with a veneer hammer and wipe away excess glue. Next, if the repair is near the edge of the work, you can lay a piece of waxed paper or plastic film over the repair, cramp a block of heated wood over it, and leave the whole assembly until the glue has set: see Fig 9:8.

Dealing with an open blister calls for the same treatment, also making sure that all dirt, wax, etc, has been thoroughly cleaned away.

Other common defects occur where the veneer has been accidentally cut, scuffed, chipped, or bruised, all of which are best rectified by inserting a patch of new veneer. This must match the old veneer as much as possible, and the ideal state of affairs exists when you can use a piece from an inconspicuous part of the job. If you cannot do this, choose a veneer that is slightly lighter in colour so that you can darken it to match when polishing – this is much easier than having to bleach it. One of the most important requirements is that the grain in the patch should match as unobtrusively as possible, and frequently you can best achieve this by making the patch diamond-shaped; or you can use the veneer punch already referred to.

REMOVING OLD VENEER

You can only use the following method on veneer that has been laid with Scotch glue, and it involves using the electric iron and cloth mentioned above.

The first step is to ensure that the heat from the iron can get through whatever finish is on the wood. This may mean stripping it off or pricking a network of holes right through the veneer and the polish to the glue beneath. Then, with the iron set at 'cool' or 'medium', place a tea cloth, or any fairly thick and absorbent cloth, wrung out in water, over the veneer and run the iron across it. When you have ironed the cloth dry, dampen it and repeat the process.

It will probably take some time for the glue to become liquid enough for the veneer to lift. When it does, slide a thin-bladed knife (a palette knife is perfect) under it to prise it loose. Don't be tempted to increase the heat of the iron because this will not speed up the job and you will risk scorching the veneer. Just keep ironing and prising with the knife until the veneer comes away easily.

If you intend re-using the veneer, wipe off as much of the old glue from the back as possible with a damp rag, and if necessary gently scrape it. It will almost certainly have buckled during removal and, having made sure it is still damp, you can sandwich it between two pieces of plastic film and press it between two pre-warmed flat boards. Leave the 'sandwich' with weights on top at least overnight. If the veneer is still buckled, repeat the process.

DEALING WITH STRESSED VENEER

This fault consists of stress marks that appear when a veneer has been laid over the joint of two pieces of wood, one of which has shrunk more than the other, as in Fig 9:9; or when a veneer has been laid over a dovetailed joint that has moved. In either case it can present a major problem.

How you deal with it depends on whether or not the piece is a valuable antique. If it is, it would probably be better not to do any more than fill in the largest cracks with coloured wax or beaumontage. If it is not valuable, you could remove all the veneer, adjust the clamps and the panel to fit each other, and re-veneer.

WORKING WITH NEW VENEERS

Veneering is a craft on its own, and there is not enough space to describe all its aspects thoroughly. The most that can be done is to outline the basic techniques that will enable you to cope with normal day-to-day veneering jobs. Those who would like to learn more, should read a book such as *Practical Veneering* (see Bibliography).

CHOOSING AND PREPARING A GROUNDWORK

A 'groundwork' is one of the terms used for the baseboard on which veneer is laid; 'substrate' is

Fig 9:9 Typical stress marks on veneer

another, more modern, term. In the old days, groundwork always consisted of solid timber – Honduras mahogany, yellow pine, and oak were all widely used at various times – but today, we are lucky enough to have a range of man-made boards that are eminently suitable.

Remember, as we look at the various kinds of groundwork, that veneer exerts a strong pull of its own when laid.

The man-made boards include plywood, chipboard, blockboard, laminboard, and medium density fibre board, which is usually referred to by its initials MDF. Their qualities are as follows.

Plywood As you probably know, this consists of odd numbers of laminations (or plies) glued together: 3-ply is not stout enough to be veneered; 5-ply is suitable for small doors and panels; but anything larger needs the $\frac{5}{16}$in (7mm) thickness as a minimum.

If you veneer one side with a face-veneer, then you will have to balance it by veneering the other side with a 'counter' veneer (also called a 'balancer'). These are usually cheaper veneers such as obeche or gaboon, and every veneer supplier keeps good stocks.

Both face and counter-veneers must be laid with their grain directions matching and at right angles to the grain of the outer face of the plywood. This could mean that you have first to lay a cross veneer on both sides before you lay the face veneer and the counter-veneer. This also applies when veneering blockboard or laminboard.

Chipboard This is now widely employed as a groundwork, and should be face-veneered and counter-veneered. Some boards have a finer grade of chips on one side than the other, and you should lay the face veneer on the finer side. Rub both sides with coarse glasspaper to form a key for the glue, and make sure that all dust is completely removed before applying it.

Blockboard consists of 1in (25mm) strips of softwood glued together side by side and sandwiched between two thick veneers. **Laminboard** is similar, except that the strips are narrower (⁵⁄₁₆in or 7mm wide). Both need counter-veneering, and are good groundworks. Laminboard is the better of the two because it has less tendency to warp.

Medium density fibreboard (MDF) This is the best of all as a groundwork because it does not warp or twist at all, and has the great advantage that the edges can be veneered as readily as the face and sides. You will need to glasspaper it with a coarse grade paper to provide a key for the glue, and also to counter-veneer it.

Solid wood If you are re-veneering antique furniture, you will be dealing with this as a groundwork, and it needs special consideration. All splits and any warping and twisting will have to be put right first, and Chapters 4 and 6 deal with most of the troubles.

There are two important factors to take into account as well. The first is that solid timber tends to shrink away from its heart side, and Fig 9:10 shows how to tell which one this is. The second is that veneer has a strong tendency to pull as it dries out, and the effect is shown in Fig 9:11, where the two opposing forces cancel each other out. Solid

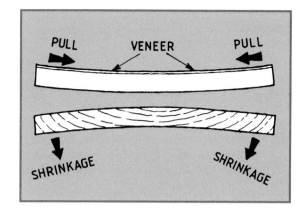

Fig 9:11 The pulling effect of a veneer as it dries out

timber also benefits from the counter-veneering of each side first before laying the face and counter-veneers.

A 'last-resort' method with difficult timber is to cut it into longitudinal strips say, about 2in (51mm) wide, and then glue them together side by side with the heart sides opposed in alternate strips, as shown in Fig 9:12.

Fig 9:12 How strips are glued side by side with heart sides alternating

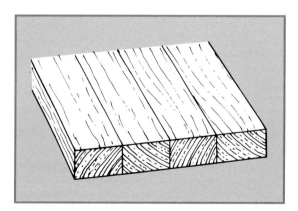

Finally, if there are any knots in any kind of groundwork, cut them out and replace them with pelleted plugs. The grain of the knots is usually at right angles to that of the timber, and when the latter shrinks, the knot will stand proud and make a bulge in the veneer.

Fig 9:10 How timber tends to shrink away from the heart side

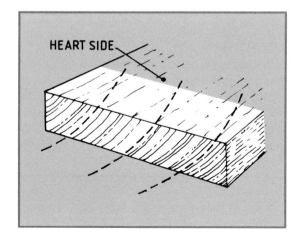

CHOICE OF ADHESIVE

(see also Appendix G for methods of use)

Scotch glue (also referred to as 'animal' glue) is the traditional adhesive for laying veneers, and has been used for several centuries. It is still probably the most versatile of all glues. It has the great advantage that, if anything goes wrong, it can be re-liquefied by the electric iron and wet cloth process, and the fault put right. It is also one of the best for laying burrs and curls; it is the preferred glue to use when hammer veneering; it helps to fill the grain and will also take stain; and it is definitely the cheapest. One more point – if you are laying a light coloured veneer such as holly or sycamore, you can lighten the colour of the glue by stirring in a little flake white powder.

PVA emulsion (polyvinyl acetate) adhesives such as Evostik Resin W, like other cold-setting adhesives, are unsuitable for hammer veneering because they lack the 'tack' of Scotch glue, which holds the veneer as soon as it has been pressed down. PVA adhesives need to be held down with weights or cramps until they set. This can take from six to eight hours, so such adhesives are more suitable for laying veneers in a press or on cauls.

UF (urea-formaldehyde) adhesives are also cold-setting, and in addition are waterproof and heat-resistant. They, too, can be used in press or caul laying and are particularly good for laying curl veneers. They are supplied in powder form, which needs to be mixed with water.

Impact adhesives are available from all DIY stores and are normally used for sticking down plastic laminates. They can also bond veneers to curved shapes without the need for cauls or cramps because, once the adhesive has dried out on both the veneer and the groundwork, the two can be pressed down by hand to achieve a satisfactory bond.

Glufilm is a proprietary product consisting of a paper-backed roll of thermoplastic adhesive which is obtainable from World of Wood (see List of Suppliers). It is ideal for laying large leaves on to flat surfaces, but is not suitable for burrs or curls.

The method of application is first to cut the Glufilm to fit the groundwork with a pair of scissors and lay it in place. Smooth over the paper backing with a domestic electric iron set at medium heat and then allow it to cool, when the backing paper can be peeled off. At this juncture,

you do not have to melt all the Glufilm but only to stick it down in enough places to enable you to remove the backing paper.

Next, position the veneer on top of the Glufilm and the groundwork, and lay the peeled-off backing paper on top of it to protect against scorching the surface. Now slowly work all over the surface with the electric iron set at medium heat; the aim is to melt the adhesive without scorching the veneer.

As you iron, press the veneer down behind it with a veneer hammer or a block of wood – 10in by 6in (250mm by 150mm) is a convenient size. Try to develop the technique of holding the iron in one hand and the hammer or block in the other so that you work both together. It sometimes helps to damp the veneer slightly if it dries out during ironing, and one of the small misting sprays used to spray indoor pot plants is ideal for this.

PREPARING THE GROUNDWORK

Whichever groundwork is used, it must be perfectly flat, and any hollows or dents must be raised flush with the surface by means of a wood filler. Plywood sometimes has knots on its exterior faces (how many depends on the grade) and although these may be sound and not loose, you should remove them with a power router and fill in with a patch of matching veneer. Such knots can absorb more or less glue than the remainder of the surface and this may cause trouble later.

You will need to tooth the groundwork to provide a key for the adhesive. For this, you can either rub it with coarse glasspaper, or scrape it in all directions with a fine-toothed hacksaw blade. Finally, make sure that all dust has been completely removed with a 'Tak' rag.

Some kinds of groundwork are very absorbent and soak up the glue like blotting paper. As a result, the veneer itself is starved of glue and cannot be laid properly. Chipboard and some softwoods are often susceptible to this. The remedy is to apply a coat of glue size (if you intend to use Scotch glue afterwards), or a coat of PVA/water mixed in equal proportions if PVA adhesive is to follow. As a urea-formaldehyde adhesive is gap-filling anyway, there is no need to pre-coat at all.

End grain always presents a difficulty because of its ability to absorb adhesive, and it's best to avoid

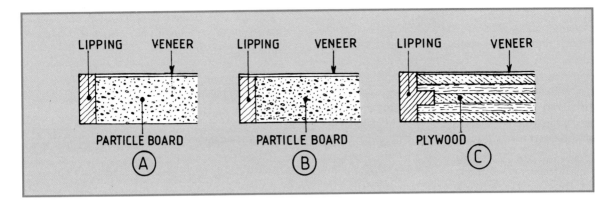

Fig 9:13 Various designs of lippings

it if at all possible by covering it with lipping; Fig 9:13 shows several types. If you do this, you will have to choose between (A) where the lipping is pinned and glued on after veneering and so protects the edge of the veneer; and (B) where the reverse applies and the lipping is fixed first with the veneer laid over it to hide it. If you can't use a lipping, you could try applying at least three coats of glue size (or diluted PVA adhesive), allowing each coat to dry thoroughly before applying the next. This should fill the grain and allow you to lay the veneer safely. Although I have not tried it, there seems to be no reason why you could not apply a coat of a UF adhesive diluted with water and, once it has dried, lay the veneer with the same adhesive used at normal strength.

Glufilm can be employed to make your own 'iron-on' veneer strips for edges by ironing it directly to a leaf of veneer and then cutting the coated leaves into strips. These are then ironed on in the normal manner.

PATTERNS IN VENEERING

There are five basic patterns for veneered panels, as shown in Fig 9:14; (A) halved or two-piece matching; (B) quartered or four-piece matching; (C) alternating square matching; (D) diamond matching; and (E) reverse diamond matching.

Today's fashions in furniture favour the use of straightgrained, stripey veneer such as sapele. (C), (D), and (E) are particularly suited to this. Pattern (C) is easy enough to achieve, but unless you are methodical in matching and cutting the pieces for (D) and (E), you could be in trouble.

The best method for dealing with these two is shown in Fig 9:15. You will need four consecutive leaves, which should be cramped together on top of each other as at (A). Fix a straightedge at 45° across one end and cut or saw through all four. Then repeat the process at the other end to produce the parallelogram w-x-y-z shown at (B). Next, arrange the uppermost pair of leaves in book fashion with y-z as the centre line (see C) and tape

Fig 9:14 Basic patterns for veneer panels

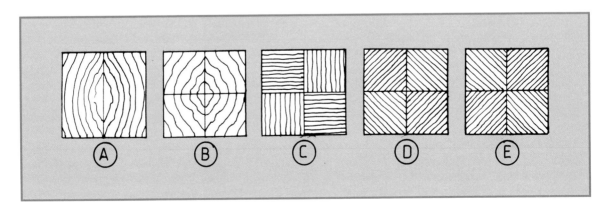

them together. Then lay the straightedge from x to x and cut off the triangle x-y-x, (D). Finally, fit this triangle into the aperture w-x-x-w and tape the edges. The result will be a rectangular panel as shown at (E).

The following is the best way to lay halved and quartered panels, (A) and (B) respectively. Both are laid in a similar manner, so we will concentrate on the quartered pattern.

You will need four consecutive leaves for this (or two leaves for a halved pattern), and you must choose them very carefully so that not only does the grain pattern match, but also the reflection of the light from the surfaces. Some craftsmen arrange the pieces in the requisite pattern and get

Fig 9:15 How diamond matching is achieved

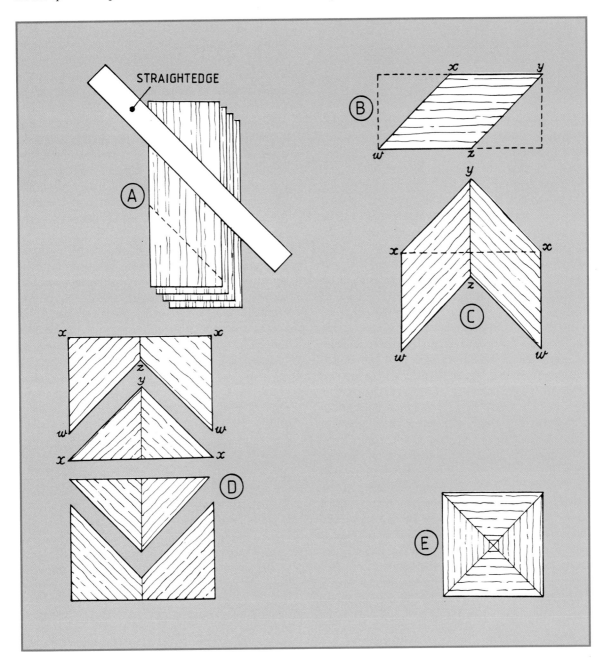

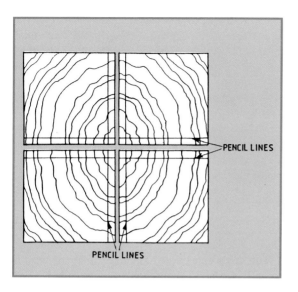

Fig 9:16 Marking out veneers for panels

a helper to hold a mirror above them so that their reflection can be studied. The whole project can be very wasteful of veneer, and you can reckon on an average of about 50 per cent wastage.

Assuming you have chosen the leaves, the next step is to mark out and cut them, and this leads on nicely to a description of the best method of making joints. Fig 9:16 shows you how each piece is marked out with pencil lines indicating overlaps at the edges of the joints. When the pieces are laid, the pencil lines should coincide with the centre lines marked on the groundwork.

The overlap of one piece of veneer on to another need only be about ½in (12mm) wide. The pieces are placed on a flat board and a straightedge is cramped over the overlap at about ¼in (6mm) away from the line to be cut. Use either a craft knife or a saw to do the cutting; a saw is preferable for thick veneers or those with a strongly figured grain. If the veneer is brittle and likely to splinter, stick a length of gummed brown paper tape over the line and cut through that. Do not use plastic pressure-sensitive tape because it will pull off tiny splinters of the veneer as you remove it – the brown paper tape will slide off if you wipe it with a damp rag. Having made the cut, lift off the upper waste strip, then lift the top veneer and peel away the lower strip. The result should be a perfect joint as in Fig 9:17

VENEERING METHODS: (1) HAMMER; (2) CAUL

HAMMER VENEERING

This method has been employed by craftsmen for many years, and is particularly suitable for laying small areas and bandings. As you will appreciate, the veneer has to stick down immediately after it has been ironed on and before the hammer is used. Only Scotch glue has sufficient initial 'tack' to allow this to be done, although PVA adhesives will give almost the same result if the water contained in them is allowed to evaporate first before ironing. The time taken for this to happen is, however, unpredictable and you would be well advised to use Scotch glue instead.

You will need an electric iron set at 'cool', plus a sponge or cloth dipped in hot water and then squeezed or wrung out. You will also need the veneer hammer and Scotch glue freshly made to the consistency of thin cream. This is important because the thicker the glue, the harder it is to press out, and the thinner it is the less likely it is to form a strong bond.

Brush an even, thin coat of glue to both the groundwork and the underside of the veneer, and lay it in place, pressing it down by hand all over the surface. This is where the tackiness of Scotch glue is an advantage because the veneer will stay down. You now have to moisten the veneer surface with the sponge or the cloth wrung out in hot water. 'Moisten' is the operative word because too much

Fig 9:17 How to cut veneers to ensure a perfect joint

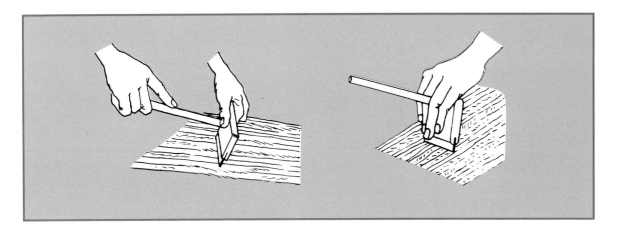

Fig 9:18 Two ways to hold a veneering hammer

water will cause the veneer to swell and also weaken the bond. Pass the electric iron back and forth over the work (do not press on it) to liquefy the glue and draw it into the grain of the veneer, and then use the veneer hammer to squeeze out surplus glue. Start at the centre and work outwards with a zigzag movement, using the hammer like a squeegee to force out any air bubbles as well as glue.

It's very likely that as you work on one area, the glue will chill on another. If this happens, you can melt it with the electric iron after first moistening the surface to prevent scorching. There are two ways in which you can hold the hammer, as shown in Fig 9:18, and it doesn't matter which one you use. Try to work along the grain as much as you can because using the hammer crosswise will tend to stretch the veneer. Take care at the edges because it is very easy to break the veneer where it overlaps. It's best to hold the hammer at an angle so that at least half of it stays on the groundwork. Wipe away surplus glue with a damp cloth.

CAUL VENEERING

This method has the advantage that urea-formaldehyde (UF) and PVA adhesives can both be employed as well as Scotch glue. In fact, they are to be preferred because all the work can be done cold and the cauls do not have to be heated, as would be necessary with Scotch glue. The process is well suited to veneering large areas, and for laying veneers that are thicker than average.

The cauls can be any kind of flat board with a smooth surface. Many books recommend solid timber (the best), but what they do not tell you is where to buy solid boards wide enough to cramp up, say, a 24in (610mm) or wider panel.

Chipboard seems to be the obvious choice, and you can use it in the ¾in (19mm) thickness. But, as you will see, it needs care because chipboard will split if put under pressure. Plywood is better, especially if you use two ⅜in (10mm) sheets at the top and two more at the bottom. One of the sheets in each case could be the coarse, cheap grade used for shuttering concrete.

Fig 9:19 shows the set-up. There are several points to note. The lower edge of the top bearer is curved slightly so that, as pressure is applied, the air and surplus glue are expelled from the centre outwards. The bottom bearers are stouter than the top ones and do not have their edges shaped. And the bearers must be opposite each other and cramped up from the centre outwards. The top bearers can be about 2in by 1in (51mm by 25mm), and the curve need only be very slight.

I cannot recommend Scotch glue because the cauls would have to be heated almost to scorching point and the bottom bearers would have to be applied quickly in case the glue should chill. This could soon lead to panic stations. The atmosphere when either UF or PVA adhesive is used is calmer, and the procedure is as follows.

The cauls need to be an inch or two (25 or 50mm) larger all round than the work to be done, and the adhesive applied to the groundwork alone. Lay a sheet of plastic film over the veneer to prevent any excess adhesive from sticking. The

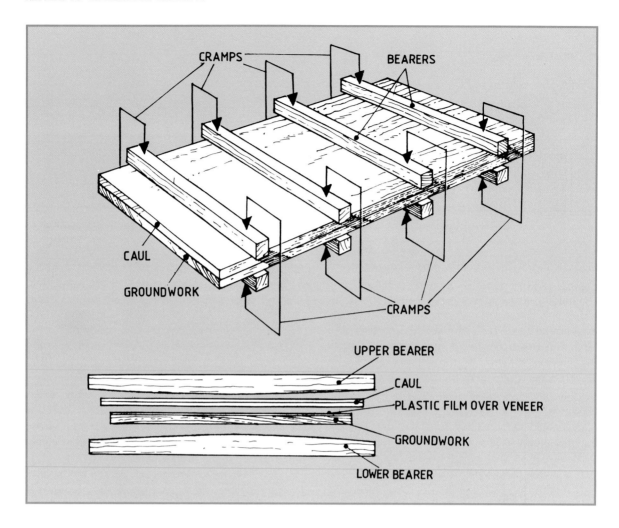

Fig 9:19 Pressing veneer by means of cauls

Fig 9:20 Laying a crossbanding with the hammer; note the taped joints

film will also compensate for any unevenness that may be caused by any gummed brown paper tapes stuck along the joints. If you can, do the job on a warm day because the temperature will speed up the setting time of the adhesive.

CROSSBANDINGS (see also Chapter 12)

These are narrow strips of veneer, usually from ½in to 1in (12mm to 25mm) wide, with the grain running crosswise. You can cut them with a cutting gauge, a craft knife, or a saw, depending on their nature and thickness.

Cutting and laying straight lengths is simple, and Fig 9:20 should be self-explanatory. Difficulties

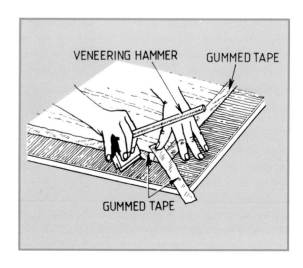

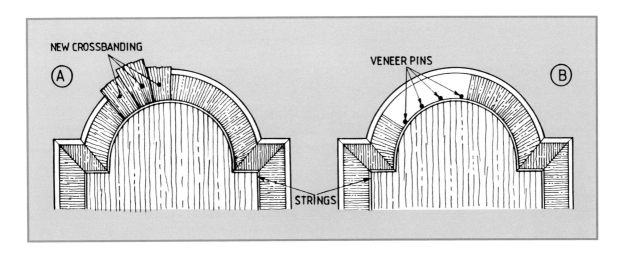

Fig 9:21 (A) Laying a crossbanding round a curve;
(B) holding stringing in place round a curve

Fig 9:22 Veneering shapes

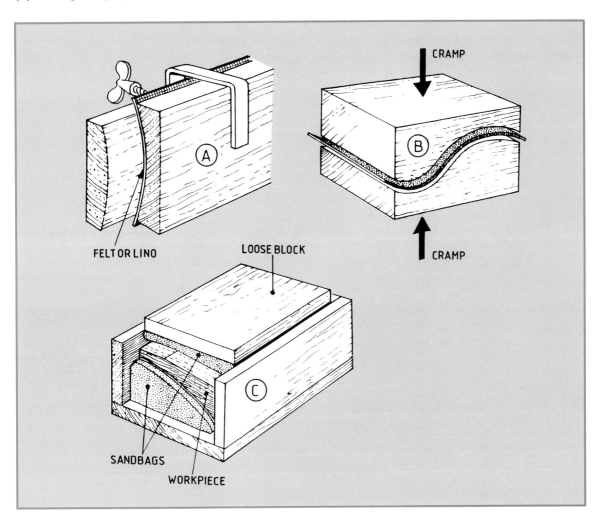

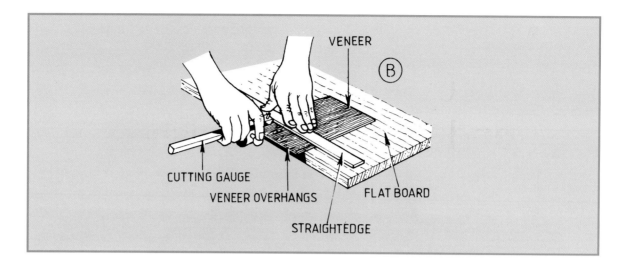

arise when crossbanding has to negotiate a curved corner, and where a stringing follows it round. Fig 9:21(A) illustrates how wedge-shaped pieces of veneer are cut to fit round the corner and are taped down, their outer ends being trimmed when the glue has set. You have to judge how many pieces are needed so that the grain runs radially; it is better to err on the side of too many rather than too few. The same method is used with herring-bone banding, which has to be cut into two halves down the middle.

Solving the problem of the stringing is shown in Fig 9:21(B), which shows how veneer pins are partly tapped in to hold it in place while the glue sets. After this, the crossbanding can be laid and held down by means of gummed brown paper strips. See further details in Chapter 12.

VENEERING SHAPES

If you are dealing with a job that calls for veneering shapes, particularly if it is a relatively modern one,

Fig 9:23 Cutting veneer with a cutting gauge

you will find the modern contact (thixotropic) adhesives by far the best to use because they make an instant bond and will hold the veneer in place without the need for cramping.

For those engaged in restoring antique pieces, life is not so easy because they have to use Scotch glue, which cannot hold a veneer round a shape without being cramped, so some kind of shaped caul is needed, as at (A) or (B) in Fig 9:22.

You can make up a simple box with a loose lid (C), and put the workpiece into it, having first glued and taped the veneer in place. Surround the workpiece with sandbags. It helps if the sand is warmed because this will prevent the glue from chilling; but it should not be hot because this could scorch the veneer. The lid can be cramped down to apply pressure.

Fig 9:23(A) shows how to cut veneer safely with a cutting gauge.

10 Stains, polishes, and traditional finishes

A basic knowledge of the various types of finishes and the periods in which they were used is not only interesting but can also be a significant pointer to the age of a piece of furniture.

Such furniture as there was before 1450 was almost always painted because this was a way of brightening up cold and damp interiors, and also allowed the dirt and soot to be washed off every spring. Fireplaces did not appear until the middle of the sixteenth century; prior to that date, smoke from the fires found its way out through holes in the roof after first depositing a layer of soot on everything. From about 1450, the 'vernacular' style of furniture used in manor houses, monasteries, inns, etc, was finished by being rubbed with an oil of some kind, usually walnut, linseed, or poppy. This often also contained a natural resin such as copal, and this kind of finish continued throughout the seventeenth century.

The opening up of trade with Oriental countries from about 1650 onwards led to the use of spirit varnish. This consisted of shellac dissolved in alcohol (then called 'spirits of wine'). The alcohol rapidly evaporated, leaving a thin film of shellac on the wood. Ten or twelve coats rubbed down with Tripoli powder constituted the higher class finishes; two or three coats and no rubbing down were good enough for inferior work. In the eighteenth century, spirit varnishes were still being used, but by the end of the period wax polishes, and linseed oil coloured with pigment for cheaper furniture, had superseded them.

About 1820 a new method of finishing arrived from France called, appropriately enough, French polish. This rapidly became so popular that during the Victorian period many old pieces were ruthlessly stripped and French polished in the name of 'improvement'. This often destroyed the patina built up over centuries. French polishing continued to be a standard trade finish until the 1930s (the factory in which I worked was still using it in 1939), but it finally fell out of favour after 1940.

It was replaced by cellulose lacquer, which was introduced in the 1930s, and became the standard finish until the 1960s. Then it, too, was superseded by the present-day synthetic lacquers.

TOOLS AND EQUIPMENT

Many of these are to be found among general workshop tools, or they can be adapted from household materials such as screw-top plastic or glass jars, empty bottles, and cotton or linen rags.

A powered orbital sander will save you hours of laborious sanding by hand, and a powered spray gun can also be handy for applying some stains, but it is not obligatory. Hand tools include a cabinet scraper; a Skarsten scraper; a selection of wire and bristle brushes for stripping; and a sanding block with a pad of felt glued to its face, or one of solid cork. A 'Tak' rag is a good and cheap investment because it will pick up all dust particles – even the microscopic ones that a brush might miss.

You will also need a selection of brushes, and this will depend on what kind of work you are doing. Fig 10:1 shows the different types; (A) is a wide (say 4in or 100mm) brush for applying stain; (B) a fitch for dealing with small corners and mouldings; (C) a pencil brush for touching in small details; and (D) a varnish brush that has longer and more flexible bristles than a paint brush. Remember that you will need a separate set of brushes for oil and water stains.

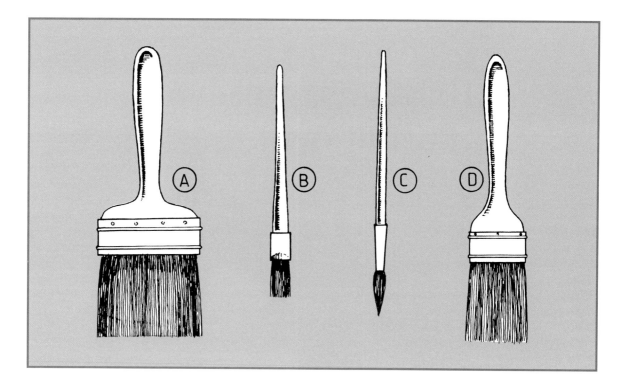

French polishing calls for one or two extra appliances, and these will be described as the process is dealt with.

IDENTIFYING A FINISH

The first point to appreciate is that no matter what the basic original finish is, it has probably been covered with wax polish as a result of normal domestic cleaning. This has first to be removed by rubbing with a cloth moistened with turpentine substitute (white spirit).

When this has been done, you are in a position to identify the underlying finish by testing as follows.

1 Try rubbing an inconspicuous part with a clean cloth moistened with methylated spirit. If this leaves a deposit on the cloth, the finish is French polish. Methylated spirit will not affect wax, varnish, or cellulose finishes.
2 Moisten a cloth with turpentine substitute and rub the surface; this will remove wax and varnish finishes but not French polish or cellulose.
3 A cellulose finish will yield to cellulose thinners; other finishes are unaffected.

Fig 10:1 Types of brushes

If none of these tests gives a result, the only conclusion you can come to is that the piece has a modern synthetic lacquer finish, and you will have to use a special stripper to remove it. There are several proprietary brands available, and you should check that the one you choose will do the job because there are some general purpose strippers that are unsuitable.

CLEANING AND REVIVING OLD FINISHES

Some antique pieces have such a dingy and woebegone look that it seems impossible to restore them to their original pristine appearance. There are, however, some comparatively simple procedures that will do so.

The first step is to get rid of loose dirt, and to clean the grime out of mouldings, carving, and awkward corners with a brush or a pointed stick. Then make a 50/50 mixture of boiled linseed oil and turpentine substitute, and brush it over the piece. Follow this by rinsing off with a solution of warm soapy water. Remember that both French polish and Scotch glue can be rapidly affected by this solution if it stays on the surface for any length of time, so deal with a small area and dry it thoroughly before moving on to the next. You will almost certainly be amazed at the transformation effected by such a simple treatment.

For revivers, look through the catalogue of any supplier of polishing materials and you will find that they go to great lengths to satisfy your every need. There is certain to be a range of 'revivers' for restoring a shine and a finish to furniture that has a faded, exhausted look.

Despite this, there always seem to be a number of polishers who like to make up their own recipes, and they may be interested in the following homemade revivers.

1 One part vinegar; one part raw (not boiled) linseed oil.
2 One part vinegar; one part raw linseed oil; one part methylated spirit.
3 Four parts raw linseed oil; twelve parts vinegar; one part terebene driers.
4 Equal parts of raw linseed oil, methylated spirit, and turpentine substitute plus a little vinegar.

STRIPPING

This is a once-and-for-all job in the sense that once you have started it you are committed to finishing it, so be sure in your own mind that it's really necessary.

Dealing first with what one could call 'dry stripping', this can be used most effectively for painted or varnished surfaces. No liquids are used because the job is done with scrapers, glasspaper, and/or a hot-air paint stripper. The methods of using them are obvious but in addition to the traditional cabinet scraper, there are also hooked scrapers (which plumbers employ for working lead pipes, but they are just as useful to us), and the proprietary Skarsten scrapers. All are shown in Fig 10:2, and you can often find them at a ship's chandler.

Now for the liquid strippers. A glance through *Yellow Pages* will show you the firms that undertake stripping in your area, but before you patronise them, think carefully. They are mainly concerned with stripping doors, windows, and painted or varnished softwood furniture, and it is unreasonable to expect them to cope with a veneered rosewood table or something equally delicate. Remember, too, that solutions containing water, acids, or alkalis play havoc with glues and polished finishes; and in most cases you would be well advised to do the job yourself.

Whichever method you employ, there are several precautions you should take. First, remove as much hardware as you can, including handles, catches, and possibly hinges as well, unless you are sure the stripper will not discolour them. Next, stand the job on several layers of old newspaper in a well-ventilated place — out of doors, if possible. Wear a pair of goggles to protect your eyes in case of splashes, and a face mask if the manufacturer advises it. Wear thick industrial-type gloves and wash your hands thoroughly after work.

You will need a motley collection of appliances

Fig 10:2 Types of scrapers

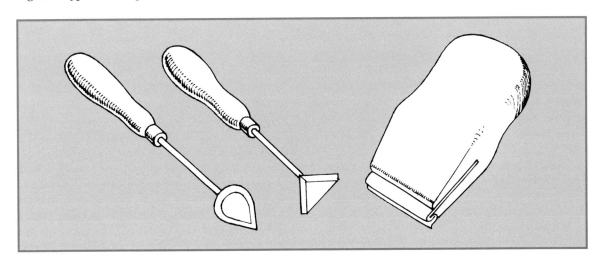

and materials. These should include a pad of wire wool; a large and a small wire brush (the latter should be the kind used for cleaning suede shoes); a couple of old toothbrushes for getting into crevices, particularly those on turned work; a fairly blunt paint scraper; and as many rags as you can get — these have to be cotton, linen, or canvas because man-made textiles are non-absorbent.

I recommend one or other of the many proprietary strippers available, which will remove all kinds of finish, including polyurethane lacquers. Some are specially formulated and are guaranteed not to harm delicate veneers or glues. You can also get pastes which can be applied to vertical surfaces without running down it. Always apply and neutralise them strictly in accordance with the manufacturer's instructions.

There will be those, however, who like to use such strippers as caustic soda (also called sodium hydroxide or lye) and the method is as follows.

Do the job out of doors if you can, or in a very well-ventilated place, and stand the piece on a strong plastic sheet. Make sure that the excess runs away into a drain because caustic soda is used as a drain cleaner and you will get the benefit of clean drains at the same time. Have a hosepipe handy for washing the stripper off, and rinse away any splashes on the skin or clothing immediately. Also, wear industrial-type heavy rubber gloves and goggles to protect your eyes.

The recipe for an average strength stripper is approximately 1lb of the crystals to 1 gallon of water (450g to 4.5 litres). Always add the crystals to the water, otherwise the mixture will foam up and spit. If you use warm (not hot) water, the action will be speeded up. The stripper will dissolve Scotch glue and play havoc with such finishes as French polish, so furniture made and finished with these materials is unsuited to the treatment. Also remove all brasswork such as handles, hinges, etc.

Caustic soda darkens the colour of many timbers, particularly oak, but does not affect softwood, so try the mixture first on test pieces of any other timber. The dark colour can be removed later by bleaching if necessary.

You can apply the solution with a piece of canvas wrapped round and tied to a piece of stick, or with a sponge, or you can simply ladle it on by means of a used tin can nailed to a stick. Some professional restorers keep a metal tank and immerse the whole job in it. Whatever you use, you will need to rinse the piece down thoroughly with running water from the hose to remove all traces of the solution because it may affect any subsequent stains or finishes. Any parts that are not reached by the rinsing can be sponged with a 50/50 white vinegar and water solution and then rinsed again.

PREPARING A BARE WOOD SURFACE

Many craftsmen like to leave a wood surface such as mahogany or walnut just as it finishes after being scraped with a really sharp cabinet scraper, and there is no doubt that when done properly such a finish possesses a sheen that is unattainable by any other method.

Most of us have to be content with sanding the job to an acceptable finish. Sanding, although widely employed in the trade, is a misnomer because glasspapers, garnet papers, or silicon carbide wet-or-dry papers are now used, sand-paper having been superseded long ago. Begin with a coarse grade, working through the medium grades and ending with the finest, which in the case of glasspaper is often referred to as 'flour' paper (another misnomer).

One of the golden rules when sanding is always to wrap the glasspaper round a block. For flat surfaces, the traditional block was made of cork, but many modern ones are of wood with a facing of thick felt – both the cork and the felt absorb any slight inequalities in the surface. Never wrap the glasspaper round your fingers or hold it in your hand while sanding because instead of smoothing away bumps, you will simply deepen hollows. This is also a certain way to dub (round off) the arrises (edges) of the work – a sure sign of amateurish sanding. When sanding mouldings, you should go to the trouble of shaping a block to the reverse profile and use that.

Both disc and drum sanders are unsuitable, although the latter may be used lightly and gently on a curved surface; otherwise both of them are too fierce. The best tool is a powered orbital sander. Its pad moves in tiny circles – hence its name – and after using it you will need to sand these away by hand with a block and flour paper. Remember that the slightest flaws or blemishes will be greatly exaggerated when the piece is polished, and you will regret not having made the effort to get rid of them.

Take great care after each sanding to brush and wipe away all dust, preferably with a 'Tak' rag, because any dust particles left on the surface may be ground into the grain by subsequent sanding and clog it. A good tip is to sponge the wood with hot water before the final sanding because this 'raises the grain' or, in other words, as the surface dries, the tiny wood fibres stand erect and can be sanded off. The hot water will also cause any depressions left from the machining of the timber to swell up level with the surrounding area.

TYPES OF STAINS AND THEIR CHARACTERISTICS

The following are the standard stains listed in the order they are dealt with: oil stains, water stains; spirit stains; varnish stains; chemical and home-mixed stains.

OIL STAINS

These are easily bought from DIY stores and polish suppliers. They are spirit-based on turpentine substitute (also called 'white spirit') and contain a binder to hold the colouring agent in suspension. You can use them on both antique furniture and modern pieces constructed from man-made boards. In all instances they penetrate the grain deeply and enhance it.

The colours available are all those of various timbers such as light oak, medium oak, golden oak, dark oak, Jacobean oak, red mahogany, brown mahogany, teak, walnut, yew, and one non-wood colour – black – for ebonising.

The advantages are many. The different colours can be intermixed, but only within one manufacturer's range. In other words, the colour produced by one manufacturer is not necessarily compatible with that from another. They can be applied easily with a brush, a polisher's mop, or a lint-free cloth always *with* the grain and never across it. They will not raise the grain. They do not give the grain a muddy appearance but, on the contrary, enhance it. The stains can be removed easily with turpentine substitute. They are fast to light and fade-resistant. They are ideal for staining large areas because you do not have to worry about a 'hard edge' where one patch dries out before you can apply another.

But there are also some disadvantages. The stain has to be sealed if it is to be followed by an oil-based varnish or a plastic lacquer, otherwise it will bleed through, because they all contain the same base, namely turpentine substitute. To seal it, apply a coat of bleached shellac or transparent French polish when it is thoroughly dry. It has a comparatively long drying time of six to ten hours and needs to be in a warm, dry place. The stains contain a tar-based ingredient that is the base of the colour, and this sometimes rises to the surface and precipitates out. To correct this, allow the stain to become touch-dry, then wipe over it with a clean rag to remove the residue. Some colours the stains impart to different woods can be unexpected. You should try out a stain on a test piece first – as an example, knots tend to resist the stain and dry out lighter in colour.

WATER STAINS

These are made by dissolving water-soluble aniline powders in water, and can be bought ready made, or you can make them up for yourself. Although tap water can be used, rainwater is better, and distilled water best of all. A few drops of household ammonia or washing-up liquid added to the solution will help it to penetrate the grain. Colours available include several shades of oak, mahogany, walnut, teak, satinwood, rosewood, limed oak, and fumed oak; also red, green, blue, grey, purple, and black. They can all be mixed with one another, thus producing a wide range. Approximate quantities for mixing are 4¼oz of powder to 9 pints of water (120g to 5 litres).

The advantages of such stains are that they are cheap. They are also easy to mix and apply – you can use a brush, a polisher's mop, or a cloth. They are fast to light and fade-resistant. They do not give the wood a muddy appearance but actually enhance the grain. Any finish can be used over them once they are dry, no further treatment being necessary.

There are also several disadvantages. The stains contain water and, as a result, they raise the grain. To prevent this, you should sponge the wood with hot water, allow it to dry and then sand it with fine grade glasspaper before applying the stain. Again, because they contain water, the stains should not be used on veneered surfaces bonded with Scotch glue or, indeed, on any veneers that might swell

135

when they absorb water. Take care when applying them, and work quickly so that hard edges and streaks are avoided. On greasy or oily woods such as teak or cedar, penetration is poor and such woods are best stained with spirit stains. They have a slow drying time of at least twelve hours, depending on the temperature. Be careful to sand the surface very lightly once the stain has dried or you could remove some of the colour.

SPIRIT STAINS

These are obtainable ready made, or you can make your own by dissolving spirit-soluble aniline powder in methylated spirit. The approximate quantities for mixing are the same as those for water stains. Remember that the function of spirit stains is to hide the grain, so you will need to adjust the mixture if you want a 'wash' coat. Some experimenting on test pieces will be needed.

As with water stains, there is a wide variety of colours, such as various shades of oak (including limed oak), mahogany, walnut, teak, rosewood, satinwood, browns, reds, greens, yellow, blue, purple, grey, and black. All colours can be intermixed.

The advantages include the following.

Because of their masking properties, the stains are ideal for touching in faults in wood surfaces. For the same reason, they can be used to simulate grain effects. They do not raise the grain. They have a very fast drying time because the methylated spirit evaporates quickly – usually in a few minutes.

The stains also have their disadvantages. Because of their fast drying time, the stains need to be applied quickly with a large brush, a polisher's mop, or a rag. Always apply *with* the grain, never across it, and try to avoid overlaps because they will dry as streaks. Normal spirit stains tend to fade and are not light-fast, but there is one type called 'Alcovar' that is resistant to ultraviolet light and therefore light-fast. Penetration can be poor, and the powder can dry out and become loose on the surface.

VARNISH STAINS

These consist of varnishes to which colouring materials have been added, and they are widely available from DIY stores, etc. Normally, they are used for inexpensive furniture and joinery such as

doors, stair handrails, partitions, etc. They are made by several manufacturers and, while the colours are usually those of woods such as oak, mahogany, teak, walnut, and the like, there are also reds and greens. Apply the stain direct from the tin by brush. Allow about three days for thorough drying, then sand off with a fine grade glasspaper. You can then brush on one or two coats of any polyurethane lacquer to produce a surface that is very resistant to heat, alcohol, acids, and general wear.

The advantages of such stains include the fact that they are easily available and reasonably priced, which are the major reasons for their popularity. Although full drying time is about three days, they can be used after six to twelve hours, depending on temperature. They do not raise the grain. The stained surface need not necessarily receive any further treatment but can be used as it is. They are light-fast and will not fade.

The disadvantages are that they have only superficial penetration; they tend to mask the grain, and they also tend to build up a surface thickness. Because of this, they are not suitable for antique restoration.

STAINING WAXES

These are ideal for the many people who like waxed finishes. One of the best is Black Bison wax which is silicone-free and can be applied by brush or with a pad of fine steel wool on to the bare wood, French polish, or varnish. They are available in eleven shades (all wood colours, plus one clear). And the shades are light-fast and can be mixed with one another.

CHEMICAL STAINS FOR MIXING AT HOME

VANDYKE CRYSTALS

Most polish suppliers stock these. They should be dissolved in warm water and the solution strained through an old nylon stocking to remove any sediment. A teaspoonful of household ammonia to a pint (0.5 litre) will improve the penetrative qualities. It is difficult to specify the exact quantity of crystals because it depends on the strength of stain you want, so a little experimenting is called for. A fairly dilute solution will give good results on oak, mahogany, and walnut, tending to make the natural colour warmer and mellower. Before subsequently polishing the surface, seal it with a thin coat of shellac.

BICHROMATE OF POTASH CRYSTALS

Again, these are sold by most polish suppliers. The stain is made by dissolving the crystals in water until you have a saturated solution – that is, a solution in which the water can absorb no more. This forms a concentrated stock that can be diluted to requirements.

Although the solution has a rich orange tint, it produces a deep brown colour on mahogany, greenish-brown on oak, but does not affect all woods. This is because it reacts only with those containing tannic acid. So if you need to stain such woods as birch, American whitewood, or pine, they must first be primed with tannic or pyrogallic acid. Your local pharmacist should be able to order this specially for you.

The stain is 'fugitive' – that is, it will fade in strong sunlight. Add to this the fact that the crystals are poisonous and can harm the skin, and it seems hardly worth the bother in making it up when there are so many excellent proprietary stains.

POTASSIUM PERMANGANATE CRYSTALS

These should also be dissolved in water, when they create a beautiful purple coloured solution. Years ago, the solution was used as a foot bath for hot, tired feet – a job it did very well. The snag was that it stained the feet a warm brown colour! It does the same thing with wood, but it is very fugitive and I cannot recommend it as a permanent stain.

ASPHALTUM

This is obtainable in small granules or chunks, which are dissolved in turpentine substitute (or preferably genuine turpentine). Warm the mixture in a pan placed inside another one containing hot water. Alternatively, bitumen black powder can be prepared in the same way. There are two further stages to making the stain. First, strain it through an old nylon stocking to remove any sediment; second, add a tablespoonful of gold size to each pint (0.5 litre) to act as a binder.

COPPERAS

There are three kinds of copperas; green (sulphate of iron), blue (copper sulphate), and white (sulphate of zinc). Only the first is of any use as a stain. Dissolve a teaspoonful of crystals to a pint (0.5 litre) of water for a medium strength blue stain, which can be diluted or concentrated as required. When used as a pale blue stain, it will kill the redness of mahogany so that it resembles walnut, and this is its main use.

It will also give oak a blue-grey colour. Possibly its most interesting feature is that it will turn sycamore grey, thus producing 'harewood'. The principal factor in its action is the strength of the solution so you must be prepared to experiment with test pieces. When used as a stain, brush a thin coat of shellac on the surface to seal it before polishing.

The following notes may be of help to restorers who want to use genuinely old stains from choice or necessity; I must emphasise that I have used none of them myself so they should be well tested on scrap pieces.

John Evelyn, in his book *Sylva* (1664), refers to beech furniture being washed over with a decoction made of the green husks of walnuts in order to make it resemble walnut. This decoction was probably made by soaking the husks in rainwater for several days, and then adding bicarbonate of soda at the rate of one tablespoonful per gallon (4.5 litres), which acted as a binder. The liquid was then heated slowly and simmered (but not boiled) for a couple of days, after which it was allowed to cool, and was eventually strained off into bottles and kept in a dark place.

Another recipe he mentions is for ebonising pearwood, which is an eminently suitable wood for the treatment because of its fine, even grain. To quote him:

> There is a black which Joyners use to tinge their Pear tree with, and make it resemble Ebony, and likewise Fir and other woods for Cabinets, Picture Frames etc. which is this – take logwood, boyle it in ordinary oyle, and with this paint them over, when tis dry work it over a second time with lamp black and strong size. That also dry, rub off the sootiness adhering to it with a soft brush or cloth.

IRON STAIN

Another old-fashioned stain was made from a handful of iron nails steeped in a quart (1 litre) of ordinary vinegar for a week or so. The liquid was then strained and produced a stain that gave oak a cold black colour.

Regarding lamp black, Charles Hayward mentions in one of his books that this was made in Victorian times by holding a piece of tinned sheet metal over a gas fishtail burner and scraping off the deposit. Unlike the deposits from an oil or candle flame, it was not oily or greasy. For those who insist on complete authenticity, the flame from a piece of burning wood gives a non-greasy black; modern gas blowlamps do not, however, deposit anything.

Logwood, also known as Campeachy (*Haematoxylon campechianum*) comes mainly from the Gulf of Mexico and is a bright red wood still obtainable from specialist hardwood suppliers. Stalker and Parker describe how to use it in their book, *A Treatise on Japanning and Varnishing* (1688), as follows:

Take log-wood and boil it in water or vinegar, and whilst very hot brush or stain over your wood with it two or three times; then take the Galls, and Copperas, well beaten, and boil them in water, with which wash or stain your work so often till it be a black to your mind; the oftener it is laid, the better will your black be; if your work be small enough, you may steep it in your liquors instead of washing it.

The Galls referred to were probably from the Gall Oak tree (*Quercus infectoria*) and were used to make ink; the Copperas was the green kind, ferrous sulphate. Incidentally, Indian ink was used in the eighteenth century by amateur japanners, so it can be regarded as a legitimate material to use. It consisted of lamp black mixed with glue size. I mention this because Thomas Sheraton in his *Cabinet Dictionary* (1803) writes that ebonising was carried out 'by a few washes of a hot decoction of galls, and when dry, adding writing ink, polishing it with a stiff brush, and a little hot wax'.

In the same book Sheraton gives a recipe for staining mahogany with 'red oil' made from alkanet and dragon's blood. Alkanet is the old name for the anchusa plant, which is a well known English garden flower. The exotically named dragon's blood is a bright red gum from the dragon tree, which grows in Malaya and other tropical regions. Until the recent advent of photosetting in the printing trade, it was used as an acid resist by printing-block makers. It is still freely obtainable from polish suppliers.

To return to Sheraton's recipe. Alkanet, he writes,

was much in use amongst cabinet-makers, for making red oil; the best composition for which, as far as I know, is as follows: take a quart (1.13 litres) of good linseed oil, to which put a quarter of a pound (112 grams) of alkanet root, as much opened with the hand as possible, that the bark of the root which tinges the oil may fly off; to this put an ounce (28 grams) of dragon's blood, and another of rose pink, finely pounded in a mortar; set the whole within a moderate heat for twelve hours at least, or better if a day and a night. Then strain it through a flannel into a bottle for use. This staining oil is not applicable to every sort of mahogany... [mahogany that is] close grained and hard and wants briskness of colour, the above oil will help it much. All hard mahogany of a bad colour should be oiled with it, and should stand unpolished a time, proportioned to its quality and texture of grain; if it be laid on hard wood to be polished off immediately, it is of little use; but if it stand a few days after, the oil penetrates the grain and hardens on the surface, and consequently will bear a better polish, and look brighter in colour.

The 'rose pink' he refers to was actually whiting dyed with a decoction of brazil wood, which is a hard timber, bright orange in colour with dark red stripes. No doubt you could substitute an oil-soluble modern powder colour.

There is another way to make red oil which you may like to try. The basic ingredient is alkanet root. You will probably have to sacrifice one of your garden plants because this does not seem to be commercially available. About 4oz (113g) are needed in the form of short strips bruised with a hammer. Steep them in a pint (0.5 litre) of raw linseed oil, to which a tablespoonful of turpentine substitute has been added, for two or three days, stirring occasionally. Finally strain it and bottle it. This makes a fairly strong colour and you may have to dilute it with linseed oil.

Finally, here is a recipe for 'The True French Polish' from a book called *The Cabinet Maker's Guide* (1830) by G. A. Siddons:

To one pint (0.5 litre) of spirits of wine (modern equivalent – methylated spirit), add a quarter of an ounce (7g) of gum-copal, a quarter of an ounce (7g) of gum-arabic, and one ounce (28g) of shell-lac. Let your gums be well bruised, and sifted through a piece of muslin. Put the spirits and the gums together in a vessel that can be close corked, place them near a warm stove, and frequently shaking them, in two or three days they will be dissolved: strain it through a piece of muslin and keep it tight corked for use.

It seems that this was simply brushed on in the same way as a varnish and not rubbered like conventional French polish.

DEALING WITH MINOR FAULTS

SURFACE MARKS

White heat marks on a French-polished surface are usually caused by placing hot plates or dishes on it, or by spilling hot water. Make up a 50/50 mixture of boiled linseed oil and turpentine substitute and apply it to the area with a cloth. Allow it to stand for ten minutes or so before wiping it off. Alternatively, you can use camphorated oil. In each case, neutralise the oils by rubbing on a few drops of vinegar afterwards. You may have to repeat the process two or three times to remove the marks completely.

You can also use the camphorated oil treatment on marks caused by cold water that has been spilled accidentally, again neutralising it with vinegar. Or you can rub the marks with metal polish, but do not let the polish dry – wipe it off before this happens.

There is another dramatic and flashy (literally) method which those with strong nerves can try. It involves standing the surface to be treated as nearly vertical as possible and wiping over the marks with a soft cloth that has been warmed. Then wet the cloth with methylated spirit, but not so much that it drips, and go over the marks again. Then set light to the spirit at the bottom of the film (never at the top or you will burn the finish) so that it flashes alight and removes the marks. Finish by applying a coat of furniture polish.

Similar marks on a varnished surface need to be tackled by some form of abrasive treatment. The mildest way is to moisten a piece of finest grade wire wool, or a cloth, with some light machine oil (the kind used for sewing machines or bicycles) and dip it into cigar or cigarette ash, or ordinary salt, and rub the marks in the direction of the grain.

There are two further methods that are particularly suitable for dealing with varnished surfaces. One is to rub the marks with a soft cloth dipped in a paste of fine pumice powder and light machine oil, working with the grain. The other is to damp a cloth with cold water, wring it out and sprinkle a couple of drops of household ammonia on to it. Rub the marks immediately, drying the surface with another soft cloth.

A simple remedy for disguising small scratches is to rub them with the kernel of a pecan nut, a walnut, or a brazil nut, all of which contain natural oils that will often hide the defect. Or you can try one of the several proprietary cleaners.

SURFACE SCRATCHES AND CRACKS

Small blemishes are easily made good, using one or other of the proprietary fillers that can be bought from DIY stores or polish suppliers. They are usually in stick or crayon form and are inexpensive. Wax filler sticks can be cut into chips which you soften by kneading with your fingers and pressing into cracks or scratches. You can also smooth off or shape the filler with the point of a hot knife. There is a knack to using a hot knife, or better still, the tip of a soldering iron. The stick should be pressed against the heated tip so that a piece melts and drops into the crack, where it can be pressed and moulded into shape.

This kind of filling is also known as 'beaumontage' and it is not difficult to make up your own. It is worth knowing how to do this because you may have to match a colour that is not in the proprietary range, and because the filler is wax-based it cannot afterwards be stained. You will need a round or rectangular tin – an empty tobacco tin is ideal – fitted with a simple handle. Place it over a gentle heat and put in it a small quantity of beeswax (either the bleached white, or the light brown, according to the final colour you want), an equal amount of rosin, a few flakes of shellac, and mix them together. Add as much powder colour as necessary while you stir. Vandyke powder is the base for walnut and dark oak, and red ochre or Venetian red for mahogany. The rosin is a stock commodity of polish suppliers. Once set, the beaumontage can be stored and small amounts extracted, melted, and applied as described above.

If you need a filler that can afterwards be stained, choose a shellac stick. This is applied with the tip of a hot knife or the bit of a soldering iron in just the same manner as the wax fillers described above. The difference is that, once set, it can be sanded down and stained.

Really deep cavities such as may be sustained while moving house, or as a result of wood decay or attacks of woodworm, need special treatment.

All polish, grease, dirt, and loose wood must be cleared away, and the area round the hole masked off with masking tape. Before applying the filler, it is advisable to provide some kind of anchorage to hold it in place. An effective way is to drive in some small veneer pins so that their heads protrude but do not stand proud of the surrounding surface. Use an epoxy resin filler (such as Araldite) mixed with sawdust of the appropriate colour, and slightly overfill the cavity so that once the filler has cured it can be sanded level. There is a stage early in the curing process when the filler assumes the consistency of hard cheese, and if you catch it at this stage you will be able to slice it level with a sharp knife.

Colouring in any filler to match the surrounding wood is a laborious process, and is best done with artists' water colours used fairly dry. Start by applying a thin coat of shellac, then brush on the water colour lightly and gingerly. You will certainly have to build up the colour with successive coats, fixing each one with a thin film of shellac. Remember, you can always darken a light colour, but it's liable to be messy and tricky to do the opposite.

FILLING THE GRAIN

This is only necessary for saving labour and materials on high gloss finishes, and the modern partiality for natural waxed finishes means that the process is not used as often as it used to be.

In the old days, the two principal fillers were plaster of Paris made into a paste with water; or whiting, also made into a paste but with pure turpentine. Both pastes were coloured to match the wood by the addition of the appropriate powder colours. Actually, the grain of any wood can be filled by polishing alone, and this is the better way of doing it. But it will involve you in a lot of work and the use of much material.

Plaster of Paris is still employed and is sometimes listed as 'superfine' plaster by suppliers. The work should first be stained and, when dry, given a couple of coats of clear shellac. This must also be allowed to dry – it will fix the stain and also prevent the filler from losing its colour at a later date. The filler should be tinted with powder colour when you are at the paste-making stage, and only enough colour is needed to tone down the whiteness. For a colour that will eventually be 'natural', the filler need not be tinted at all.

Plaster of Paris sets quickly, so you should only deal with a small area at a time. Rub it on as a thick paste with an old rag or a piece of loosely woven canvas in a circular motion, using plenty of elbow grease, and then rub it off across the grain. There are bound to be corners and crevices where the filler dries as a thick deposit, and these have to be cleaned out with a brush, a pointed stick, or both.

Once this has been done and all is dry, apply a coat of oil with a piece of wadding, followed by a sanding with glasspaper. This will create a thick paste of plaster and oil on the surface which should be wiped off with a rag. What oil you use depends on whether the finish is to be natural or coloured. For the former, use white oil (also called white mineral oil); for the latter, linseed oil.

There are also proprietary fillers such as 'Wheeler's' which are readily obtainable. Apply them in accordance with the maker's instructions. They are made in several colours, so there should be no problem in using them.

SEALING THE GRAIN

A sealer is to a polish finish what an undercoat is to a paint finish; the sealer provides a bond between the stained surface and the final polish and it also prevents the polish from sinking into the surface.

There are several kinds, all available from polish suppliers. There are shellac-based kinds for subsequent French polishing; cellulose-based for cellulose lacquers; those for use under oil varnishes; and a general purpose one for use with French polish, cellulose lacquer, and polyurethane lacquer. It also protects the colour from the fading effect of ultraviolet light.

They can all be applied by brush or a rag with no difficulty. You can dilute a polyurethane lacquer with thinners (usually turpentine substitute) in the proportion of 5 to 1, and use that as a sealer.

MATCHING IN A REPAIR

How you tackle this depends to a great extent upon the size of the repair. As a general rule, if the area is less than ¾in (19mm) square you should not need to stain it. Larger areas do need staining, however, and it is a job requiring a delicate touch. You can apply a water stain by brush or rag, and in both cases they should be just moist; otherwise a hard line will develop between the old and the new work that will be difficult to disguise.

Brush a light film of shellac over the stain to fix it. If the colour is too dark after everything has dried, dip a piece of fine steel wool in methylated spirit and rub the area until the colour becomes paler. You are now ready to match in both the grain and any figure in the wood, and this is best done with a pencil brush and artists' water colours. The important thing is to use the brush in short strokes with the minimum of water and colour. Don't overdo it, or the area will appear too dark and too obvious. Finally, wait until the colour is dry, and then brush on a coat of shellac. You can then go ahead with normal polishing.

FRENCH POLISHING

Before describing the traditional method of French polishing, mention must be made of several proprietary finishes such as Furniglas, Duraxalin, Wuncote, and others that give the appearance of French polish without the labour or the need for special skills. Many of them also confer extra resistance to domestic hazards. They are perfectly acceptable to those who are not restoring antiques and have no need of authenticity. They should be applied in accordance with the manufacturer's instructions because methods vary with differences in formulation.

Turning now to traditional French polish, you must appreciate that, like upholstery, it is a skilled trade on its own, and while the information given should enable you to make a reasonably good job, only plenty of practice will produce results of consistently high quality.

Probably no other finish gives such a hard brilliant shine combined with a deep lustre that shows wood off to its best advantage, and for these reasons it has retained its popularity over the years. Unfortunately, it is easily marked by water, heat, or spirits. Spilt alcohol dissolves it, but any accidents can usually easily be put right.

TYPES OF FRENCH POLISH

Basically the polish consists of shellac dissolved in industrial alcohol, which is only available to the trade. Methylated spirit is the same thing but with additives such as pyridine, wood spirit, and methyl violet dye to make it unpalatable.

You could make up your own polish by dissolving shellac in methylated spirit, but as there is a wide range of colours and grades offered by polish suppliers at reasonable prices, it is really not worth it. The standard types are given below; most of them are available in either hard or soft quality.

So-called as it is made from shellac shaped like translucent buttons. It is best used for warm golden brown shades. If it is applied to a dark stain, it will tend to give a muddy colour.

Garnet polish This is a dark polish and is the one most frequently used for antiques.

French polish A medium brown colour.

White polish A light-coloured, almost clear polish made from bleached shellac.

Transparent white polish Colourless and very hard; made from bleached and de-waxed shellac.

Black polish Used for jet black finishes.

Brush polish Contains an additive to slow down the drying time, thus allowing the polish time to flow. Normally brushed on to turned work.

EQUIPMENT

You can store the polish in plastic or glass bottles, labelling each with its contents. Choose bottles with screw-on caps that can be pierced with small holes. Pierce two holes per cap, so that one allows the polish to be shaken out drop by drop, and the other enables replacement air to enter. You will also need several screw-top jars – the kinds used for instant coffee are ideal – for storing 'fads' and 'rubbers', which should be kept separate.

A fad is a piece of wadding employed to apply and build up the polish. Buy the special wadding sold by polish suppliers because ordinary cotton wool is useless. To prepare it, take a piece of wadding about 10in (250mm) square and soak it in polish. Allow it to dry, soften it with methylated spirit, and wring it out. This will stop loose threads from sticking to the work. Now look at Fig 10:3 which shows the stages in folding the wadding to make a fad. Because this is rather complicated, it's

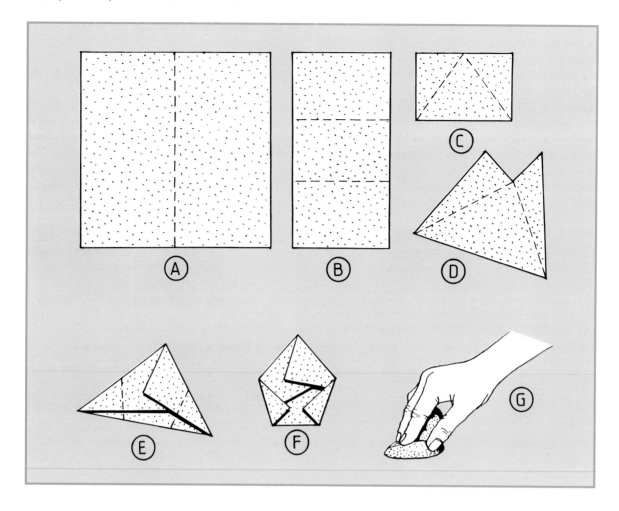

Fig 10:3 Stages in making a fad

a good plan to try a few practice runs first, damping the wadding with water instead of polish. Shape the fad to fit your hand; (G) shows the way to hold it.

The rubber is used to give a final finish to the surface once it has been built up by the fad. A rubber is simply a fad covered with a piece of rag, which should be folded over it. You must choose the right kind of rag, which should ideally be linen but can be cotton. Man-made mixtures are not suitable because they are not absorbent enough.

You will also need a small quantity of oil, say, about half an eggcupful. It can either be raw linseed oil or, preferably, white oil (sometimes called 'mineral oil' or 'white mineral oil'), because this does not thicken so easily and is less greasy than linseed.

FADDING

Arrange the work against the light (for instance, in front of a window) so that you can see the marks where the fad has been. Try to make your strokes towards and away from your body, because moving your arm from side to side means that the stokes will be in the shape of an arc, which is undesirable. Charge the fad by opening the folds and dripping in enough polish to make it fairly wet; then press it on to a piece of paper or cardboard to spread the polish evenly.

Start fadding by working backwards and forwards along the grain, pressing down firmly to force the polish into the pores all over the surface. Repeat the process two or three times until there is a thin film all over, recharging the fad when necessary. Fig 10:4(A) shows what the path of the fad should be during this stage. Allow the film to dry and then flatten it by sanding lightly with the finest grade of glasspaper held in the hand: this is one of the few occasions when such a method of holding the glasspaper is recommended.

Now recharge the fad, but before using it, flick a few drops of oil on the surface of the work. Then spread the oil all over with the fad, pressing down very lightly and moving it in wide arcs. You should be able to see an oily smear following the path of the fad, the purpose being to lubricate its passage over the polish. If the fad skids, you are using too much oil, so wipe it off with a clean rag and go over the surface again until the oil is evenly spread.

Fig 10:4 Using the fad – the various strokes

Keeping the fad charged with polish, go over the surface as shown at (B) by making small circles round the edges and filling in with large loops. At first the fad will move easily because the oil acts as a lubricant, but it will gradually become stiffer to use, so apply plenty of pressure and recharge it from time to time. The polish will gradually take off the oil. You will see bright patches appearing, and the pores should appear well filled with polish. You may find at this stage that ridges form round the path of the fad (they are called 'whips'); this is caused by excess polish oozing out. Try to rub them down with the fad immediately. If this is unsuccessful, allow the polish to dry thoroughly and rub them down with fine grade glasspaper

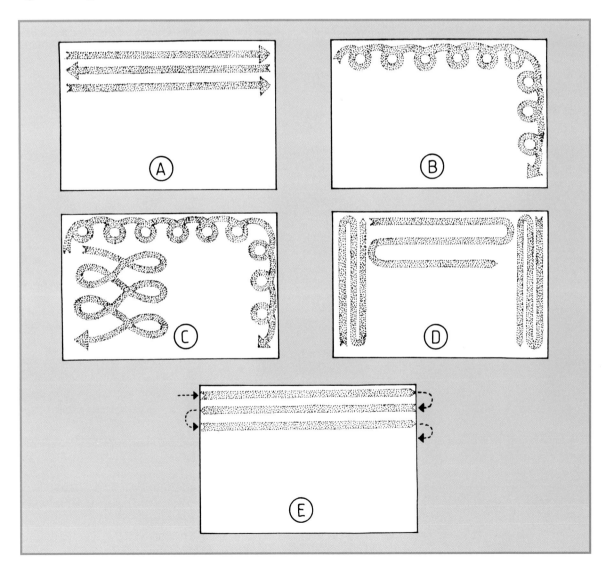

lubricated with a few spots of oil. Then wipe away the dust and oil and go over once again with the fad.

Now change the path of the fad to that shown at (C); namely, long figures-of-eight, and gradually transform them to the straight strokes shown at (D). You need to use a rubber next instead of a fad, moving it in long parallel strokes with the grain (see E). Glide the rubber on and off at the ends of the strokes and never dab it down on to the surface or you will ruin it.

The rubber must be charged with polish by unwrapping the outer folds and dripping in just enough polish so that when you pinch the point, the polish just oozes through the cloth. As a result of all this exertion, the surface should be bright and quite free from oil. Now leave it for 24 hours to harden. This is the time to fill any small holes or cracks with a shellac stick as already described, and once this has been done you can get on with the process called 'bodying up'.

Begin this by flicking a few drops of oil on to the

surface of the work and glide on your rubber, charged with polish. Distribute the oil evenly all over with strokes as shown at (A), Fig 10:5, making small figures-of-eight round the edges and larger ones in the centre. Next, gradually change to the long figures-of-eight shown at (B), charging the rubber as necessary (normally about three times). Continue by gradually changing to the movement shown at (C), when the surface should be smooth and glossy. There will probably be some oil still left on it which you can wipe off with a clean rag moistened with methylated spirit. It will dull the surface slightly, which does not matter at this stage.

Finally, having finished the basic bodying up, we come to the finishing. You will need to make up a separate rubber for this, which should be kept for this particular job. Also, make up a 50/50 mixture of polish and methylated spirit to be used for this final bodying.

Flick a few drops of oil on the surface and spread it evenly with the rubber which has been charged with the 50/50 mixture. Use light, even pressure until the rubber dries out, moving it in circles with an occasional straight stroke along the

Fig 10:5 The technique for using a rubber

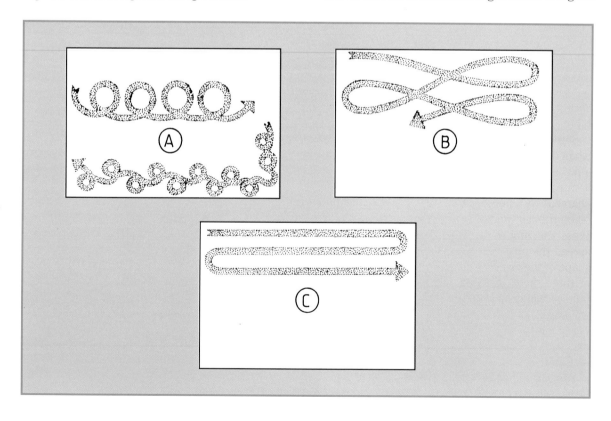

grain until the rubber is dry. You should then be left with a surface that carries just a very thin, delicate film of oil.

Carry on immediately by 'spiriting off'. You will need another new rubber for this, which should be kept for the job and no other, and it should be charged with a few drops of methylated spirit applied to the fad. Test for the right amount of spirit by touching it to your lips – it should not be wet, but cold and sharp. Wrap the fad in its cloth to make a rubber, and glide this on to the surface, moving it rapidly with firm pressure in long figures-of-eight and circles. This will not only remove all traces of oil but also achieve the desired aim – that of burnishing the surface so that it looks lustrous and mirror-like. As a finishing touch, dip the face of the rubber into Vienna chalk and rub with long strokes that will improve the finish even more.

As I said at the start, to become proficient calls for a great deal of practical experience, because a professional French polisher develops a 'feel' for handling the fad and the rubber, and knows intuitively just what needs to be done to the surface at any particular stage. A first-class book on the subject is Charles Hayward's *Staining and Polishing* (see Bibliography).

POLISHING MOULDINGS
These are awkward to polish, not least because of the problem of holding them while doing it. The easiest way is by means of double-sided adhesive tape.

Start by applying some polish with a fad, and when dry apply a thin coat of varnish. Next, tear off a piece of used fad and wring out any polish. Fold it in a piece of rag to make a small rubber, and charge it with polish, continuing by putting a little oil on the face and dipping it into pumice powder. Press the rubber on to a piece of cardboard to spread the mixture evenly; then mould it into the shape of the profile. Rub it along the moulding two or three times, applying steady pressure, and the pumice will cut back the varnish while the polish will burnish it to a shiny finish. Finally, run a clean rag along the moulding once or twice to remove

the last traces of oil, and the job is done.

POLISHING TURNINGS
One problem is how to hold these while polishing them. A single turning can be left in the lathe and turned by hand, but if you have several to do, try making up a few 'cradles' as shown in Fig 10:6.

Another problem is, that by their very nature, turnings are bound to have end grain showing somewhere which, if you are not careful, will absorb more than its fair share of polish. To combat this, use a weaker solution of stain than normal and apply it with a rag. Wipe off the stain before it penetrates too deeply into the end grain and, at the same time, apply a little more to the areas of straight grain. When you are satisfied that the stain is as evenly distributed as possible, brush on two coats of brush polish and sand them lightly. Brush polish contains a special additive that slows down the drying time so that it can flow easily.

Then, with a used fad charged with the brush polish, apply a coat to the workpiece while rotating it by hand; allow the polish to dry and follow with another coat. Finally, spirit off in the manner described for French polishing but use a ¾ polish to ¼ methylated spirit mixture instead of half and half.

POLISHING INSIDE SURFACES
These do not call for special care and, in general, a couple of fads of shellac will suffice to give a clean

Fig 10:6 A simple cradle for holding turned work while polishing

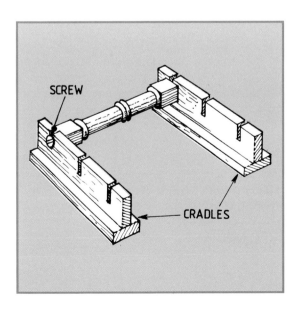

SCREW

CRADLES

finish. A good alternative would be two coats of hard spirit varnish, rubbed down between coats.

WAX POLISHES

These impart beautiful finishes to wood and they improve with age and being re-waxed from time to time. Such a finish can, however, become grubby on pieces that are constantly handled, and these should first be sealed with a coat or two of shellac. Unfortunately, this does mean that the wax cannot enter the grain of the wood and, although you will get a good shine, you will not get the depth of lustre.

You can make up your own polish to one or other of the following recipes.

Basic polish Shred yellow or brown beeswax (a potato peeler or nutmeg grater will be useful for this) and dissolve it in pure turpentine. You can speed things up by standing the container in a saucepan of hot water; the completed polish should have the consistency of a thin cream.

Light coloured polish Make as above but use bleached beeswax.

White coloured polish Mix in white powder colour to the light-coloured recipe; this polish will leave traces of a white deposit in the grain of the wood.

Black polish Add lamp black powder to the basic polish and mix thoroughly. But modern wax polishes are so good and easy to apply, and can be obtained in so many different colours, that to make your own is only worth doing in extraordinary circumstances. In addition, such polishes can be used for staining the wood, thus avoiding the need for the conventional staining process. Should you nevertheless want to apply a separate stain, then it can be either water or oil. In the case of oil, you will have to seal the coat with an application of shellac.

Avoid silicone and quick-drying wax polishes, which both have their uses but are not to be recommended for this kind of work. Rather, use a wax that does not dry too quickly – say, in less than an hour. Apply it freely and evenly with a cloth or a brush of the shoe-brush type – the latter is particularly useful for carvings and mouldings – and rub off the excess with a piece of coarse rag or canvas. Allow the polish to dry for an hour or two, then repeat the process. Should you require an antique effect, rub the excess off the main central areas but allow a build-up round the edges and in the crevices of mouldings and carvings. Don't overdo it, however, because the effect can quickly assume a laboured and contrived appearance.

After three or four applications, you can put on a coat of quick-drying wax polish with a wad of soft cloth, working a small area at a time and buffing it up with a clean, soft, lint-free rag before moving to the next one. A polishing bonnet tied over a disc sander in a power drill will soon bring up a brilliant shine. Move it lightly and rapidly first across the grain and then finish by sweeping it along the grain.

Any subsequent blemishes caused by spilling water, or exposure to heat or sunlight can be removed by rubbing with turpentine substitute on a cloth and then made good by re-waxing.

LINSEED OIL FINISH

This is a straightforward finish and does involve a lot of hard work, but it is not marked by heat or water. Because of the way in which it is applied, it is only suitable for large flat surfaces such as table tops.

You will find raw linseed oil more successful than the boiled kind, which does not dry so well. Put the oil in a double-boiler and heat it until it begins to simmer. Then take it off the heat, but watch the oil all the time you are heating it because it is inflammable. Add pure turpentine to ⅛th of the volume of oil, and a teaspoonful of terebene driers for each ½ pint (0.28 litre) of the mixture. Apply it with a brush of the shoe-cleaning type and scrub it well into the grain. Now comes the hard work: wrap a piece of felt or soft lint-free cloth round a weight such as a house brick and rub the surface long and hard. Do the same thing every day for three or four weeks. This should bring up a superb glowing surface that can always be revived by re-oiling and rubbing.

The treatment is good for mahogany, especially if the oil is tinted red. Do not use it on walnut, however, unless you want a very dark brown, almost black, colour.

MODERN SYNTHETIC FINISHES

Under this heading come polyurethane varnishes, and teak oil. There is little point in describing how to apply them because the manufacturers go to great lengths to make them as fool-proof as possible, and give full instructions on the can or in accompanying leaflets.

POLYURETHANE LACQUER (VARNISH)

This is probably the most popular wood finish used by woodworkers, particularly for modern furniture. Deservedly so, because it is straightforward to apply (full instructions are given by manufacturers), is reasonable in price, and easy to obtain, and it gives a finish that is resistant to all the normal domestic hazards. It will even resist a burning cigarette for some time. It is unwise to apply it in cold or damp conditions, and you must make real efforts to keep the surroundings as dust-free as possible. The old-time coach painters used to work almost naked so that no fluff or dust could come from their clothing. You don't have to go to such lengths but it·makes sense not to wear a woolly cardigan or hat, and also to sprinkle some water on the floor to stop dust from being kicked up.

Neither a grain filler nor a sealer is necessary. In fact, the lacquer is viscous enough in its own right to fill the grain, and when the first coat is thinned with white spirit as recommended by the manufacturers (usually 30 or 50 per cent), it is readily absorbed by the outer layers of the wood.

You can use water, spirit, naphtha, or bicarbonate of potash stains before you apply the lacquer, but not oil stains. Always wipe off any deposits that may lie on the surface after staining because they can cause muddiness. Another good method is to colour some French polish with a spirit dye and colour the wood with it. In that case, the first coat of lacquer should not be diluted.

Apply the lacquer with a perfectly dry varnish brush or you may find the bonding of one coat to the next will suffer. You can dry a slightly damp brush by dipping it in methylated spirit which, when it evaporates, will take the water with it. Allow six hours for the solvents in the lacquer to evaporate before applying another coat (the complete curing process actually takes several days), but do not delay the re-coating more than twelve hours or the coats will not bond properly.

A standard and very effective finish results from applying three coats (the first one being diluted according to manufacturer's instructions), sanding down lightly between each, and rubbing down the final one with steel wool dipped in wax to give a warm, satin-like sheen.

TEAK OIL

This is specially formulated for use on teak, which has a naturally greasy composition that can give problems when using other finishes. The oil can be used to restore the natural colour of other hardwoods; it gives a matt sheen finish. Apply as instructed.

CELLULOSE LACQUER

In almost all second-hand furniture showrooms it's a safe bet that most of the pieces will have been finished with this kind of lacquer because it was the standard industrial finish used between about 1925 and 1970. It provides a heat- and waterproof surface, which can also withstand hard knocks and abrasions, although not to the same degree as polyurethane lacquers, which are rapidly replacing it.

I have the greatest hesitation in recommending anyone to use it except in controlled factory conditions. When you realise that its basic ingredient is nitrocellulose, that its flashpoint is below 22°C (72°F), and that it is highly inflammable and can be explosive, you can understand why. In my years in the industry I saw enough spectacular factory explosions and fires to convince me that this is a finish best left to the experts.

If you have a piece of such furniture, you can remove the finish quite easily with cellulose thinners (from polish suppliers). Follow the instructions precisely and work in a well-ventilated place.

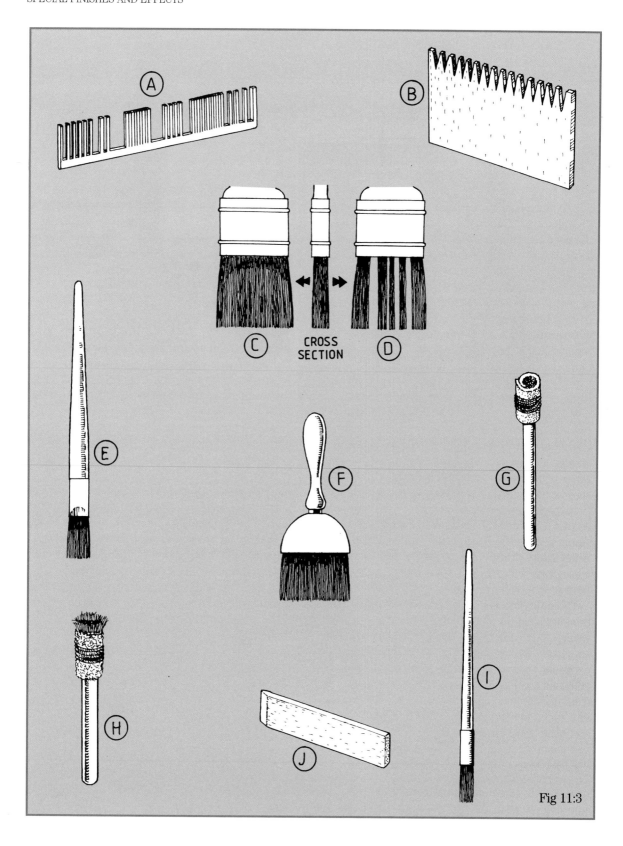

Fig 11:3

11 Special finishes and effects

This chapter is for those who, because of choice or the need to match another piece of furniture, have to work with special finishes.

FUMING WITH AMMONIA

In its simplest terms, this consists of exposing raw wood to the fumes of ammonia. The timbers that best respond are those which contain natural tannin such as oak and chestnut and, to a lesser extent, mahogany. Greasy timbers such as teak cannot be fumed.

It follows, then, that if you want to fume other timbers, they will need to be primed with either tannic or pyrogallic acid, or else they will not change colour at all. Before applying the acid, remove any metal fittings, particularly iron or steel screws, nails, and hinges because the acid will turn them black. Then wash the wood with warm water so that the pores will absorb the acid more readily. Apply the acid liberally with a sponge, taking the usual safety precautions to protect the hands and eyes. Wipe off excess acid and leave the piece to dry.

The next step is to fume it with ammonia – not the kind used for household cleaning, which is too weak – but with .880 ammonia as sold by polish suppliers. Remember that ammonia fumes are extremely penetrating and will affect all parts. If you want to fume, say, only the drawer fronts of an oak dresser, it is no good putting the whole drawer into the ammonia because the sides, end, bottom, and back of the drawer front will all be affected. If you cannot dismantle the drawer fronts, then you will have to mask the parts you do not want fumed

by taping plastic film or masking tape over them. You should also make sure all traces of glue or polish are completely removed, or the ammonia will be unable to do its job.

In the 1930s a fumed oak finish was a recognised and popular one in the trade, and some firms built special cabinets in which the work was done. If you wish, you could build something similar for yourself on the lines of the one shown in Fig 11:1. This incorporates a useful feature, namely a hole in which a test-stick can be inserted and withdrawn from time to time to check progress; the stick

Fig 11:1 A fuming cabinet

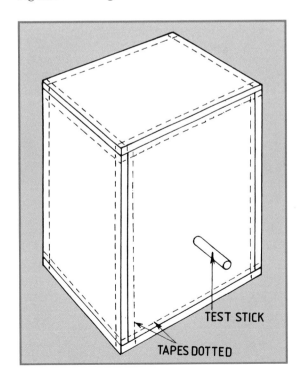

TEST STICK

TAPES DOTTED

Fig 11:3 The tools needed for 'faux bois'

should be made from the same wood as that being fumed. There is no need to go to great pains to make the cupboard, but you should stick adhesive plastic tape over the joints to stop the fumes escaping.

For the occasional job, you do not require anything so elaborate. An open framework supporting a plastic bag, preferably transparent so that you can see progress, is adequate, provided the plastic is held clear of the work, with its edges well weighted down. Again, insert a test piece that you can withdraw and replace easily, especially if the bag is not transparent.

Ammonia gives off pungent fumes that can damage your respiratory tract and lungs if you inhale it. Wear rubber gloves while you are handling it; pour some into a saucer and slip it carefully into the box or frame. How long it will take to produce the effect you require depends on how much tannin there is in the timber, how concentrated the fumes are (the less unoccupied space there is, the quicker the fumes will do their work), and how deep a shade you require. It's unlikely that you will get much effect in less than four or five hours, and twelve to twenty-four hours is quite common. Test every hour or so and replenish the saucer with fresh ammonia if necessary.

If you intend to undertake fuming as a regular practice, it is worth treating some offcuts of the kinds of timber you will be using as test-pieces, making notes of the time taken, whether acids were used or not, and so on. Should any timber contain too much tannic acid it can be neutralised by washing it with an alkali such as borax.

Finally remove the workpiece carefully. It will still smell strongly of ammonia so leave it in a well-ventilated place for a day or two for it to air. You may find that pieces that were washed with tannic acid have a dark purplish-black deposit on them. You can remove this by rubbing with a pad of wire wool dipped in methylated spirit.

The recipes for making tannic acid and pyrogallic acid are: 1oz tannin powder to 1 quart of water (28g: 1.1 litres); ¾oz pyrogallic to 1 quart of water (21g: 1.1 litres). Store the acids in plastic bottles and use plastic brushes or sponges, and do not allow them to touch metal. As old acid that has been in store will turn black, it is best to make up a fresh solution for each job.

BLEACHING

Different woods respond in different degrees to bleaching, and the following note includes the most common woods. You will need to experiment on offcuts of those not mentioned.

Bleach easily: ash, avodire, beech, birch, chestnut, elm, lime.

Two or more applications: mahoganies, maples, oaks, walnuts.

Very difficult: cherry, ebony, iroko, padauk, pines, poplars, rosewoods, satinwoods, teak, zebrawood.

HOME-MADE BLEACH
Although there are excellent proprietary bleaches, which will be described later, some readers may like to make their own from oxalic acid crystals (obtainable from polish suppliers) and water. To do so, dissolve 2oz (57g) of the crystals in one pint (0.5 litre) of very hot water. This solution can also be used to remove ink marks and the black stains that develop round iron or steel screws and nails in oak.

You will need stout rubber gloves, a rubber or plastic apron, and goggles, because oxalic acid is a poison. You should also wear a face mask if you have to sand down a surface that has been treated with the acid because the dust could irritate your lungs. Apply the solution while it is hot, using a large brush followed by a sponge to distribute it evenly into all cracks and crevices. Let it stand for half an hour and then wipe it off with a rag. You should then be able to see how effective the bleach has been and, if necessary, repeat the process.

When you are satisfied, neutralise the bleach by washing the workpiece down with a solution made in the proportion of 1 part .880 ammonia to 10 parts of cold water. Follow this by washing down with cold water, and allow the workpiece to dry out thoroughly. An alternative neutralising agent is white vinegar, used undiluted, and it should be followed by the wash-down with clean water and the subsequent drying out. A half-strength solution of the bleach can often be useful for cleaning off stripped furniture.

PROPRIETARY BLEACHES
The domestic bleaches sold for household cleaning are not strong enough for serious work but can be

used to get rid of small stains by being dribbled on them, undiluted. Wear rubber gloves and work in a well-ventilated place so that the fumes can disperse easily. To neutralise the bleach, wash it off with cold water.

TWO-PART BLEACHES

These are very powerful and are always accompanied by the manufacturer's instructions for use, which should be followed precisely. Generally, the first part of the bleach is applied and allowed to soak into the grain. The second part is then applied while the first coat is still wet and the wood is turned white. The surface is neutralised according to the manufacturer's instructions.

LIMED OAK

You can achieve this finish either by using oil paint or a proprietary liming wax; both methods are straightforward and effective. Brushing along the grain with a wire suede-cleaning brush to open it up will enhance the effect in both cases.

Dealing with the oil paint method, the first requirement is to stain the wood to the background colour against which the limed effect of white flecks in the grain will stand out. A medium brown colour looks best because the white does not contrast enough with a light or natural colour, and appears startling and contrived against a very dark one. You can use water or naphtha stain (but not oil or spirit). Naphtha is to be preferred because it is non-grain raising – referred to in the trade as NGR.

When the stain has been applied and has dried, apply two coats of clear shellac, which will prevent the grain from absorbing the paint while allowing it to remain in the pores.

Next, brush on a thick coat of white paint all over the surface and allow it five or ten minutes to become tacky. Then wipe it off *across* the grain with a piece of canvas or hessian, which should leave a white deposit in the crevices of the grain but none on the surrounding areas.

Allow it to dry thoroughly overnight and then sand it off with fine glasspaper, rubbing along the grain. Remove the dust and apply a couple of coats of clear shellac. This can be the final finish or you can, if you wish, wax polish it.

PROPRIETARY LIMING WAXES

The first step, after having brushed along the grain with a wire brush, is to stain in the background colour in the manner described. Then apply a coat or two of clear shellac and, when dry, rub on the liming wax liberally. After a few minutes, rub off the excess *across* the grain, thus leaving deposits of wax in the pores. Once the liming wax has dried, you can apply ordinary clear wax polish over it in the usual way.

EBONISING

How you tackle this job depends on what kind of finish you want, whether a polished black one with no pretensions to being ebony or one which is a definite simulation.

For the first, you can stain and fill the grain of whatever timber you have chosen with a thin paste made up of superfine plaster (plaster of Paris), a black water-soluble aniline dye, and water. The surface will need rubbing down with fine grade glasspaper afterwards because the water will have raised the grain. It can then be given a couple of coats of clear shellac prior to waxing with a black wax, or French polishing. Any parts, such as edges, that show white after the sanding can be touched in with Indian ink.

True ebonising is rather more complicated, because ebony is an exceptionally closegrained timber, and unless you choose a wood with the same characteristics, the filler will sooner or later sink into the grain and the surface will not resemble ebony at all. Timbers that respond well are apple, beech, cherry, sycamore, and also true mahogany. African pseudo-mahoganies such as abura, afrormosia, afzelia, agba, gedu-nohor, guarea, iroko, sapele, etc, do not respond well because most of them have irregular or interlocked grain.

You can stain and fill the grain as described above, and then continue with conventional French polishing, using black polish. Use a barrier cream before starting work because you cannot stop your hands getting in a terrible mess. This method will give the wood a beautiful deep black shine.

True ebony, however, has a satin-like eggshell gloss, so the shine has to be reduced. Do this by working a series of superfine parallel scratches on

151

the surface with a soft-bristled, wide brush dipped in dry pumice powder. What you have to do is to imitate the grain effect, so keep the scratches as straight as possible and, in the case of rails or legs, make sure they run along the length and not across it.

PAINT FINISH

You may be surprised to learn that much of the furniture of the sixteenth and early seventeenth centuries was painted, often in quite garish colours. So if you are contemplating doing the same to brighten up some second-hand furniture, you are in good company!

Modern paint manufacturers go to a great deal of trouble to make their paints easy, convenient, and fool-proof to use, and they have been so successful that to describe methods of application is unnecessary. There are one or two points, however, that you should know. First, if you are painting softwood, all knots should be given a couple of coats of knotting, which is prepared from shellac and prevents the natural resin in the knot from bleeding through the paintwork later as a brown patch.

Second, how to avoid 'fat edges' and 'curtains'. A fat edge is caused by stroking the brush the wrong

Fig 11:2 How 'fat edges' and 'curtains' are caused

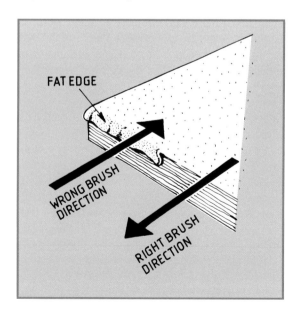

way over an edge as shown in Fig 11:2. Curtains are the runs of thick paint that result from not brushing the paint out evenly.

Apart from these small reminders, the manufacturers always give full instructions and, provided you follow them, it will be difficult to go wrong.

DISTRESSING

This is the treatment (or perhaps maltreatment) of furniture to make it look well worn and therefore, to many people's eyes, antique. Many readers may regard the practice as faking, but this is not necessarily so. After all, if a restorer is presented with three authentic antique chairs and asked to make a fourth, or a table that requires a new top, it is his job to see that everything matches.

The commonest fault with distressing is that it is overdone, and it is this that often confirms a fake. Indeed, one can occasionally find a genuine antique that exhibits very few signs of wear-and-tear because it has always been situated in an out-of-the way place. This is often the case with church furniture, and credence tables are a good example because their only purpose was to hold the bread and wine for Holy Communion.

The upper edges and corners of table tops are often worn, particularly on old oak furniture of the sixteenth and seventeenth centuries. This applies also to the centre parts of the stretcher rails, where many feet have rested over the centuries. Bearing in mind that these tables could well have stood on rushes or on a damp stone floor, it's not surprising that people preferred to rest their feet on the rails rather than on the floor. Similar remarks apply to chairs of the same period, except that it is the parts at the front that show most wear.

Another feature of this period of furniture is that the feet of tables and chairs are more often than not in a decayed state, having been subjected to years of damp and dirt. This can be imitated by wire brushing any replacement timber. The wood round knots is often worn away and leaves them standing proud, and this is another characteristic seized on by the faker.

Spurious wear-and-tear can be reproduced by means of rasps, wire brushes, metal chains (to make dents), a brick dropped from a height, or any other instrument your imagination can devise. And you can always resort to imitation woodworm holes but, again, this should not be overdone. It would be silly to riddle the new replacement part with holes if the rest of the piece is free of them. The holes are actually flight holes from which the fully developed beetle has emerged, and the only time you can see the tunnels and galleries they bore is when the outer casing of wood collapses. Some fakers slip up over this because they incorporate a worm-ridden piece of old timber that exposes the tunnels in a completely unnatural way. Finally, woodworm has never been found in genuine mahoganies from Cuba or Central America.

Furniture of the eighteenth and nineteenth centuries was comparatively well treated, probably because of the finer timbers used (walnut, mahogany, satinwood, etc), and because manners and behaviour were less rumbustious. Typical damage includes missing parts of mouldings, bandings, or beadings; chipped or cracked veneers and ink stains on writing tables and bureaux. All of these defects can easily be imitated.

RUBBED ANTIQUE FINISH

This was popular in the 1930s for mass-produced oak reproduction furniture in the style that has aptly been christened 'Jacobethan', and many examples were ludicrously overdone.

The idea was to imitate the appearance of some antique furniture where centuries of dusting and polishing by servants had built up a darker border of dust and wax round a lighter central area, such as on the panels of a door, or the high parts of carvings and mouldings.

Should you wish to do it, the easiest way is to sand the central areas more heavily than the borders after they have been stained, but please exercise restraint or the result will be an unnatural and contrived effect.

LACQUERING AND JAPANNING

These terms are often used indiscriminately as if they were one and the same thing – they are not. The confusion probably arises because English and European craftsmen unsuccessfully attempted to reproduce Oriental lacquer, although some beautiful work was turned out by both Oriental and occidental schools. The principal difference between them lies in the basic material used, and a short explanation should be helpful.

True Oriental lacquer was known to the Chinese at least as long ago as 2000BC. By the fifteenth century, Japanese craftsmen, who had been taught by the Chinese, were producing better lacquer ware than their teachers. It was this work that was imported by the European trading companies in the seventeenth and eighteenth centuries. The various names for lacquer such as Bantam, Canton, and Coromandel refer to the ports whence it was shipped and not to the places where it was made.

The raw material for Oriental lacquer was the sap of *Rhus vernicifera* (also called the 'Japanese lacquer' or the 'varnish' tree). It grows well in England but, because the sap is highly toxic, it is usually confined to private tree collections.

Japanning uses shellac instead of Rhus sap. This comes from the incrustations of sap caused by the feeding habits of an insect called *Coccus lacca*, which attacks several kinds of trees in India. The incrustations are processed to become shellac, which is obtainable today. In the seventeenth and eighteenth centuries shellac was called 'seed lac'.

Repairs to genuine Oriental lacquers should be left to specialist conservators because the work is extremely delicate. In particular, the gilding is likely to be exquisitely thin and one false move could ruin it.

Japanning, however, can be tackled, but again it needs extreme care and imposes heavy demands on your patience. Because of the time involved, it is also very expensive. You can use ordinary artists' oil paints to touch up any coloured parts. In the course of your work, if it is English or European lacquer, you will notice that most of the colours are painted on to raised areas built up with a material called gesso, and this has a bad habit of crumbling away over the years, particularly if the lacquer has been wetted at some time.

This must be put right and all loose debris taken away. You will then have to rebuild with gesso (the Italian word for gypsum), and the method of preparing it is as follows.

RECIPE FOR GESSO

You will need about ¼lb (112g) of parchment cuttings, which can be obtained from gilders' suppliers. Cut them into 1in (25mm) strips and put them in a bowl with enough cold water (say, 2 pints: 1.1 litres) to cover them well, because they will absorb it, and leave them to soak overnight. Next morning, strain off any surplus water and transfer the cuttings into an oven-proof bowl that is large enough to hold them plus three times their volume of cold water. Put the bowl into a saucepan of boiling water and adjust the heat so that the mixture just comes to the boil and then simmers for an hour or two. Then strain the mixture through an old nylon stocking into another bowl and leave it to cool.

As it cools, it will coagulate into a jelly; the degree of gelling is critical. Judging it is largely a matter of experience, but it should be the consistency of a dessert jelly and, if you hit the side of the bowl hard with your hand, the jelly should craze and break up. If you push your finger into it and it does not crack but feels springy, it is too strong. In that case, add a little cold water, put it in its bowl back into the saucepan of boiling water and warm it up, stirring gently, until you achieve the correct consistency.

What you have just made is 'parchment size' and to convert it into gesso you need to warm it up and gradually add gilders' whiting. Stir carefully all the time and try not to create any air bubbles because they will appear as pin holes when the gesso is applied. Overheating the mixture and applying it too thickly produce the same result. As you stir, press out any lumps, and finally strain the mixture through an old nylon stocking; you may have to push it through with a spoon. The result should have the consistency of milk and be completely free from lumps or particles. In this state it is called 'clearcole' and can be brushed on to fine delicate work as a first coat while it is still warm. The gesso proper, however, needs to be thicker, so you should add parchment size until the mixture assumes the consistency of cream from the top of the milk. Then add a few drops of linseed oil and stir them in.

You can apply this with an artist's flat brush in thin coats, keeping the mixture warm in a saucepan of hot water. Most work needs six to eight coats, and each one must be dry before the next is applied. All coats must be completed in one day. Do not attempt to force the drying because it will do neither the gesso nor the wood any good, so try to estimate the total amount you will need for the day's work because it must be applied fresh.

Once the whole job has been coated and set you

can lightly rub it down with finest glass- or wet-or-dry paper, and also touch up any incised patterns or sculptured shapes with a craft knife, chisels, or files. We have already described how you can paint it with artists' oil paints, but you may have the added complication of touching up gilt decoration, or matching in areas that are speckled with gold. Small, fine gilt lines and details can be delicately lined with an artist's fine brush and bronze paint. There is a range of tiny brushes used by photographic retouchers and one or other of them should be ideal, particularly the ones called 'spotters'.

Before sprinkling on the gilt speckles (use bronze powder for these), the area to be treated is lightly coated with gold size. Once it has become tacky, you can take the advice of John Stalker and George Parker in their *Treatise on Japanning* (1688), as follows:

To lay Speckles on the drawing part of Japanwork, as Rocks, Garnets, Flowers, &c.

Before you can proceed to try this experiment, a little Sieve must be framed after this manner. Take a small box, such as Apothecaries employ for pills, something larger in compass than a Crown-piece, about half an inch deep; strike out the bottom, and in its place bind very straight about it fine Tiffanie, and to prevent coming off fasten it on the inside of your box with thread, and reserve it for your necessities.

Now when your work expects to be adorned with Rocks, Flowers, or the like, use first your Pencil to varnish those places with, and whilst it is still wet put some of your strewings into the Sieve, and gently shake it over the place designed for your Rock, until it appears answerable in Speckles to what you intended; but especially when for Rocks, call for a pencil about the bigness of your finger, one that is drie and new, and with it sweep all those stragling [so spelt] Speckles, that lie beyond the wet or varnished part, into the sides and top of the Rock that is thus moistened; for there it will not only stick, but render your work, thicker Speckles in those places, more beautiful, and oblige it with a kind of shadow and reflection.

Then follows this stern admonition: 'This work admits of no idle hours, no interludes and vacations, for as soon as one part is compleated, the other desires to undergo the skill and contrivance of the Artist.'

Substitute 'nylon' for 'Tiffanie', 'brush' for pencil, and 'gold size' for 'varnish', and you have the information straight from the Masters of English Japanning. You can protect the work by applying a thin coat of French polish once everything is dry.

Large areas of damaged gilt work will probably mean laying gold leaf, so this is an appropriate point at which to describe the technique.

REPAIRS TO GILDING ON WOOD

The following notes are not an explanation of the craft of gilding, which is a skill of the highest order, but a summary of various methods of repairing and restoring small areas of damaged or missing gilt work. The golden rule (no pun intended) is that if you have the slightest doubt of your ability, don't do it. Leave it to a professional gilder – and he will probably tell you that much of his work is putting right errors made by over-enthusiastic but unskilled repairers.

There is, nevertheless, quite a lot you can do without running the risk of doing irreparable harm, and luckily there are several useful preparations you can buy from art shops or gilding suppliers (see Suppliers' List).

There are two kinds of gilding, namely water gilding, and oil gilding. The first is more difficult to apply but has a finer appearance and can be burnished, while oil gilding cannot; often both kinds were used on the same job. As far as we are concerned, it is all academic because we shall only be dealing with small areas that should not need burnishing.

Avoid using gold paint – the effect soon wears off and it is doubtful if the manufacturers would recommend it for serious restoration work but only for art and craft subjects.

'GOLD' POWDERS

These are not gold at all but bronze and, while they can be used on unimportant work, should not be employed for authentic restoration. Even if you protect them with a coat of clear shellac after application, they will still tarnish eventually, although this may possibly be acceptable on small areas. They are sold in a range of tints from the colours of brass to copper, and the tints can be further shaded either before or after application, as we shall see shortly.

First, the powder is mixed in the proportion of 1 part to 4 parts of quick-drying size (from gilders' suppliers or art shops). If the mixture has brown streaks on the surface, there is too much size, so a pinch or two of powder should be added. As its name implies, the size coagulates quickly when stored, so buy it in small quantities as you need it. A couple of drops of pure turpentine (not substitute) will help to delay the gelling, and the cap should be kept tightly closed.

You can tint the size before applying it with artists' 'earth' oil colours – so called because they are made from natural clays and are not chemically synthesised. Place a dab of the selected colour into a china palette and mix it with the powder and size solution. If it will not bind properly, add a drop or two of flatting oil, which comprises 1 part boiled linseed oil to 6 parts turpentine substitute, and mix it again. The earth colours are yellow ochre and raw sienna (both yellow); burnt sienna (warm reddish brown); and burnt and raw umbers (brown).

Alternatively, you can allow the powder/size mixture to dry, and then brush on shellac tinted with one or other of the earth colours already mentioned, or a combination of them. This method has the advantage that it confers a good degree of protection to the surface, and it can be adjusted in colour to confer an antique effect as well.

GILT VARNISHES, CREAMS, PENCILS

Red varnish A sealer and primer that should be brushed on before applying gilt varnishes, pencils, or creams.

Gilt Fontenay non-tarnishing varnish Available in eight colours, all of which can be mixed with each other.

Gilt cream A non-tarnishing wax that can be applied with the fingers; used to restore small areas of damage. In eight colours.

Gilt pencil Another way to touch up small repairs; simply rub it on and allow to dry. In six colours.

POWDER GOLD

This is an expensive way of retouching small areas with a paste of real gold, particularly places where it is impossible or difficult to lay gold leaf. The gilding can be burnished if required.

To make the paste, grind some pieces of gold leaf with a pestle in a mortar, adding a small quantity of honey so that you make a stiff paste. The honey must be natural honey and free from additives. You will probably have to improvise a pestle and mortar by using something like an oval-shaped pebble for the former, and a thick ovenware bowl for the latter. When the gold has become very fine, add a little hot water to dissolve the honey. Allow the gold to settle, pour off the honey/water, and dry the gold on a piece of kitchen paper. Apply it as a paint, using a 50/50 mixture of shellac and methylated spirit. You need a lot of gold leaf to make a small amount of paint, so you can understand why it is expensive.

REPAIRS WITH OIL SIZE

The following method of gilding with oil size is likely to be needed when you have to gild a replacement piece of ornament or moulding that must be authentic. This kind of gilding cannot be burnished.

First, fix the replacement piece with either Scotch glue or PVA adhesive if the groundwork is wood; or parchment size if it is gesso or 'compo' (this will be described later). When the adhesive has dried, paint the piece with two, three, or even four coats of yellow ochre artists' oil paint. When this is dry, inspect it carefully and remove any specks or nibs of dust. Then apply a thin coat of 18 hour gold size. Allow this to become tacky, and then lay on the gold leaf. This should be 'transfer' gold, which has each leaf attached to a wax paper backing. As soon as the gold touches the size, it will adhere and you will be able to pull away the wax paper as you go. Once everything is dry, brush on a coat of parchment size to protect it and to help any future restorer to remove dirt and stains by dissolving the size away.

You may come across the term 'ormolu size', which is a special size brushed on to protect the gilt finish. It can be obtained from gilders' suppliers.

WORKING WITH COMPO

'Compo' was a substance employed by the Adam brothers in the eighteenth century. It could be cast in patterned moulds and used instead of expensive carved wood for picture frames, fireplace surrounds, ceiling decoration, etc. They did try to patent it but were unsuccessful, although many of the actual pattern moulds they designed still exist today. The basic difference between gesso and compo is that, whereas gesso is self-supporting and can be fashioned into shapes, compo needs to be cast in a mould.

Making compo is straightforward enough, and cheap; but it is undeniably a messy business. Here is the recipe. Boil 1lb (450g) of Scotch glue in ½ pint (280ml) of water; mix separately 7oz (200g) of white resin to ½ pint (280ml) of raw linseed oil, stirring them well together. Take the glue solution off the heat and add the resin/oil mixture to it, stirring well. You now have to boil this mixture for half an hour or so in a double-boiler (that is, a larger container of boiling water), giving it an occasional stirring. Allow the mixture to cool until it is lukewarm, and then turn it out on to a bed of whiting, where it can lie while you are working. From time to time you should knead it into a doughy consistency.

One of the most common uses of compo is for renewing missing pieces of mouldings or borders by taking a cast from an undamaged portion. To do this, you will need to make up a small box to contain the moulding material. This box can be of wood because it does not have to be flexible.

Many restorers use plaster of Paris made up with warm water as the moulding material to take the impression. But there are others, such as Vinamould (from craft shops) or Paribar, which is obtainable from dental laboratories, because it is used to take impressions for dentures. Paribar can be softened by heating it gently in hot water, but beware of leaving it over a flame or it will congeal into a sticky mess. It can be used time after time so you will not need much of it.

The compo is, of course, poured into the mould and takes up the impression. You should not need a release agent but, if you are in doubt, a thin smear of petroleum jelly on the mould will help. The replacement compo pieces can be fixed down with PVA adhesive or Scotch glue.

EPOXY RESIN PUTTY

This is a versatile material which, although it should not be used for authentic restoration because it is non-reversible, can often solve some tricky problems. One such, which shows its capabilities perfectly, is the question of how to fashion those pendant icicles, waterfalls, and festoons characteristic of the Chinese Rococo style and later, Victorian, designers. A convenient and quick solution is to fashion some of this putty round a wire matrix, because it will adhere readily and can be shaped and carved easily.

The putty is made by mixing an ordinary slow-setting epoxy resin adhesive, such as Araldite, with an 'extender' which can be kaolin powder or rye flour. The latter is widely used to make the adhesive go further in commercial work. Simply mix the epoxy resin with the hardener in the usual manner (the manufacturers supply full instructions) and sprinkle on the extender, mixing it thoroughly. This is important because inefficient mixing is the principal cause of poor adhesion, and the presence of any kind of grease or oil is another. A short time after it has been applied, the mix assumes a cheese-like consistency that lasts long enough for you to be able to shape it with your fingers, or sculpt it with clay-modelling tools.

The length of time mentioned depends upon factors such as the temperature and the amount of extender used, so the obvious recommendation is to do some experimenting. Check the consistency after quarter of an hour or so, and then every ten minutes until it is as pliable as you require. Methylated spirit will get the mixture off any tools you have used, provided it has not cured. Once this happens, there is no solvent, for this is the purpose of the resin.

PAINT EFFECTS ON WOOD

In many Victorian houses and public buildings you will often find that much of the woodwork – particularly doors and panelling – has been painted to simulate wood grain. The most usual practice was to paint pine to resemble oak. The results varied enormously, from the crudest and most obvious imitation up to work that needed to be examined with a magnifying glass to tell it from the real thing.

The practice was called 'graining' and was viewed with horror by aesthetically minded purists. Nevertheless, it can transform an otherwise shabby and everyday piece of second hand furniture into a handsome object if done properly.

There are two extensions of it that can prove useful to the professional restorer, namely, imitating marble, and tortoiseshell.

FAUX BOIS (GRAINING)

This was the name given by the French to the highest quality wood graining, and it was employed in such exalted places as Fontainebleu in France and the Villa Borghese in Rome, and also to decorate *poudreuses* and similar delicate furniture throughout Europe and America.

Graining can be rendered on an oil-painted base either by applying overpainting (scumbling) in artists' oil paints, or by means of a water-based paint. The latter is the one that will be described because mistakes can more easily be rectified, the nuances of colour more effectively enhanced, and the final appearance rendered more delicately than with oil paint.

THE TOOLS

The majority of these are brushes, but there are others; a complete kit is shown in Fig 11:3 (page 148). Here, (A) is a metal comb of the type used for pets. As you can see, several of the teeth have been removed in a completely random fashion. (B) is a stout piece of leather about ⅛in (3mm) thick, in which a serrated edge has been cut. (C) is an 'overgrainer' of which you will need to make two. Use a couple of old 2in (50mm) paint brushes with the softest bristles you can find, and cut them away with a razor blade until the section of each one is thinned down as shown. Keep one in that state, but cut away some of the bristles on the other to give a random gap-toothed appearance as (D). The brush (E) is an artists' oil paint brush called a 'fitch' and should be about ⅜in (10mm) wide; while (F) is an ordinary dusting brush, which can be used as a softener.

The tool at (G) is used to simulate knots and is simply a strip of felt bound to a dowel. Its size depends on the size of the knot – you will also find it helps if you tease out the fibres at the tip. A small version can be employed to imitate the eyes in bird's-eye maple. A piece of fur with the hairs teased out and tied to a dowel is the 'softener' shown at (H). The veining fitch at (I) is a narrow ¼in (6mm) artists' flat oil painting brush; and the thumb piece (J) is a piece of leather about 3in by

⅝in by ⅛in (75mm by 16mm by 3mm) with the end bevelled off.

This is certainly a motley collection of tools, and you can make it even more so by adding such things as pieces of sponge, different sizes and shapes of feathers, rough-textured towelling, a toothbrush for 'spatter' effects, and so on. Some craftsmen swear that using a dead pigeon's wing is the only way to imitate figured walnut!

THE PAINTS

You will need two kinds – the ground colour, and the graining medium.

The ground colour can be ordinary household medium gloss paint such as you would buy at any DIY centre for painting doors, windows, etc. An alternative paint, if you cannot obtain medium gloss, is undercoat to which you add about ⅛th by volume of linseed oil to give it the necessary gloss. This ground colour must match well the background colour of the timber you are simulating, and here is a list of suggested colours for various woods.

American walnut – medium beige; bird's-eye maple – dark cream; Honduras or pale mahogany – dull orange; Spanish (Cuban) mahogany – bright orange; natural oak – pale, warm cream; light oak – pale beige; medium oak – nut brown; dark Jacobean oak – dark leather brown; satinwood – pale yellow; sycamore – ivory white; tulipwood – salmon pink; dark walnut – dark leather brown; English walnut – dull medium brown; French and Italian walnuts – warm medium brown.

The graining medium consists basically of any water-soluble pigment powder, or even artists' water colours, dissolved in hot soapy water to make a fairly thick paste; hot water dissolves the soap flakes better than cold. Use a good quality white toilet soap shredded finely – a potato peeler or nutmeg grater is handy for this – and make sure it is all thoroughly dissolved. Allow the mixture to cool and then dilute it to a thin cream with a diluent of half water and half beer. Because beer varies in its consistency, you may like to use oatmeal stout instead. Both act as a binder for the graining medium.

Suggested colours for simulating various woods are: American walnut – burnt umber, Vandyke brown; bird's-eye maple – raw sienna, burnt umber; Honduras or pale mahogany – Vandyke brown, burnt sienna; Spanish (Cuban) mahogany – Vandyke brown, mahogany lake; natural oak – raw sienna, burnt umber, dark red, black; light oak – burnt or raw umber, raw sienna; medium oak – burnt umber, burnt sienna; dark Jacobean oak – burnt sienna and black; satinwood – yellow ochre, burnt sienna; sycamore – Vandyke brown, cream; tulipwood – Indian red, Vandyke brown, burnt sienna; dark walnut – Vandyke brown, black; English walnut – Vandyke brown, burnt sienna, black; French and Italian walnuts – Vandyke brown, burnt sienna.

These are suggested component colours, and you will need to mix them in varying amounts for each different wood. Quite often a mere trace will be enough.

APPLICATION

The wood to be painted must be satin-smooth and free from dust, and the first step is to give it three or four coats of the ground colour. Allow each coat to dry overnight and rub it down lightly with the finest grade of wet-or-dry paper. This should be wetted and rubbed on a piece of soap to make a lather while you are using it. The lather should then be rinsed off.

Before you can apply the graining medium, you have to prevent 'cissing', which is the tendency of water-based paint to creep and run in all directions when applied to an oil-painted surface. You can do this by lightly sponging some of the beer/stout and water mixture, into which you have dissolved a little whiting, on to the ground colour.

PAINTING THE GRAIN PATTERNS

To describe how to do this is almost impossible, and all that can be done is to give you outline recommendations of how to proceed, plus the illustrations of various brush strokes shown in Fig 11:4, and ask you to practise your own interpretations of different configurations of grain. Some actual examples to follow are essential and, in default of the real thing, you could make use of colour photographs or illustrations from books. There are also some good grain patterns included in the ranges of various plastic laminates that can be regarded as authentic because they are reproduced photographically.

As a final protection, the graining medium must be sprayed with a coat or two of the fixative used by artists to protect watercolour paintings. When this has dried, the whole job can be given a coat of transparent varnish of the kind supplied by art shops for varnishing oil paintings.

MARBLE AND TORTOISESHELL

In order to reproduce these two effects you use the same tools and ground colour as for faux bois, except that extra aids such as chamois leather strips and pieces of crumpled-up tissue or kitchen paper can be employed to create special effects, such as mottling, when marbling.

Instead of the water-based graining colour employed with faux bois, artists' oil paints are normally used for creating the patterns. These can be thinned, when necessary, with a diluent of half linseed oil and half pure turpentine, adding a little methylated spirit when a particularly thin wash of colour is called for.

Again, the greatest aid to success is to have a good example to work from, but try a little experiment or two before you begin marbling, as follows. Fill a flat tray (a metal or ovenware baking dish is ideal) with cold water to a depth of two or three inches, then pour on several small spoonfuls of differently coloured and thinned-down oil paints at various places on the surface. You can also try dripping one colour on top of another from the tip of a paint brush. Stir the water gently so that the colours swirl and intermix. Slide a piece of thin white card into the water under them and lift it out gently. Let it dry, and study just how the swirls and eddies can be imitated by overpainting the ground colour.

In simulating both marble and tortoiseshell, it is often necessary to float colours on to one another, and the paint must be worked while it is wet. This is particularly true with tortoiseshell, which in its

Fig 11:4 Basic brush strokes when graining

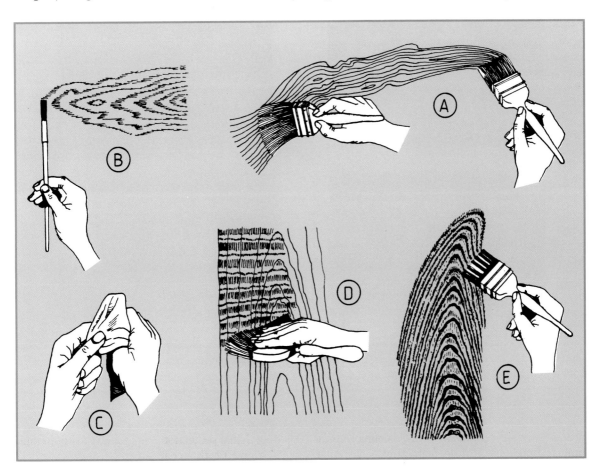

natural state has a translucent glow that can only be created by allowing the ground colour to shine through the overlaid colour washes. Once the painting is finished, it can be protected with a coat of transparent varnish, as with the faux bois.

GRAINING AND MARBLING WITH WATER-BASED ACRYLIC VARNISHES

These are a recent introduction, of which Cuprinol 'Enhance' clear and coloured varnishes are probably the best known. They are easy to apply, dry out in minutes, and brushes and other tools can be washed out in ordinary water.

WOOD GRAINING AND MARBLING

If you have to deal with a large area, brush a very thick layer of coloured varnish on to one section at a time, and use one or other of the brushes or tools already described in the section on traditional graining and marbling to achieve the effect you require. When the work is dry, apply two coats of clear acrylic varnish to give a steel-hard gloss finish. Rubbing down with the finest grades of steel wool or glasspaper can be done between coats when they are dry, but you must use a very light hand or you could remove the pattern you have just built up.

Fig 11:5 How to hold brush bristles when spattering

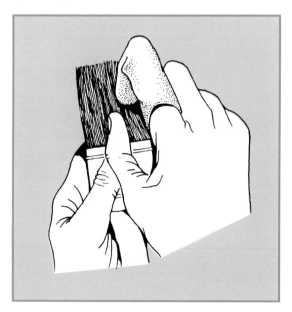

SPATTERING

Although by its nature this technique is bound to give a random effect, it is surprising how much it can be controlled by observing a few simple guide lines.

First, the brush. A suitable one is a 2in (51mm) wide paint brush with the stiffest bristles you can find – cut them down to about 1in (25mm) long.

Now, how to hold the brush and manipulate the bristles to give different kinds of spatter. Fig 11:5 shows the way to hold the brush if you are right-handed. Hold the ferrule in the palm of the left hand with the thumb on top of it; then place the tip of the right thumb on top of the left thumb to keep it steady, and stroke the bristles with the right forefinger. You should wear a finger cut from an old rubber glove to protect it. This will create a spray. With a brush that is just moist and a slow release of the bristles, you can make a fine spatter, while more liquid and a quicker stroke will give a stronger one. An even heavier spatter will result if you hold a block of wood about 1in (25mm) away from the work and tap the ferrule of the brush against it.

STENCILLING

For this you need a brush with short stiff bristles. You can make a serviceable one by using a ½in (12mm) wide brush and binding some strong twine or thread around the bristles where they enter the ferrule. This will compress them into a tight, stiff bundle.

You can buy ready-made stencils from art suppliers, or cut your own from medium weight cellulose acetate film (called 'cell'), which is also obtainable from art suppliers. Leave a 2in (51mm) margin at top and bottom of the design motif so that you can pick it up easily without smudging the pattern.

OTHER TECHNIQUES

These consist of either applying colour or, on the other hand, removing it, by using a sponge (which must be a natural one), or a rolled-up wad of newspaper or chamois leather. They can, however, only be used on work that is laid flat, otherwise the colours will run.

With all these random effects it pays to experiment on pieces of spare wood or paper first, to find the best way of creating an effect.

12 Associated materials and techniques

The path of the restorer often leads him to the fringes of other crafts such as metalwork and leatherwork, and to working with exotic materials such as mother-of-pearl and tortoiseshell. This chapter attempts to cover the special techniques involved.

BANDINGS, INLAYS, LINES, AND STRINGINGS

BANDINGS
These are bands of either one variety of wood, as used for crossbandings, or several woods glued together and sawn in such a way as to display a coloured pattern. As you can see from Fig 12:1, there is a wide range of them. Bandings vary in width, but are normally veneer thickness (0.6mm) and are sold in lengths of either one metre (39⅓in) or half a metre (19¾in).

You may need to make up your own, either to match those already on a job, or because it has to be a special thickness. This is not difficult, and is quite satisfying because of the attractive designs that can be produced easily, plus the fact that you can use up spare offcuts.

Start by gluing strips of wood of roughly the same thickness together side by side as shown in Fig 12:2(A), interposing a sheet of plastic film between them and a baseboard. A convenient width for the block would be about 12in (305mm). The lower faces of the strips must be flush, and you will need to plane the upper faces flush as well. The next step is to square off one edge on a circular-saw bench.

You may wish to sandwich the block between two outer veneers as in (B); the individual bandings can then be sawn off as shown at (C). Herringbone bandings can be made in a similar fashion, and the method is illustrated in Fig 12:3 (A, B, and C). Always make the bandings slightly thicker than the finished size to allow for sanding down.

Fig 12:1 Some typical bandings

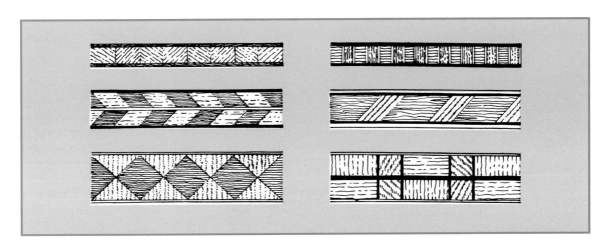

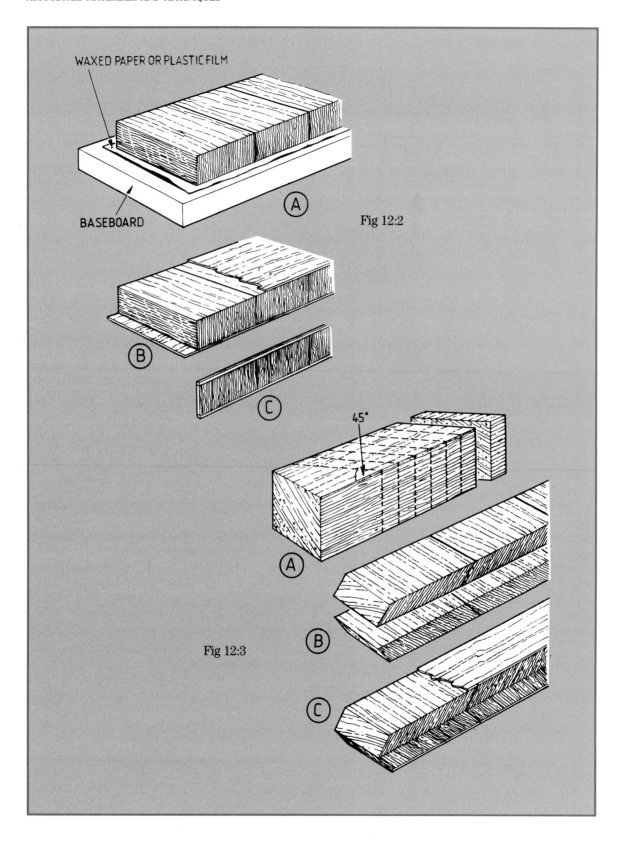

WAXED PAPER OR PLASTIC FILM

BASEBOARD

(A)

Fig 12:2

(B)

(C)

45°

(A)

(B)

Fig 12:3

(C)

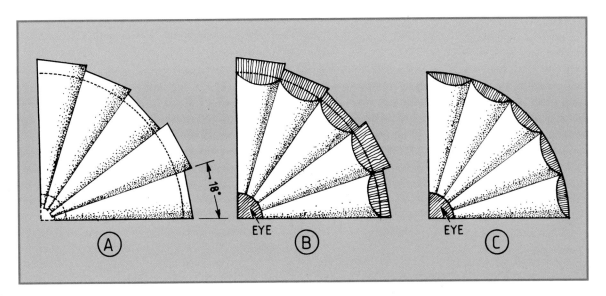

Fig 12:4 Stages in making a fan

DECORATIVE INLAYS

The inlays supplied by World of Wood (see Suppliers List) are attached to a paper backing that should be laid uppermost and dampened, and peeled off once the adhesive (Scotch glue or PVA) has set. You can apply them in one or other of three ways: (1) by letting the inlays into the veneer assembly before it is laid; (2) by gluing them directly to the surface so that they stand proud as overlays; and (3) by routing out the beds for them to the correct sizes and shapes but making them slightly less in depth than the thicknesses of the inlays. This gives you a margin of thickness for sanding off.

MAKING FANS AND SPANDRELS

These are more fiddling than difficult to make, and both are made in a similar manner.

Taking the fan shown at Fig 12:4 as an example, having cut or sawn the tapered pieces to size, the next step is to shade the edges by holding them with tweezers and dipping them in hot sand. Assemble the pieces as shown at (A), holding them in place with gummed brown paper tape which can

Fig 12:2 Gluing wood strips together to create a banding

Fig 12:3 Making herringbone bandings

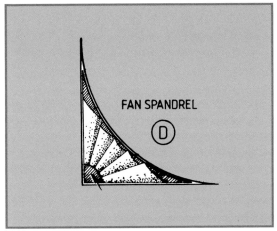

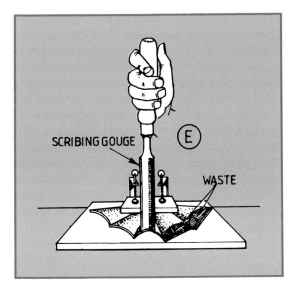

be dampened and removed later. You now need to cut or saw the quadrant-shaped outline and the smaller one for the eye, followed by shaping the scallops. The latter job is best done by cramping the assembly to a block and chopping away the waste with a scribing gouge as at (E). The same gouge can be used to chop the curved ends of the pieces of darker veneer, and once these pieces have been taped on and the eye dealt with in a similar fashion, you can saw or cut the final shape. The spandrel shown at (D) can be made up in a similar manner.

REPAIRS TO MARQUETRY

These can often involve you in a lot of intricate work – not just in plotting and cutting out replacement pieces, but also in identifying and obtaining the veneers required. Things can be made more complicated by the fact that some veneers will have been dyed so that only an expert can make an informed guess as to what they are. Again, on much antique furniture the veneers will have been sawcut and are consequently thicker than those of today. This can mean sawing your own veneers (never a popular pastime), or using two, or possibly three, modern thin veneers laminated together like plywood. In other words, examine the job carefully while bearing these points in mind, and consider if it would not be wiser to send it to a professional marquetarian who has the necessary resources.

If you decide to do the work, the first task is to plot the shape of the missing piece or pieces. Lay a sheet of carbon paper over the gap with the carboned side uppermost and cover it with a piece of white paper. Trace round the edge of the gap with your fingernail so that an impression is left by the carbon on the white paper that can be used as a pattern. Stick the pattern on to the piece of replacement veneer with a touch of Scotch glue, which will prevent the veneer splitting, and saw round it. The gap where it is to fit will need all old glue and dust cleaned out before bonding down the new veneer with either PVA adhesive or Scotch glue. Clean off any excess adhesive and lay a sheet of plastic film over the repair, and lay a heavy weight on top. Once the adhesive has set, the paper pattern can be removed by wiping it with a lightly damp cloth to loosen the glue.

If no pieces are actually missing but some have lifted, insert a thin-bladed knife under them and prise them away as far as possible. Then clean the underside of the veneer and the bed with something like a cotton bud. Once this has been done, introduce fresh adhesive and cover the repair with plastic film, and weight it down as already described.

Some restorers favour damping the lifted veneer slightly to make it more pliable but, if it has been polished, the water cannot penetrate it unless you strip off the polish or make a series of tiny pin holes. Both methods cause problems such as having to repolish the surface or disguise the pin holes.

LINES AND STRINGINGS (WOOD AND BRASS)

These terms tend to be used interchangeably, but in fact a 'line' is a thin strip of wood (often boxwood) and can be flat and of veneer thickness (0.6mm), by widths from $\frac{1}{16}$in to $\frac{1}{4}$in (2mm to 6mm); or it can be square in the same range of dimensions. It is supplied in the same lengths as bandings. Stringings, on the other hand, are very fine and delicate, and are the thickness and width of veneer.

You can make your own lines and stringing of veneer thickness by cutting along the edge of a piece of veneer with a cutting gauge. This is a marking gauge fitted with a chisel-pointed pin, as described in Chapter 9. The larger sizes of lines can be sawn by hand and trimmed by pulling them through the sizing gauge shown in Fig 12:7. This uses an old plane iron or a piece of cabinet scraper steel to trim the wood, which is held down by the spring.

Now we have to consider the different ways to work the groove that contains the line or stringing. By far the easiest method is to use a portable power router fitted with a one-flute cutter with bottom cut. These are available to cut grooves $\frac{1}{16}$, $\frac{1}{8}$, $\frac{5}{32}$, and $\frac{3}{16}$in (1.6, 2, 3, 4, and 4.8mm) wide up to a maximum of $\frac{1}{2}$in (12.7mm). When deciding the width, remember that the groove should always be just a hairsbreadth thinner than the banding, line, or stringing so that they are a tight fit.

There are several other hand methods for

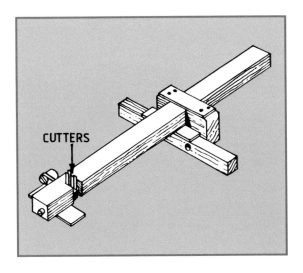

Fig 12:5 A proprietary inlay cutter

cutting the channel. One is an ordinary scratch stock of the type already mentioned. Another is a double knife that is particularly suited to cutting round curves. This can be made in the workshop by fitting two craft knife blades side by side into a wooden handle, with a washer acting as a distance piece. For those who intend to do a lot of this kind of work, a proprietary veneer inlay cutter of the type shown in Fig 12:5 would be worth buying. It has twin blades for cutting the sides of the channel and another for scooping out the waste, and can

also be fitted to an extension bar for cutting round curves.

FITTING LINES AND STRINGING

These are rubbed into their channels which, as we have described, are made a trifle narrower than the line or stringing, with a veneering hammer. To avoid bruising them, old-time craftsmen glued veneer facings to their upper surfaces with Scotch glue and rubbed down on them. Once the lines were in place, they lightly damped the veneer to soften the glue, but not so much as to cause the lines to swell and lift, and then peeled the veneer away.

A problem can arise when a line or stringing has to be taken round a curve. However, you can bend either of them by immersing it in hot water for a few minutes and then working it backwards and forwards across a round object such as a pipe until it is curved. Fig 12:6 shows how it can be helped to fit round a curve by means of strings looped round the pins on the battens. If the string is first wetted, it will shrink as it dries out and exert greater pressure.

FITTING BRASS LINES

The channels for brass lines and stringings should be wide enough so that they are a sliding fit. They

Fig 12:6 How to bend a line or string

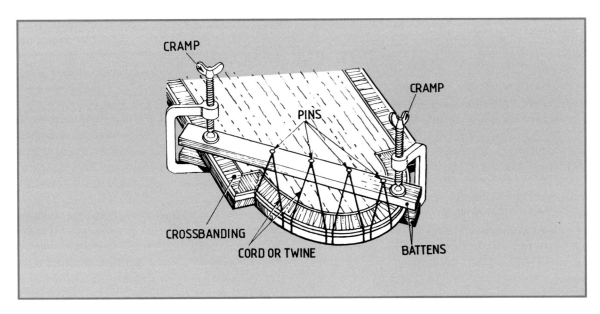

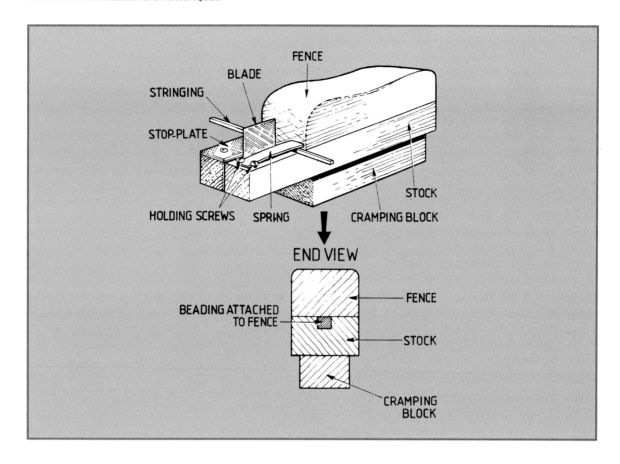

Fig 12:7 A sizing gauge that can be made
in the workshop

can then be glued down with an epoxy resin
adhesive. In the old days the brass was rubbed
with a clove of garlic, which removed grease and
acted as a mordant, and it was then glued down
with Scotch glue mixed with plaster of Paris.

A common fault with lines made of brass is that
the wood in which they are fixed, shrinks. As a
result, the brass rises in loops that cannot be
pressed down but persist in springing back. The
remedy is to lift the line locally round the loop and
cut it with a fine metal-cutting saw blade. Often the
amount removed by the saw kerf is enough to
allow the line to be fixed flush with the surface but,
if this is insufficient, the ends will have to be filed
carefully. Once the line has been glued in, a block
of wood and a piece of protective plastic film
should be cramped over it until the adhesive has
set.

PARQUETRY

This is a type of veneering where small shapes are
assembled to create a geometrical pattern, and the
most obvious example is a chessboard. This is
made from strips of veneer of contrasting colours
and, although you could cut the strips by means of
a craft knife and a straightedge to their finished
sizes, it is better to cut them slightly oversize,
cramp them between two battens with the surplus
just showing, and shoot the edges with a finely-set
plane. By doing this, you will ensure an accurate fit
and avoid making slight errors that could throw
the whole pattern out of balance.

Assemble the nine strips, alternately dark and
light, side by side, Fig 12:8(A), and hold them
together with gummed brown paper tape. Turn the
assembly through 90° and cut the eight strips in
the same fashion to exactly the same slightly
oversize width as the first nine; a metal template to
cut against is handy at this stage. Plane the eight
strips between battens to the precise finished width.

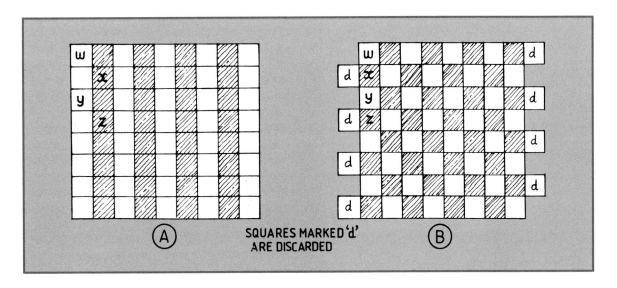

SQUARES MARKED 'd' ARE DISCARDED

Fig 12:8 Stages in making a simple parquetry design

Now you can reassemble the strips, bringing alternate strips forward one square (which can be cut off and discarded) so that you achieve the required effect as at (B). The brown paper tape can easily be peeled off if it is lightly dampened first.

DIAMOND PATTERNS

There are two of these that are traditional, namely the diagonal diamond in Fig 12:9 (A and B), and the right-angled diamond at (C) and (D) in the same illustration. The dotted lines indicate where the strips are cut. The diagrams are self-explanatory, and the manner of marking, cutting, and taping the strips has already been described for the chessboard pattern.

Fig 12:10 shows the Louis XV style parquetry that is noted for its optical illusion.

BRASS DECORATIVE INLAYS

These were popular in the Regency period, and consisted of ornamental brass shapes inlaid into a veneer such as rosewood. In those days, the veneer would have been sawcut and therefore of a thickness comparable with sheet brass. Modern veneers are too thin, and you would probably need to glue two or three together (like plywood) to get the necessary thickness.

If the brass has lifted at one corner, carefully prise it up with a flexible knife such as a palette knife, and clean away any dust or grime. Then slide in a small piece of Glufilm (see Chapter 9) with the backing paper removed, press the brass down on to it and apply a soldering iron set at a low heat. The purpose of this is to heat up the brass so that the Glufilm melts and forms a bond. As an alternative you could use a small flake of shellac instead of the Glufilm.

You can adopt the following method when a new inlay has to be made. The brass sheet should be of the soft kind – you can identify this because you can turn up a corner of it with your fingers and it will stay turned up. Gilding metal is an alternative but this is golden in colour rather than yellow. Yet another material is hard brass that has been annealed, which is not difficult to do yourself. Anneal the brass by rubbing ordinary household soap on one surface, then hold it in a pair of pliers over a gas ring until the soap turns brown or bubbles and sizzles – this indicates that the brass is annealed. Don't attempt to quench it but allow it to cool naturally.

Next, make up a 'sandwich' of the veneer (with the design marked or pasted on it) at the top, the brass under it and glued to it, and a piece of ⅛in (3mm) hardboard at the bottom. The last-named supports the brass while it is being sawn and takes the swarf. In order that the brass should adhere to the veneer, roughen it with coarse glasspaper and rub it with a clove of garlic to act as a mordant and

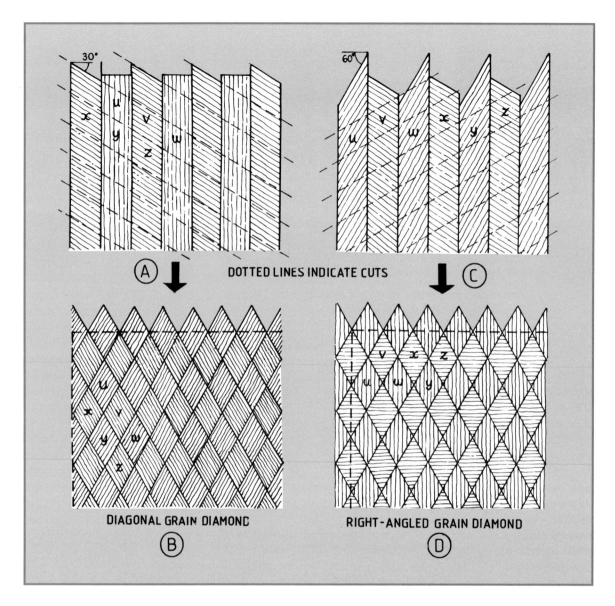

Fig 12:9 Making diamond-patterned parquetry

remove any grease.

The glue that holds the sandwich together must be easily dissolved after the cutting has been done, so modern epoxy resin adhesives are no good. Scotch glue mixed with plaster of Paris (often called 'Salisbury' glue) is used instead because it will dissolve easily. Some craftsmen dispense with glue altogether and hold the sandwich together with veneer pins. If you do this, make sure you know where they are or they will ruin your saw. By far the best machine for the job is a modelmaker's powered fretsaw fitted with a metal-cutting blade. It can also be done with a hand fretsaw but this needs a good deal of patience and concentration.

Fitting the inlay is done by using an epoxy resin adhesive, or Salisbury glue in the case of restoration. You will often find that a few pins here and there will fix down any recalcitrant pieces. Make the pins from thin brass wire cut into ½in (12mm) lengths with one pointed end made by holding the pin in a pair of pliers against a grinding wheel. Insert them after the inlay has been glued down with a wooden block cramped over it, and

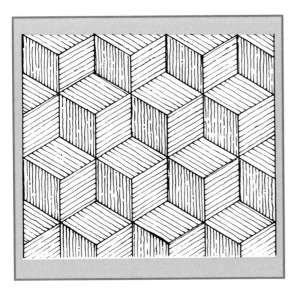

Fig 12:10 The Louis XV parquetry pattern

after the glue has set.

It is possible to make up a missing backplate for a bail handle in just the same way as a brass inlay. If you do, remember to round off the cut edges with either a file or emery powder, or both, to make them smooth.

COLOURING BRASS

New brass can be dulled down to an antique colour by one or other of the following methods. If you are dealing with brass that has been coated with a protective lacquer, it will have to be removed first with a stripping fluid.

1 The brass can be fumed with .880 ammonia, taking care not to allow it to touch the liquid or to stay in the fumes too long, otherwise it will become pitted. After fuming, wash off all traces of ammonia and polish it with fine steel wool to give it an antique appearance.

2 Brush on a solution of equal parts of common salt and sugar dissolved in wine vinegar. Make repeated applications to arrive at the required colour.

3 Make up a mixture, by weight, of 10 parts sodium hyposulphate (photographers' hypo), 1 part citric acid powder, and 40 parts cold water. Dip the brass (or gilding metal, or copper) in the mixture and the metals will change colour, taking five to ten minutes to make the complete change.

Keep the mixture moving and remove the metal as soon as it has reached the colour you want; then wash and dry it thoroughly.

REPAIRS TO BOULLE WORK

Boulle is a form of marquetry employing thin pieces of sheet brass and tortoiseshell developed and perfected by André Charles Boulle (1642–1732). It is sometimes referred to as 'Buhl' which should be, strictly speaking, confined to the pieces made at the beginning of the nineteenth century when the technique was revived.

Basically, the procedure is to hold together a sheet of brass and another of tortoiseshell while they are sawn out together to follow a pattern stuck to whichever sheet is uppermost. When they are separated, the sheets are interchangeable. If the brass sheet is predominant, the design is called 'première-partie'; while the reverse – tortoiseshell predominating over the brass – is called 'contre-partie'. Other materials such as silver or mother-of-pearl were sometimes introduced into the designs, and the brass itself was often engraved and the lines filled with a coloured paste to enhance their appearance.

There are many beautiful examples of Boulle work in Scone Palace, near Perth. They include two commodes that complement each other, one being 'première-partie' and the other 'contre-partie', and the whole collection is well worth a visit if you are in the area.

The problem that bedevilled the old-time craftsmen was how to ensure good adhesion, and the most common faults you are likely to be confronted with are pieces of brass that are lifting, and loose or missing patches of tortoiseshell. Scotch glue with lime and glycerine added was used to bond down the brass, which had been annealed and rubbed with garlic as already described. The tortoiseshell was held in place with a clear fish glue.

When dealing with loose pieces of either material, the first step is to clear away any adhesive that remains, remove the pieces, and clean up the cavities. Both glues will soften readily if warm water is applied to them as sparingly as possible, and all old glue and dirt must be thoroughly cleaned out. Roughen the underside of the brass with coarse glasspaper or a file to provide a key for the glue. Then stick it down with an epoxy resin adhesive, or the Salisbury glue already referred to if it is part of a true restoration.

Working with tortoiseshell is more complicated, because you may find that it was either painted on the underside, or that it was laid on top of coloured paper. The purpose in both cases was to impart a coloured glow that shone through the shell. The paper should come away easily if you wipe it with a cloth dampened in hot water; or, in the case of paint, you can touch it up with artists' colours. You will need a clear adhesive because the tortoiseshell is translucent. A modern adhesive such as UHU is suitable as it is water-clear.

Tortoiseshell itself is brittle but it can be rendered flexible by soaking it in hot water. In order to coax it to negotiate a curve, you often have to steam it and then use a sandbag containing warm sand as a caul to hold it in place while the glue sets. You can glue strips of linen to the outside of the shell with Scotch glue to prevent its cracking. The glue and strips can easily be removed with a rag damped in hot water afterwards. It helps if you can slightly roughen the surface to be glued to provide a key, but this has to be done gently with nothing coarser than medium glasspaper, because deep scratches might show through.

Fig 12:11 How to incline the saw blade at an angle when cutting Boulle inlays

Tortoises are a protected species, so their shells are no longer on sale. If you do have some pieces, look after them carefully by rubbing them once a week with a paste of senna powder and olive oil on the palm of your hand .

CUTTING BOULLE INLAYS

These are cut in the form of a sandwich in the manner already described for brass decorative inlays. If you hold the cutting-out saw vertically, you will inevitably have a tiny gap equal to the thickness of the saw blade all round the pieces when you come to assemble them. The easy way to get over this is to do as Boulle sometimes did and fill the gap with a coloured paste to form part of the decoration – a coloured wood filler is as good as anything.

There is, however, another way to avoid the problem altogether, as shown in Fig 12:11. Here, the saw blade is angled slightly so that the cut-out pieces fit snugly. The angle is just enough to compensate for the thickness of the saw blade, and if you are using a power fretsaw, the table can be tilted accordingly.

MOTHER-OF-PEARL, IVORY AND BONE

There are several varieties of mother-of-pearl, the commonest being the 'goldfish' pattern, which has a wavy figure in different colours. These change with the angle of viewing but are, generally, pink, white, yellow, green, and pale blue. Another pattern is the 'iris' which is speckled green with

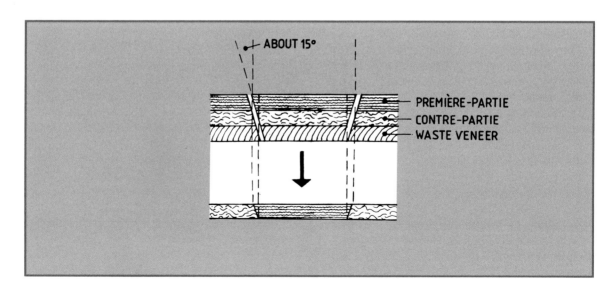

twists of blue, grey, black, and red. Pure white and black are by far the rarest.

Mother-of-pearl is usually about $\frac{1}{16}$in (1.5mm) thick and in random shapes from 1in to 2in (25mm to 51mm) wide. It is so delicate that even light pressure will crack it. This means that it has to be reinforced before you can saw or file it, and the best way is to back it with a stiff veneer and a paper interleaf applied with Scotch glue, so that both can be removed easily when the work has been done. For the same reason, it should be protected by a wrapping of leather or thick felt if you need to hold it in a vice.

Before gluing mother-of-pearl down, which can be done with fish glue or a mixture of Scotch glue and plaster of Paris, roughen the back with a file, and also prick the groundwork on which it is to be laid to form a good key. Apply hand pressure to achieve the initial bond, then lay a comparatively light weight such as a small plane on the work to hold it down. Anything heavier is likely to crack it. Normally the face is so smooth that no polishing is needed but, if it is, rub it very lightly with rottenstone or finest pumice powder. Old mother-of-pearl can be revived by lightly rubbing it with almond oil.

Many of the small knobs and handles on antique furniture, especially Victorian pieces, which at first sight appear to be ivory are, in fact, bone. Often the only way to tell the difference is to look at a cross section when you will see that ivory has growth rings like a tree, while bone does not.

One of the most common troubles with ivory veneer is that it tends to curl up if the glue beneath has perished, and any attempt to force it to lie flat will probably crack it. If you can get the veneer off, it can be softened by immersion in hot water for half an hour or so, otherwise you will have to direct a jet of steam against it for a few minutes. In both cases the work should be cramped up (but not tightly) and left overnight. Both materials can be glued down with the same adhesives as used for tortoiseshell.

Should you have to turn up some ivory or bone knobs on the lathe, you will find that a slower speed is needed than for wood, and the action is one of scraping rather than cutting. Recommended speeds are 300rpm with high speed steel tools, or 150rpm with carbon steel.

CLEANING ORMOLU

The world 'ormolu' is derived from the French term 'bronze dorée d'or moulu', or gilt bronze, and the metal was employed on French furniture, clocks, candelabra, picture frames, doors, and fireplace surrounds in the eighteenth century. Its use also spread to England, where Matthew Boulton (1728–1809) was instrumental in making and distributing it to the trade from his works in Soho, Birmingham. The Adam brothers were among his best customers.

Briefly, to make an ormolu mount, a model was first produced in wood or wax and then cast in bronze. This was then tooled and chased to a perfect finish, and gilded by means of fire gilding. The method has not been used for many years because it was dangerous to the health of the workers and also very expensive. Today, the gilding is applied by an electrical process.

The best and safest way to clean grimy gilt ormolu is to shred some good quality toilet soap into a jug of hot water, adding about half a cupful of domestic quality ammonia. Stir the mixture thoroughly until the soap has fully dissolved and, when it has cooled, wipe the ormolu with it, brushing gently with an old toothbrush in the crevices. Rinse off with clean water. You will need to wear rubber gloves. Small areas of damage to the gilding can be restored by the methods described in Chapter 11.

The one thing you must not do is to use metal polish because this will remove some of the gold and ruin the piece. Nor should you use this kind of polish on bronze mounts because it will remove the highly prized patina that has built up over the years.

CABINET LOCKS

Before dealing with repairing them, a description of the various types of locks that are available today will be helpful. There are four of them, as shown in Fig 12:12.

The straight cupboard lock (A) is screwed on to the inside of a door without needing to be recessed in, and as the bolt can be shot both to the left and to the right, there is no worry about 'handing'. The cut cabinet lock (B) fulfils the same purpose, but it has to be housed in a recess on the inside of the

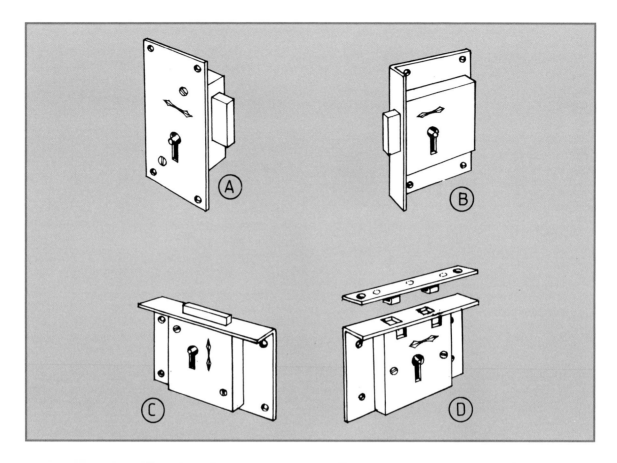

Fig 12:12 The four basic locks for cabinets

door. Its bolt shoots in one direction only, either to left or right, depending on which 'hand' it is. To determine which 'hand' is required, face the door from the outside and if the lock has to be fitted to the left-hand side, you need a left-hand lock. The drawer lock (C) is used on drawers and needs to be housed into a recess. So does the box lock (D) which, as its name implies, is used on small chests and boxes. It has a matching locking plate that is let into the lid, and this is fitted with two metal loops which engage with teeth that rise from the lock when the key is turned.

REPAIRING LOCKS

The first thing to do with any lock that will not work is to clean both it and its accompanying key, and squirt in some light lubricating oil. Don't forget to prise out any accumulated fluff and dust from the hollow end of the key, if it has one (this kind of

end is called a 'pipe'). Frequently this is all that is needed to restore the lock to working order.

Locks on antique furniture fall into two categories, namely the 'ward' lock, and the 'lever' lock. The former is usually found on eighteenth-century pieces, and the latter on those of the nineteenth century.

A typical ward lock is illustrated in Fig 12:13(A) and operates by the pipe of the key fitting over a pin, so that when it is turned a notch in the 'bit' (the working blade of the key) rides over a 'ward' (a protruding flange on the lock plate) and engages a shaped recess in the end of the bolt, thus causing it to shoot outwards.

Fig 12:13(B) shows a lever lock, which in some ways resembles a ward lock. The main difference is that the bolt cannot move until a set of levers fixed on top of it has been moved aside by the teeth on the bit of the key. Each lever has a differently shaped 'gate' or pattern cut into it to correspond with a tooth on the key, and all the levers are mounted on the 'stump' on the bolt. Although a

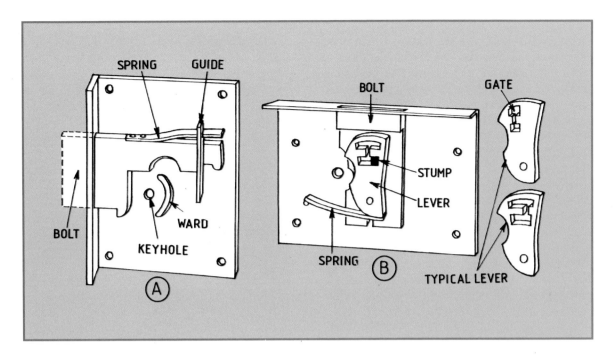

Fig 12:13 (A) a ward lock; (B) a lever lock

three-lever lock is illustrated, four-lever ones are also common. In both kinds of lock, the component parts are usually either screwed or riveted in place. If riveted, the rivets will have to be punched through and replaced when repairs have to be done.

Broken springs are the most common fault with ward locks, and usually it is a matter of soldering the broken piece back into place, or making a new one altogether. With a lever lock, the most likely trouble is that one of the levers has become worn or a piece has broken off, both of which mean making a new lever of the same thickness of metal, and shaping it by means of round or triangular files.

A replacement rivet can be made from an ordinary nail of the appropriate diameter; if necessary you can enlarge the hole to fit the nail. Cut off the head and point of the nail with a hacksaw, and then cut it off to a length that is the combined thickness of the parts to be joined plus one and a half times the diameter of the nail itself. This means that when it is inserted into the hole, threequarters of its diameter will protrude from each side. When you have inserted the rivet,

support the work on a solid slab of metal and burr one end over with a ball-pein hammer. Then turn it over and burr the other end. It's best to use a succession of light hammer blows because if you strike the rivet too hard, it will distort the burr. If you want the head of the rivet to be flush with the surrounding surface, you will need to countersink the hole first, then file the rounded burr flat.

Making a new key is relatively straightforward if you can open up the lock and take it to a locksmith; he will then sell you a suitable blank. You file this as necessary and, though it can be time-consuming, at least you can see how things are progressing. If it is a matter of making a new key for a lock that cannot be opened, your best plan is to take it to a locksmith. The job can be done in the workshop, but it is all a matter of trial-and-error, and only too likely to go wrong.

LAYING LEATHER

If you are replacing old leather with new, the first requirement is that all old stuff should be removed, and splits and other damage to the recess in the wood made good. In particular, make sure that the corners have all accumulations of glue, dust, etc, cleaned away so that the edges of the leather will lie flat and snug.

173

ORDERING THE NEW LEATHER

Normally, this will be 'skiver' leather, which is the skin of a sheep and may carry small blemishes or scars from incidents that occurred to the animal during its lifetime. If the blemishes are unobtrusive, they are accepted by the trade and can be regarded as proof that the leather is genuine and not an imitation based on plastic. In any case, no reputable supplier would venture his reputation by supplying substandard material.

Because the leather comes from sheep, there is a limit to its size. This is usually about 33in by 24in (840mm by 610mm), and to cover areas larger than this, the material will have to be joined. This can be done by the supplier. There is a range of five colours – red, green, gold, blue and brown – but others are available at extra cost, namely, bottle green, lime, tan, maroon, black, and parchment. Fig 12:14 shows the range of tooled borders offered by World of Wood (see Suppliers' List), which can be either gilt or 'blind' – that is, impressed but not gilt.

If the piece required is a true rectangle, give the supplier the exact finished dimensions. He will always allow you a margin for trimming and fitting, whatever the size or shape. Make a paper or card template if the piece is shaped or curved, and mark the upper side 'face side'. You can also show on it the position of any tooling that may be required.

Fig 12:14 The range of tooled borders available from World of Wood

LAYING LEATHER

The traditional adhesives for this are diluted Scotch glue or paperhangers' cold water paste made rather thicker than normal. A more convenient way is to use a PVA woodworking adhesive diluted in the proportion of four parts of adhesive to one part of water.

Fig 12:15 Directions in which to stroke the leather, when laying it

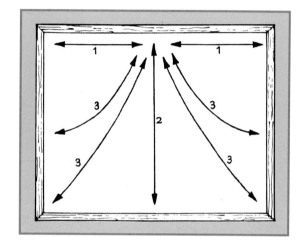

Before you spread the adhesive, check exactly how the leather is to be trimmed in order to centralise any tooling in the recess, and mark a line lightly along the margin; then start by cutting one long edge. Apply the adhesive with a brush all over the recess, and locate the long edge you have just

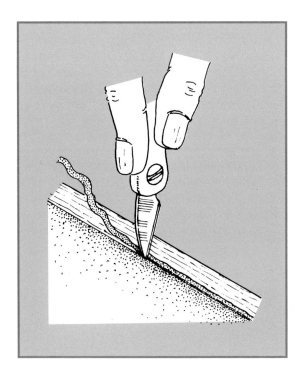

Fig 12:16 Trimming the edges of the leather

cut tight up to the edge. Rub it down with a clean soft cloth and follow on by rubbing across the centre, and then in curves towards the outside; Fig 12:15 shows the directions in which to rub. You will find that the leather tends to stretch a little and, although the aim is to produce a taut surface free from wrinkles and trapped air, at the same time you must try to ensure that it is not stretched or under tension.

The next step is to trim the remaining edges; this is done with a really sharp craft knife. Feel for the edge of the recess and run your fingernail along it. Then insert the point of the knife, angling it as shown in Fig 12:16 so that the edge of the leather is bevelled and consequently does not show the unstained side. As you cut, ease the waste away gently, and keep the knife blade slightly twisted as well as at an angle, so that it tends to cut towards the wood rather than to the leather. When you come to a corner, hold the waste out of the way at right angles, and make the next cut into the corner from the opposite direction to produce a neat job. Press the edges down with your thumbnail and leave the work to

dry. Return after half an hour or so to rub out any bubbles of trapped air or wrinkles that may have developed.

In certain circumstances, for example with some designs of portable writing desks, the leather will be subjected to continual opening and closing, so a piece of linen may be glued (with PVA adhesive) along the back of the folding line to reinforce it.

The surface of the leather may well have been treated with a protective lacquer before you receive it, and sometimes a white bloom appears because of changes in humidity. All you need do is to direct a current of warm air at it from a hair drier or a fan heater and the bloom will disappear. Finally, keep the leather supple by occasionally rubbing it with a little good quality clear or white leather polish.

DECOUPAGE

This technique consists basically of gluing black and white or coloured prints to a wooden, glass, or china surface and then coating them with many coats of varnish so that they vaguely resemble Chinese or Japanese lacquer ware. The technique was enormously popular as a hobby with ladies of the leisured classes in the eighteenth century, and 'penny plain, twopence coloured' prints could be bought at many stationers.

The obvious first step is to make sure that the surface of the wood is satin-smooth, and one of the best ways of testing this is to wipe it with an old nylon stocking, which will catch on any roughness.

What kind of print you choose depends on your taste, and you can fix it temporarily with Blutak or Plasticine while studying the effect. Should the print have printing on the back, it will have to be prevented from showing through by sealing it with a coat of PVA white adhesive slightly thinned down with water. You can cut the outline with scissors, or tear it, or cut it first and then char the edges with a lighted cigarette to soften them. In all cases it is helpful to feather the edges by sanding them on the back with fine glasspaper because you should not be able to feel them with your fingertips when the job is finished.

ANTIQUE METHOD
First, seal the wood with a coat of clear French polish to prevent colours from the print bleeding

into it. Then stick the print down with gum-arabic and roll it smooth with a rubber roller as used by photographers. When dry, brush on a coat of glue size and, when this in turn is dry, begin applying spirit varnish. This is a long job because you must allow twenty-four hours for each coat to dry, papering it down lightly with fine glasspaper. Leave the last one untouched. Up to twenty coats may be needed, and the varnish should overlap on to the adjacent wood so that the edges of the print are undetectable.

MODERN METHOD
Begin by sealing the wood with two or three coats of spray-on acrylic sealer of the kind sold by art shops; then stick the print down with PVA adhesive. When the adhesive has set, apply coats of polyurethane clear lacquer – again, you will probably need about twenty. Leave each coat for about eight hours to dry (it will be touch-dry after an hour or two, but ignore this). You need not glasspaper any of the coats until the tenth, followed by every third until the last coat, which is left as it is.

In both methods the great enemy is dust, which can either be airborne or the result of glass-papering. Protect the job from the former by erecting a temporary tent over it during the intervals when you are not working on it. In the latter case, wipe the dust away with a 'Tak' rag.

13 Historical guide to decoration and fittings

Any professional restorer will tell you that he has to acquire a comprehensive knowledge of antique furniture styles as an essential requirement. The reasons are obvious, such as the need to supply authentic replacement parts where pieces have been broken off; having to make a piece to match existing furniture; or having to alter pieces to make a 'marriage'. The last-named is an antique dealer's term for two originally separate pieces which have been combined to create a new one.

There is only one way to acquire this knowledge and that is by visiting museums and stately homes, supplemented by studying the many books on the subject.

PROPORTION AND DESIGN

No doubt you will have read, or heard the comment, that the old-time craftsman had an instinctive feeling for good proportions. Although this may or may not be true of the designs of some rural makers, it is certainly true of professional cabinet-makers from the early seventeenth century until the end of the Regency period, about 1830. They worked either to a set of rules based upon the classical orders of architecture, or on an even earlier concept known as the Golden Mean, or Divine Proportion. Inigo Jones (1573–1652) was the first architect and designer to apply the system of proportion in design represented by the classical orders, which include the Doric, Ionic, and Corinthian (all Greek), and the Tuscan and Composite (both Roman). The Greeks never used the Roman orders, but the Romans adopted those of the Greeks, particularly the Corinthian.

In his book *The Gentleman and Cabinet Maker's Director* (1754), Thomas Chippendale illustrated all the orders and was at great pains to establish a 'module' for each. The module was a dimension equal to the diameter of the shaft at its widest point, and was divided into sixty parts called 'minutes'. The column of each order had a definite mathematical relationship between the size of its module and the sizes of its various mouldings and decorations.

He also gave full size profiles of the mouldings for many of his designs. Sheraton also dealt with the subject in his *Cabinet-Maker and Upholsterer's Drawing Book* (1791), and considered that the knowledge was necessary to all men of culture and all cabinet-makers. Nevertheless, the subject seems to be little regarded today and rarely appears in books on woodwork and design, nor (as far as I know) is it taught as a basic theory.

THE GOLDEN RULE

This has been known since the time of the Ancient Egyptians and has been used over the centuries by architects and designers. Le Corbusier, the renowned French architect, used it constantly in his work.

There is no need for us to go into how it was originally calculated. The mathematical definition is that it relates to the proportion of three magnitudes so that the first part (or magnitude) is to the second part, as the second is to the whole, or the sum, of the two parts. Because this is difficult to visualise, it is illustrated in linear form, and also as a rectangle, in Fig 13:1. What it amounts to is that a rectangle with each of two sides 1 unit long, and the other two sides each 1.618 units long, is in perfect proportion (it was called 'Divine Proportion' in Renaissance days).

Because the units are in proportion to each other, they can be measured in any kind of units

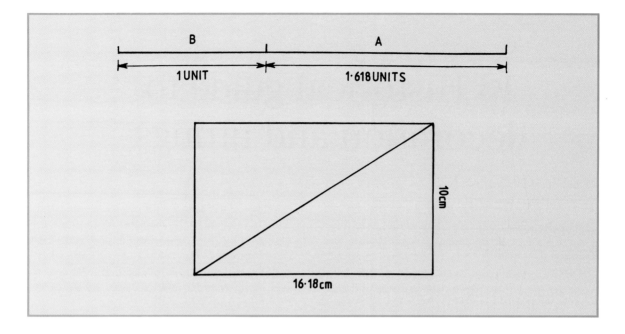

Fig 13:1 Rectangle illustrating the 'Golden Rule'

you like – inches, centimetres, yards, metres, miles, kilometres, etc. To make calculation easier for practical workshop purposes, the ratio can be regarded as 8 units to 5 units, or 8:5.

To apply the ratio, you can use a simple formula. As an example, let us suppose you want to make a cabinet 40in (1,015mm) wide that conforms to the Golden Rule. How tall should it be?

Our working ratio is 8:5

Ratio of width of cabinet to height is 40:X

The formula can be cross-multiplied with the result that 5 times 40 equals 8 times X, or 200 = 8X, from which X is obviously 25in (635mm). Actual examples are illustrated in Fig 13:2 which shows the outline of a Chippendale-style chair dating from 1755, and in Fig 13:3 that of a bureau-bookcase of the same period. By applying the formula mentioned above to the measurements, you will find that both designs are based on the Golden Rule. Thus, in the front elevation the extreme width of the chair over the front legs is 27in (686mm), and the overall seat height is 17in (432mm). Applying the formula to this rectangle we get

8:5
27:17

and by cross-multiplying, $8 \times 17 = 136$ and $5 \times 27 = 135$, the amounts being almost the same to within an inch.

CHIP CARVING

This was a favoured decoration on furniture of the early 1500s, and consisted of geometrical shapes based on circles, squares, rectangles, diamonds, and occasionally, simple Gothic patterns. The patterns were never complicated because at that period all furniture was made by carpenters who were not skilled enough to carve ornate designs.

Although such work can be done today with chisels and carving gouges, there is little doubt that at that time knives were the most usual tools, and one or other of the several kinds of modern craft knives should enable you to make perfect cuts.

Fig 13:4 shows a typical motif at (A). The design must be drawn out accurately because the slightest deviation will show badly. Note, too, that the centre lines of the pockets need to be marked

Fig 13:2 The 'Golden Rule' applied to a Chippendale-style chair

Fig 13:3 The same 'Rule' applied to an eighteenth-century bureau-bookcase

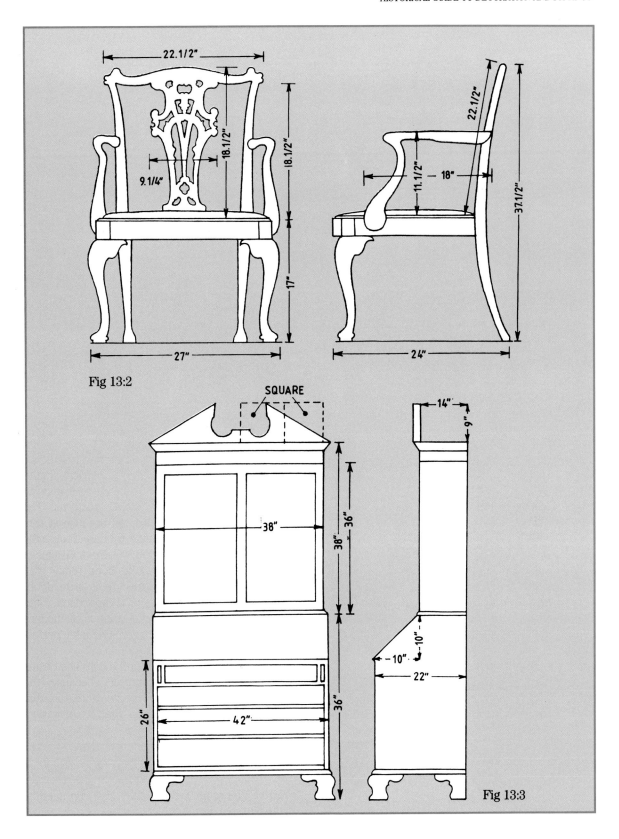

Fig 13:2

Fig 13:3

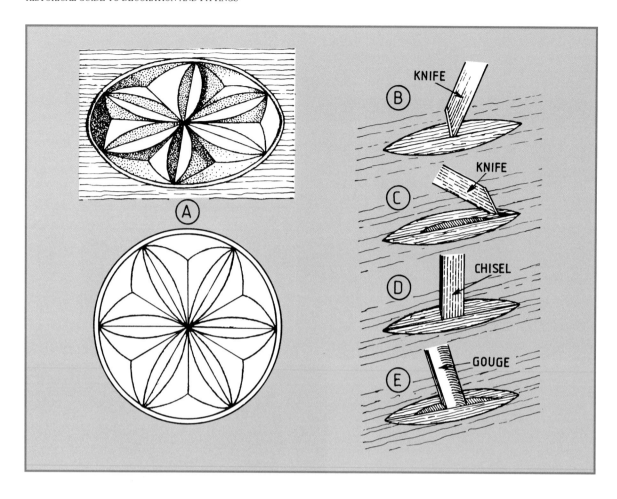

Fig 13:4 A typical chip-carved motif

in. Begin cutting with the knife on the centre line as at (B), gradually increasing the depth of the cut in the middle. Then slice away the edges as at (C), keeping the knife at the same angle throughout. The drawings at (D) and (E) show how a chisel and a gouge may be used instead of a knife, but whichever you use, make as few cuts as possible to achieve a clean crisp finish.

CHISEL AND GOUGE CARVING

These two kinds of carving are done with simple cuts of the chisel or gouge, and are well within the ability of any restorer or cabinet-maker.

CHISEL CARVING

This was used originally in the sixteenth and seventeenth centuries, and enjoyed a new lease of life during the Gothic Revival in the nineteenth century. Three typical designs are shown in Fig 13:5 and, in all cases, you should plot the pattern to suit the widths of your chisels.

In design (A), work the groove first so that it is slightly wider than the width of the chisel being used. Mark out the steps and square a line across at each one. Then cut down across the grain with the bevel of the chisel facing the deeper part of the step and held slightly out of vertical away from it. You will also need to hold the chisel at an angle when cutting the sides, so that it cuts deeper at one corner than the other.

Note in design (B) that the lines forming the corners of the squares do not quite meet. You will need to hold the chisel at a slight angle, as described in (A), so that it penetrates more deeply at the centre than at the edges.

Design (C) has to be worked in two separate

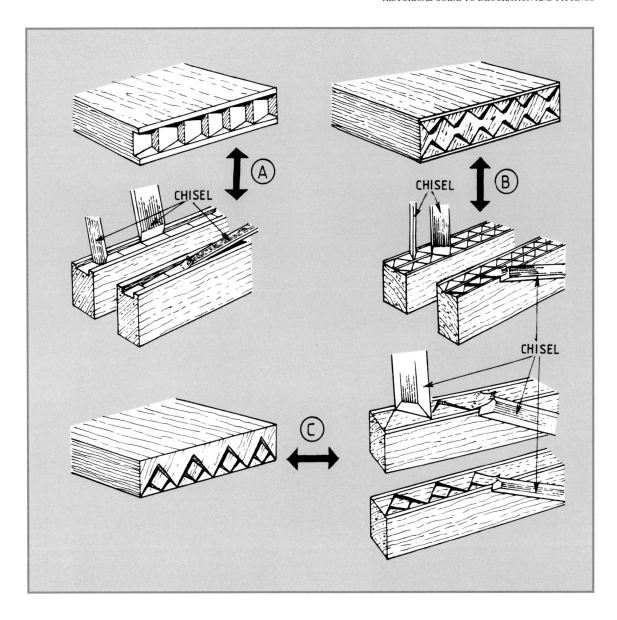

Fig 13:5 Some designs of chisel carvings

stages. Mark out the main angled lines first and cut them, noting that the floor of each depression slopes. Then mark out and cut the smaller squares in the depressions and pare away the waste.

GOUGE CARVING

Examples of this are shown in Fig 13:6, and the methods of cutting them should be self-explanatory.

CHAMFERS AND MASONS' MITRES

The chamfer is a feature that the sixteenth-century joiner borrowed from the stone mason. The latter worked a sloped bevel on the lower edges of windows and other openings so that rainwater could drain away easily. In imitation of this feature, some chests and cabinets had chamfers on the top edges of the panels or framing rails but none on the lower edges. The joiner would work the chamfers with his plane, although he had to stop short at a corner where the rail met a

181

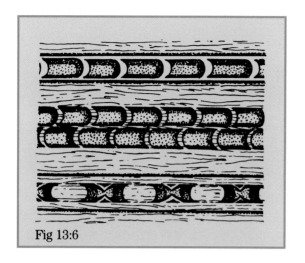

Fig 13:6

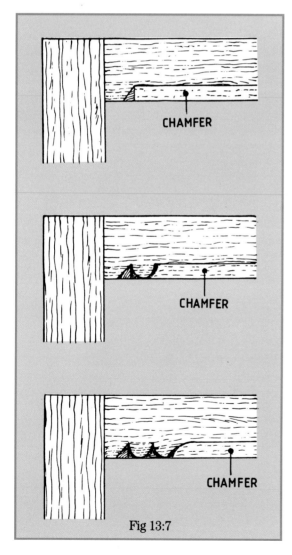

Fig 13:7

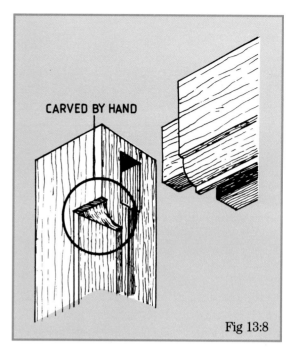

CARVED BY HAND

Fig 13:8

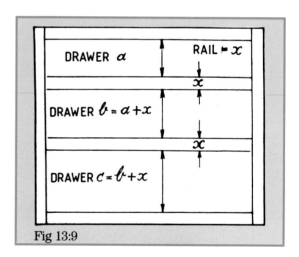

Fig 13:9

Fig 13:6 Some designs of gouge carvings

Fig 13:7 Methods of stopping chamfers

Fig 13:8 The masons' mitre

Fig 13:9 How to determine drawer depths

Fig 13:10 (A) Some of the better-known designs of English period mouldings and (B), overleaf, some French patterns

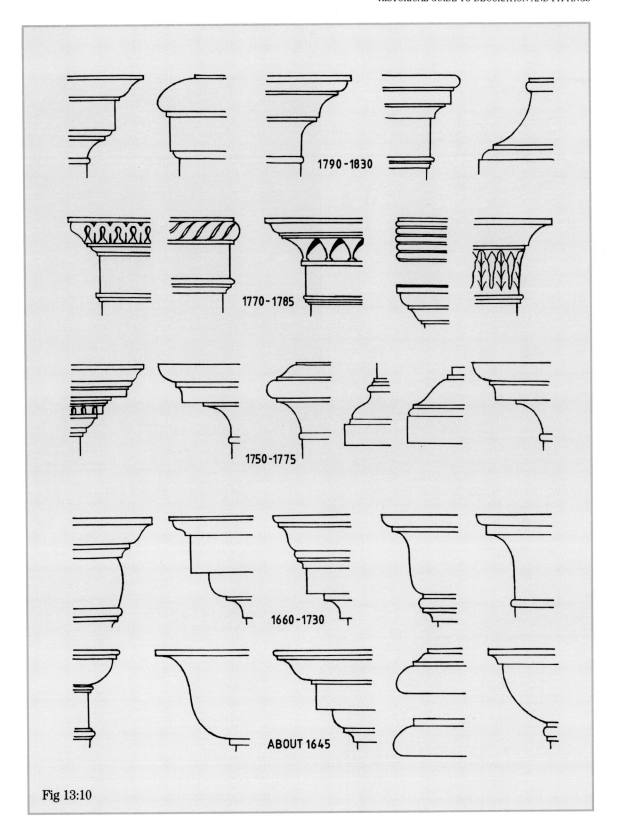

1790-1830

1770-1785

1750-1775

1660-1730

ABOUT 1645

Fig 13:10

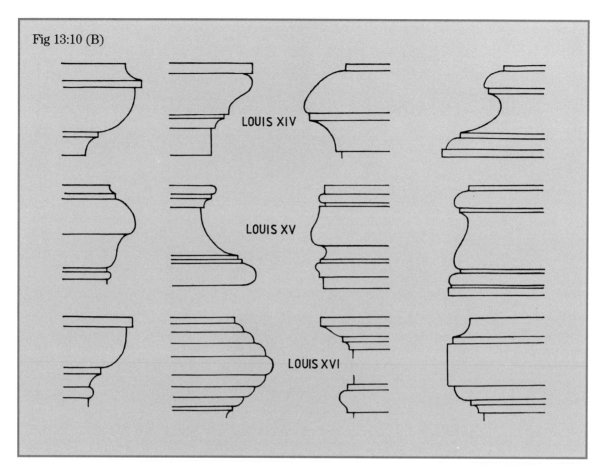

Fig 13:10 (B)

LOUIS XIV

LOUIS XV

LOUIS XVI

vertical. These 'stops' were at first made by a straightforward chisel cut as in Fig 13:7, but later became decorated with carved shapes as shown.

MASONS' MITRE

This is another device that joiners borrowed from the stone masons who, because they were working in stone, were compelled to adopt this form of mitre wherever two components with moulded edges met at right angles; see Fig 13:8. The joiners made their version of the mitre by running the moulding on the edge of the rail right through, and continued the moulding into the mitre by carving it.

DRAWER FRONT DEPTHS

As a guide, each drawer front (for example, in a chest of drawers) should be as deep as the one above, plus the thickness of the rail supporting it; see Fig 13:9

PERIOD MOULDINGS

Mouldings have already been discussed in Chapter 8, but some typical examples of English period mouldings are shown in Fig 13:10(A), and French in Fig 13:10(B). Fuller details of various styles are included in Thomas Chippendale's *The Gentleman and Cabinet Maker's Director*; George Hepplewhite's *The Cabinet-Maker and Upholsterer's Guide*; P. and M. A. Nicholson's *The Practical Cabinet-Maker*; and Thomas Sheraton's *The Cabinet-Maker and Upholsterer's Drawing Book*.

PERIOD CASTORS, HANDLES, AND HINGES

CASTORS (Fig 13:11)
These were first employed on English furniture towards the end of the seventeenth century. The earliest ones were small hardwood rollers (often

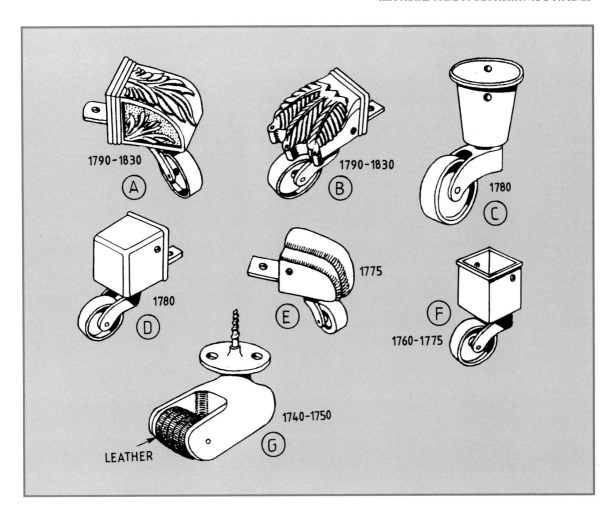

Fig 13:11 Some designs of period castors

boxwood) revolving on metal axles and could not swivel laterally. This defect was soon remedied and, from about 1710, the horns holding the rollers were fixed to the end of spindles, which allowed them to swivel through 360°.

The next development was to use leather discs threaded on to a metal axle, as in Fig 13:11(G). These can be difficult to remove if the threaded screw is firmly embedded in its hole because the body of the castor cannot be used to give leverage while unscrewing it. The best way is to remove the fixing screws from the circular plate; then insert a thin screwdriver into one of the holes and gently punch it round in an anti-clockwise direction.

Some typical examples of the various periods are also illustrated and it is encouraging to know that very good reproductions of most of them are still obtainable from reputable suppliers.

HANDLES (Fig 13:12)

The earliest examples were cast-brass drop handles, and these were usually fixed by means of a 'snape' which resembles the modern style of paper fastener in that it had forked tangs. These tangs were inserted through the hole in the door or drawer front and then hammered back on themselves to provide a secure fixing.

Loop handles, which are also called 'bail' handles, first appeared about 1650, and the first ones had snape fixings. These were soon supplanted by threaded rods with nuts that were tightened up against the inside of the door or drawer front. These handles often had back plates

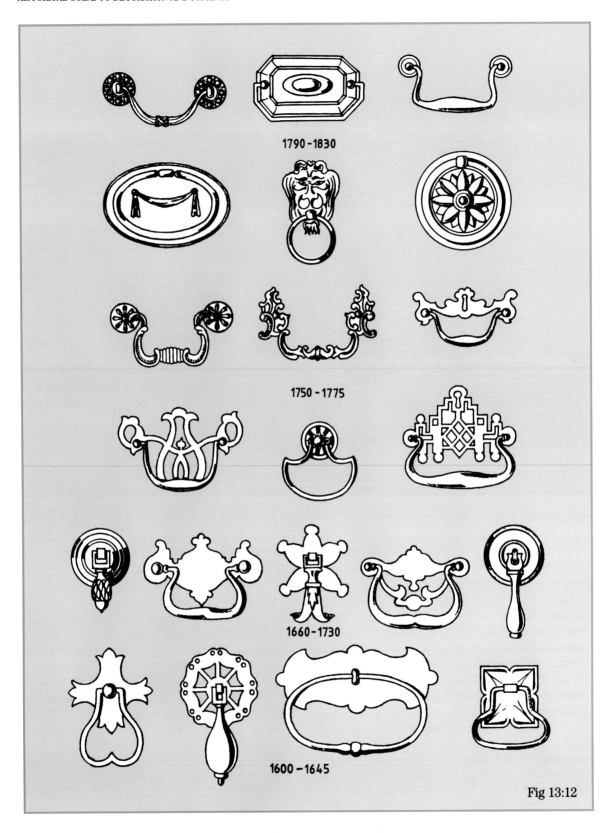

1790 - 1830

1750 - 1775

1660 - 1730

1600 - 1645

Fig 13:12

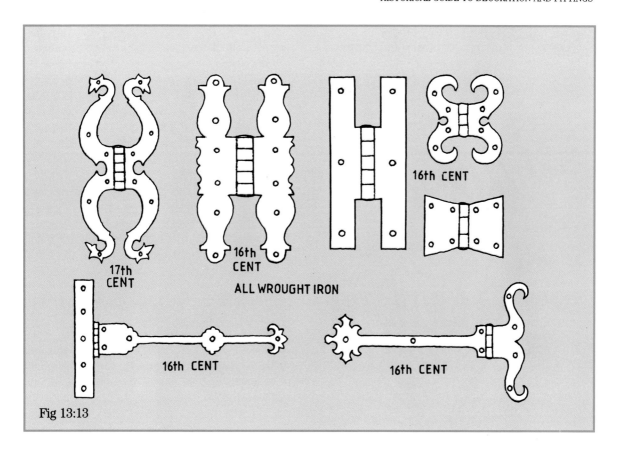

Fig 13:13

Fig 13:13 Typical period hinges

Fig 13:12 Typical period handles

either engraved or punched with patterns and, from 1720 onwards, with cut-out scroll work.

Again, it is quite easy to buy reproduction handles that are faithful copies of the originals. Most of them will probably need to be 'antiqued' in colour and finish, and this has been dealt with in Chapter 12. In addition, you may have to use a fine file on the bevelled edges, because on modern reproductions they are usually too obviously regular and need to be made less so.

HINGES (Fig 13:13)

On early English furniture of the twelfth and thirteenth centuries, hinges were usually of the 'pin' type, made in wood or metal. From the fourteenth century, they were made in wrought iron. The butterfly hinge was the most widely used pattern up to the fifteenth century, and its design gradually developed into the H-hinge and the cock's-head hinge. Strap hinges were always the most favoured ones for cupboard doors and chest lids, where strength was needed. These were made in wrought iron.

Solid brass hinges of the modern style came into use at the beginning of the eighteenth century, but without any countersinking of the screw holes. This was because screws were still handmade, and did not conform to any recognised standard patterns of head-countersinking, thread diameters, or screw points.

The brass industry in Britain did not exist until the 1570s, although brass and latten (an alloy of copper and zinc resembling brass) had been imported from the European continent for many years. In 1566, copper ore was discovered in Cumberland and calamine, which is the ore of zinc and essential for making brass, was found in the same year near Bristol.

ILLUSTRATED LIST OF DECORATIONS AND ORNAMENTS

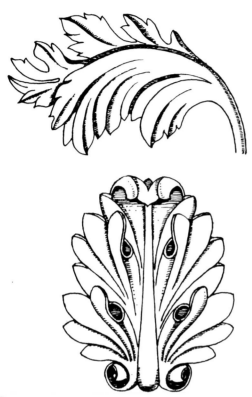

Fig 13:14

Acanthus (Fig 13:14) Based on the leaves of *Acanthus mollis* (bear's breech), this ornament was used on Greek and Roman architecture, and its first use in England was about AD800. It did not appear on English furniture to any extent until the sixteenth century, and was widely used until about 1860 when, like other carved ornamentation, it fell into disuse because of the popularity of cheap mass-produced furniture.

Fig 13:15

Anthemion (Fig 13:15) A series of formalised honeysuckle flowers and leaves linked by scrolls or a continuous decorative band. The design is derived from Greek architecture and was applied to English furniture from 1760 to 1830, when interest in all things Grecian was at its height. Some chairs called 'anthemion backs' or 'honeysuckle backs' used the motif in the form of a shaped splad with curved bars in the back, from about 1780 until 1820.

Applied facets These were thin pieces of wood shaped like diamonds, lozenges, or triangles, which had their edges heavily bevelled off or faceted. They were applied to the flat surfaces of the panels and framing of chests, cupboards, and the like in the late sixteenth and seventeenth centuries. They were often used in conjunction with strapwork (*qv*) to create a style of decoration called 'strap and jewel' work.

Acorn turning Ornaments, usually finials, which resembled acorns in shape, were used to decorate furniture mainly in the late sixteenth century and to a lesser degree during the seventeenth and eighteenth centuries.

Arcading A series of linked arches with semi-circular heads, employed widely as a decoration on chair backs, chests, cupboards, etc, during the late sixteenth and the whole of the seventeenth century. The basic design of the arch is thought to have been based on early (eighth century) pictures of the Temple at Jerusalem. The 'Franks Casket' made in Northumbria about AD700, has a panel that includes this feature, with an Ark of the Covenant in the middle.

Baluster (Fig 13:16)(A) Architectural term for a turned column that usually forms one of several similar supports for a balustrade. Although in many cases the design is used upside down, the illustration shows it right way up.

The motif was widely used on chair and table legs of late sixteenth- and seventeenth-century furniture, for the splads of many early eighteenth-century chairs, and for the splads of some Windsor chairs either in solid or pierced form. It was also used on chair and stool legs from 1580 to 1640, combined with bobbins and rings.

Bead and reel (Fig 13:16)(B) Usually found in conjunction with egg-and-dart moulding (*qv*), and mainly employed on late sixteenth- and seventeenth-century furniture.

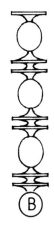

Fig 13:16

Blind fret Also called 'card cut'. A kind of lattice or strapwork that does not fully penetrate the thickness of the wood and thus appears in low relief. It can either be carved from the solid (card cut), or a strip of fretwork glued on to a background. Frequently used by Chippendale and his contemporaries, particularly for the Chinese style.

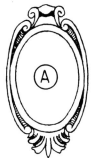

Fig 13:17

Cabochon (Fig 13:17)(A) An egg-shaped, circular, or oval convex ornament, usually enriched round its edges with either strapwork (sixteenth and seventeenth centuries) or formalised acanthus foliage (eighteenth century).

Card cut See Blind fret.

Cartouche (Fig 13:17)(B) An ornamental tablet, usually oval in shape, with its surrounding edges carved to resemble cut or rolled parchment. The tablet is often carved or painted with a coat of arms or a monogram. Usually incorporated in the pediments of late seventeenth- or early eighteenth-century furniture.

Chinoiserie General term for decoration and ornamental work in the Chinese style. There were two separate periods of interest: the first from about 1660 until 1700, and the second from about 1750 to 1790.

Colonnette A column of circular or rectangular section of one of the orders of architecture in miniature, often with a fluted shaft. Used on late eighteenth-century chairs where a set of four or five of them were inserted in each chair back, particularly in several Hepplewhite designs.

Fig 13:18

Crocket (Fig 13:18) A carved ornament with retroflected leaves, usually situated at the angles of pinnacles, gables, and canopies in Victorian Gothic furniture; also occasionally found on fifteenth- and sixteenth-century pieces.

C-scroll As its name suggests, a carved scroll in the shape of the letter C. It was introduced during the early eighteenth century and continued to be popular, particularly with Thomas Chippendale, until 1770.

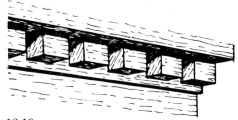

Fig 13:19

Dentils (Fig 13:19) An ornament in the form of small rectangular blocks spaced out along a cornice or pediment moulding. See illustrations of Period Mouldings.

Echinus A carved moulding on a Greek Doric

column, which was often decorated with the egg-and-tongue motif (*qv*).

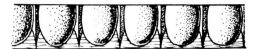

Fig 13:20

Egg-and-tongue (Fig 13:20) Also referred to as 'echinus' or 'egg-and-dart'. A decorative feature occasionally used on seventeenth-century furniture, but more widely during the early nineteenth century on Greek Revival designs.

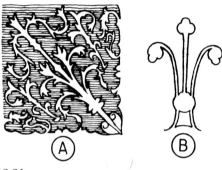

Fig 13:21

Endive leaf (Fig 13:21)(A) Formalised designs of the leaf were used in marquetry (seventeenth and early eighteenth centuries), and also in the form of a foliated scroll on mid-eighteenth-century furniture.
Fleur-de-lys (Fig 13:21)(B) A formalised interpretation of the flower of the garden lily. Occasionally used in painted or carved decoration in the sixteenth and seventeenth centuries.

Fig 13:22

Gadroon (Fig 13:22) Also called 'nulling'. A carved decoration on the curved surface of mouldings on the edges of tables and cabinets; also on the bulbous legs of Elizabethan and Jacobean tables and on bedposts. It is one of the best known decorative ornaments, and continued to be used in every furniture period up to the present day.

Fig 13:23

Grecian key fret (Fig 13:23) The pattern was cut out as a fret and then glued to the work. It was especially popular during the later years of the Greek Revival period, about 1810 to 1830.

Fig 13:24

Guilloche (Fig 13:24) Consists of two or more bands intertwined to form a running pattern, usually with a decorative floral motif included in the loops. Like the gadroon, it was used in all the furniture styles from the sixteenth to the middle of the nineteenth centuries.

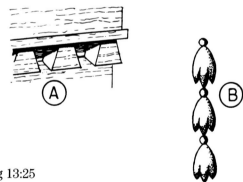

Fig 13:25

Guttae (Fig 13:25)(A) An architectural feature borrowed from the Greek Doric order, and consisting of small wedge-shaped ornaments. It was occasionally used by both Thomas Chippendale and George Hepplewhite.
Husks (Fig 13:25)(B) Carved ornament based on the flowers of the shrub *Garrya elliptica*. Widely used during the latter half of the eighteenth century, often combined with a shell motif. A

similar design in the USA was called the 'bell flower'.

Imbrication Formalised representation of fish scales, which was used as an ornament. For instance, where carved dolphins acted as supports for a table.

Fig 13:26

Ionic capital (Fig 13:26) This was commonly used as the topmost member of turned table legs and bed pillars in the late sixteenth and early seventeenth centuries.

Key pattern See Grecian key.

Knop A rounded knob used in conjunction with turned rings or reels to form a series of ornaments on a leg or support.

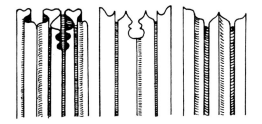

Fig 13:27

Linenfold (Fig 13:27) Carved representations of linen hanging in vertical folds, probably originating in Flanders. The earliest examples in England seem to have been on doors at Hereford Cathedral in 1492, but its use on furniture was mainly between the years 1500 to 1560. There are scores of variations on the theme but, generally speaking, early designs had the linenfold extending to the bottom of the panel, with the decorative return at the top only. The carved details were often crude and shallow. After 1525, the design was returned at the bottom as well as the top, and the whole thing became more sophisticated and delicate. See also Parchemin.

Fig 13:28

Lunette (Fig 13:28) A semicircular decorative motif, either carved or inlaid, and found on early and mid-seventeenth-century furniture.

Mace Alternative name for a split turning of baluster shape applied to a surface as decoration during the late sixteenth and the first half of the seventeenth century.

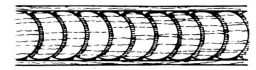

Fig 13:29

Money carving (Fig 13:29) A strip of overlapping discs carved to resemble coins. Occasionally used on furniture of the first half of the eighteenth century, and also on some pieces of the Arts and Crafts style in the late nineteenth century.

Nulling See Gadrooning.

Fig 13:30

Parchemin (Fig 13:30) A design resembling part of a linenfold panel, which was widely used from about 1550 to 1630.

Patera A circular or oval ornamental disc that could be painted, inlaid, carved in wood, or cast in brass. Used from about 1750 to 1830, the later examples on Regency furniture being mainly brass.

Pounced background Also called 'punched', 'stamped', or 'stippled'. Very small patterns pricked or stamped to fill in the background on a carved surface. Used intermittently during all period styles.

Punched background See pounced background.

Fig 13:31

Romayne carving (Fig 13:31) Male or female heads in profile and carved in low relief as ornaments on furniture and panelling during the years 1520 to 1600.

Fig 13:32

Rose-and-ribbon (Fig 13:32) Continuous carved decoration used on the edges of some tables in the mid-eighteenth century.

Roundels When applied to furniture, this term refers to chip-carved circular ornaments on the fronts of thirteenth- and fourteenth-century chests.

Scratch carving A primitive form of carving of incised lines to form simple patterns, used on country-made furniture not later than the end of the seventeenth-century.

Scroll See Vitruvian scroll.

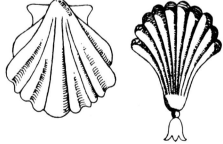

Fig 13:33

Shell-carved motif (Fig 13:33) This was often used during the Queen Anne and early Georgian periods (1700 to 1730) to embellish the knees of chair and table legs. It was frequently combined with a husk ornament (qv). The motif was also used in the late eighteenth century as the centre piece of the cresting on the backs of sofas and chairs, particularly those designed by Robert Adam. It also took the form of a concave cove on the upper parts of some corner cupboards of the same period.

Stamped background See Pounced background.
Stippled background See Pounced background.
Strap-and-jewel work Term used to describe the combination of split turnings, applied lozenge, and faceted diamond shapes, with strapwork (qqv).

Fig 13:34

Strapwork (Fig 13:34) Carved in low relief, this consisted of interlaced scrolls, arabesques, and similar motifs contained in a long rectangular border that vaguely resembled a strap. Widely used between 1550 and 1640.

Fig 13:35

Swags (Fig 13:35) A carved or painted representation of flowers, fruit, or foliage interlaced with ribbons. A popular form of decoration between the mid-eighteenth and early nineteenth centuries.

Trophy A tasteful arrangement of objects devoted to a particular activity such as hunting, music, painting, or fencing. Often carved in wood, but sometimes inlaid or painted.

Fig 13:36

Tudor Rose (Fig 13:36) A formalised version of the Lancastrian red rose and the Yorkist white rose, combined in one ornament. Used on early sixteenth-century furniture and resurrected on Victorian mock-Tudor and modern 'Jacobethan' furniture.

Vitruvian scroll (Fig 13:37) A succession of linked scrolls that gives the impression of a running wave. Used about 1730 to 1830.

Fig 13:37

Wave scroll See Vitruvian scroll.

'SHORTWOOD CARVINGS'

These are made by Sefco Ltd (See Suppliers' List) and are true reproductions in plastic of carved period designs such as shells, paterae, swags, husks, and acanthus ornaments. There are also complete sets for fireplaces and pelmets. The range is very wide and is contained in their catalogue.

They offer a quick and easy way of completely transforming an otherwise mundane piece of furniture into something more sophisticated and glamorous. Fixing is by pinning and gluing with an ordinary PVA adhesive, but the wood background must first be stripped of wax, polish, or varnish. The carvings can be joined end to end, and also bent if necessary by applying gentle heat. Finishes are confined to emulsion or oil paint, although there seems no reason why they could not be gilded. Full instructions are included in the catalogue.

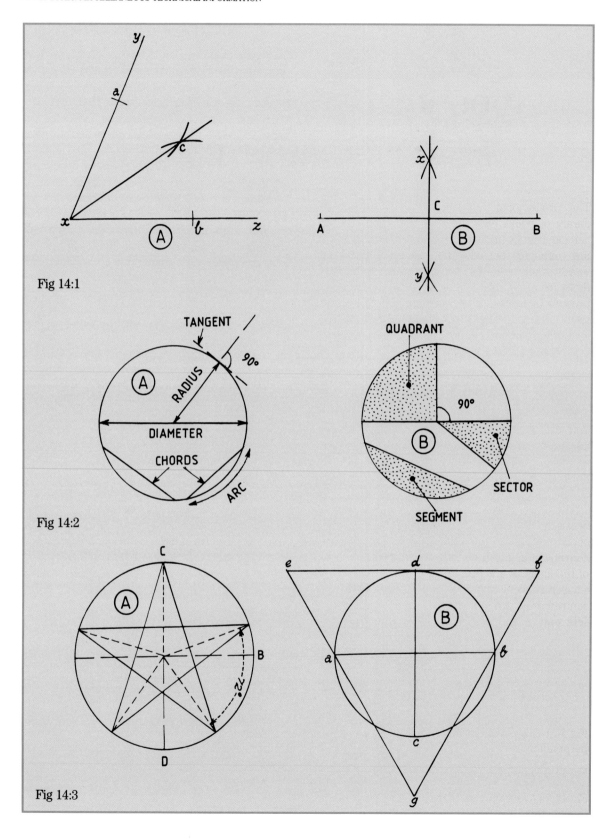

Fig 14:1

Fig 14:2

Fig 14:3

Appendices: Miscellaneous technical information

The professional restorer inevitably collects a library of books containing technical information and can usually find what he wants in a matter of a few minutes, but the amateur or occasional woodworker often has to buy books or borrow them from a public library. Although they don't pretend to answer all technical problems exhaustively, the following pages deal with many that occur in repair and restoration work.

APPENDIX A
SETTING-OUT GEOMETRY

BISECTING AN ANGLE

You can use a protractor to do this in most instances but sometimes an awkward angle such as, say, 69½° has to be halved. The answer is obviously 34¾°, but this can be difficult to read off accurately on a protractor.

The diagram in Fig 14:1(A) shows how to do it precisely. The angle is lettered x,y,z: use x as the centre and with your compasses opened to any convenient angle, draw two arcs that cut the arms of the angle at a and b. Reset the compasses to a smaller convenient radius and, using a and b as centres, draw two more arcs to cut each other at c. Join x and c, and this line will bisect the angle.

BISECTING (AND ERECTING A PERPENDICULAR TO) A STRAIGHT LINE

In Fig 14:1(B) A–B is the straight line. Set your

Fig 14:1 How to bisect an angle and erect a perpendicular

Fig 14:2 Parts of a circle

Fig 14:3 (A) plotting an inscribed star; (B) finding the length of the circumference of a circle

compasses to a convenient angle and draw arcs with A and B as centres so that they intersect both above and below the line at x and y respectively. Join x and y and the point C will bisect the line A-B, and the line x-y will be at right angles to it.

PARTS OF A CIRCLE

These are shown in Fig 14:2 (A) and (B).

STARS INSCRIBED IN CIRCLES

This type of pattern frequently occurs on veneered table or cabinet tops, and on sixteenth- and seventeenth-century oak furniture, and needs to be set out carefully.

Fig 14:3(A) shows a five-pointed star. Draw in the vertical and horizontal diameters A-B and C-D first; where they intersect is the centre of the circle. Mark off 72° divisions as shown, and the points where they meet the circumference are the points of the star. The 72° is arrived at by dividing the 360° of the circle by five. Six-pointed (60° divisions) and eight-pointed (45° divisions) stars can be set out in the same way.

FINDING THE LENGTH OF THE CIRCUMFERENCE

The usual mathematical way is to multiply the diameter by pi, which is approximately 3⅐ or 3.14. Because it is a recurring decimal, the figure cannot be precise. A more exact method (and one for those whose mathematical ability is a little rusty) is shown in Fig 14:3(B).

Given the circle, the diameter of which is a-b, draw the tangent e-f at right angles to c-d and, using a 60° set square, draw the triangle g-e-f so that its sides just touch the points a and b. Then the length of the line e-f will be half the circumference of the circle.

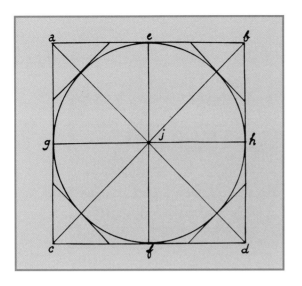

Fig 14:4 Drawing an octagon in a square

DRAWING AN OCTAGON IN A SQUARE

Fig 14:4 shows how to do this. Start by drawing the square a,b,c,d, then join the diagonals a-d and b-c; next draw the vertical and horizontal lines e-f and g-h. Where these lines all intersect at j is the centre for the circle, and this is drawn next. At each point where the radiating line cuts the circle, draw a line at right angles to it. Doing this all round the circle gives you the octagon.

Fig 14:5 Plotting a trefoil

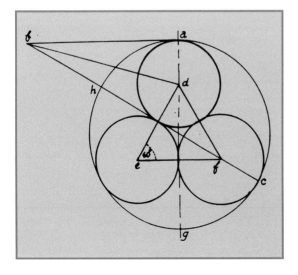

DRAWING TREFOILS AND QUATREFOILS

These patterns were often employed in medieval furniture and a knowledge of how to set them out is bound to be useful.

Referring to Fig 14:5, draw in the vertical diameter a-g, and make the tangent a-b at right angles to it. Using your protractor, draw another diameter c-h at 60° to the vertical one and extend it to b. Bisect the angle a,b,c so that the bisecting line b-d intersects the first vertical diameter a-g at d. This point, d, is the apex of the equilateral triangle def, which you can now draw with a 60° set square; this in turn gives you the centres for the smaller circles.

Fig 14:6 Plotting a quatrefoil

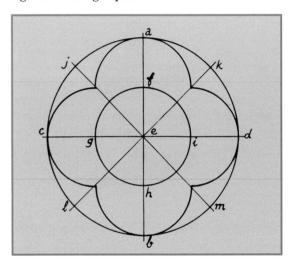

Fig 14:6 shows how to set out a quatrefoil. First, draw the vertical and horizontal diameters a-b and c-d; then bisect the distance a-e at f. Set your compasses to a radius e-f and, using e as the centre, describe a circle that cuts the diameters at f,g,h, and i. These points are the centres for the small arcs (or 'foils'). Drawing in the diameters from e to j,k,l, and m at 45° determines the points of the cusps.

SETTING OUT
VARIOUS SHAPES AND ARCHES

These are illustrated in Fig 14:7 and, although the

Fig 14:7 (opposite) Patterns of arches and how to plot them

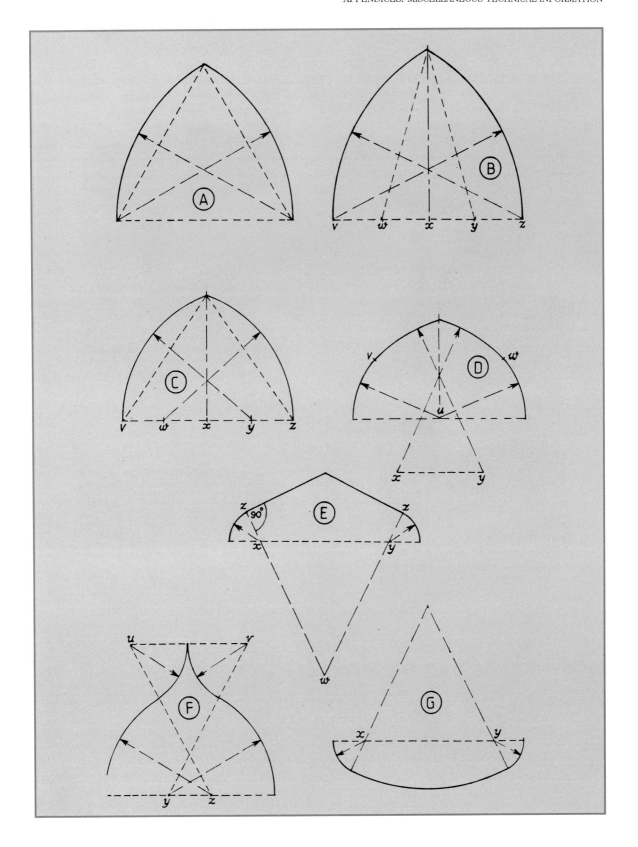

drawings are more or less self-explanatory, the following notes may help.

In geometry there are three kinds of triangles – equilateral, isosceles, and scalene. In an equilateral triangle, the three sides are equal, as are all the angles (60°). In an isosceles triangle, two sides and the two adjacent base angles are equal. In a scalene triangle, none of the sides or angles is equal.

(A) is an equilateral arch based on an equilateral triangle of the required size.

(B) is a lancet arch based on an isosceles triangle. The divisions between v,w,x,y, and z are all equal, and x is the centre point of w-y.

(C) is a drop arch, again based on an equilateral triangle; the divisions on the base line are equal and are all contained within the arch.

(D) is a three-centred arch. The base line x-y can be any convenient length, and the points x and y are the centres for the upper curves. The centre for the lower curves is at u. The curves meet at v and w.

(E) is a four-centred arch. The centres and proportions can be arranged to make different designs. Points x and y are the centres for the curves. Note that the lines x-z and y-z must be at right angles to the flats of the top.

(F) is an ogee or, more correctly, an ogival arch. Points u and v are the centres for the upper curves; y and z those for the lower.

(G) is a 'depressed' arch. The centres x and y must always coincide with the intersections of the sloping lines with the base.

PLOTTING A SCROLL

This is shown in Fig 14:8, and the design is frequently needed on antique furniture, particularly for the ends of the arms on chairs.

First divide the overall width of the scroll, which is a-b, into eight parts, and from a draw a-c at right angles so that its length is equal to one of the divisions; join c to b. From point No 4 draw an arc that is tangential to b-c, and where this intersects a-b, mark in point d. Now draw a line downwards from d at right angles to a-b, and draw c-e parallel

Fig 14:8 Plotting a scroll

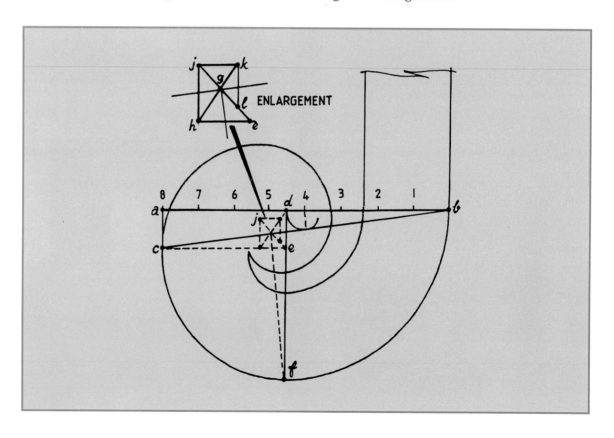

to a-b. Taking point d as a centre, draw an arc from b to cut the extension of line d-e at f. Then with point e as the centre, draw the arc fc.

From f, draw a line c-b and at right angles to it, thus giving you point g. Draw a line from d through g and extend it to c-e, thus locating point h, which is the next centre. From h draw a line vertically upwards to locate point j; a line drawn from j to d-h gives the centre point k. Draw a line vertically downwards from k to locate centre point l, which will enable you to complete the drawing of the outer scroll. The inner one can be drawn parallel to it.

PLOTTING THE ARCHIMEDEAN SPIRAL

Fig 14.9 shows the way to do this, and once you have grasped the principle involved you will find it straightforward.

Start by dividing the circle into twelve sectors and number them as shown, using either a 30° set square or a protractor. Then divide the vertical radius into twelve equal parts. Starting at division 1 and working downwards, draw an arc from each division to meet the radius with the same number – division 1 to radius 1, division 2 to radius 2, and so on. This will give a series of points that you can join freehand.

REDUCING OR ENLARGING MOULDINGS

Draw a full-sized section of the sample moulding as at abc in Fig 14:10 and also a base line x-l of any convenient length. Draw another line x-b and extend it to any convenient length.

Let us assume that the height of the sample

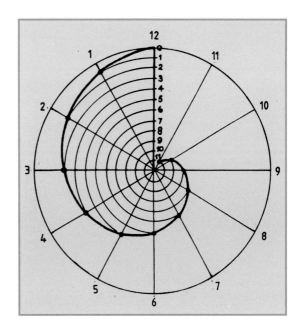

Fig 14:9 Plotting an Archimedean spiral

moulding is 2in (51mm), and that you need to produce a smaller one 1in (25mm) high, and a larger one of 3in (76mm). Draw a vertical line j-g upwards and 1in (25mm) long to meet x-b – this locates the smaller moulding. Similarly, draw a vertical line f-k upwards, 3in (76mm) long, to meet the extension of x-b at k.

Now join the salient points of the sample moulding abc to x and extend the lines to e-l. The intersections will give points that you can join up freehand.

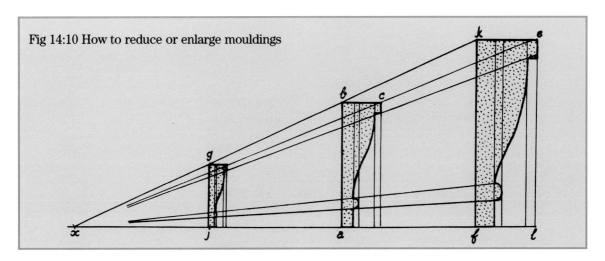

Fig 14:10 How to reduce or enlarge mouldings

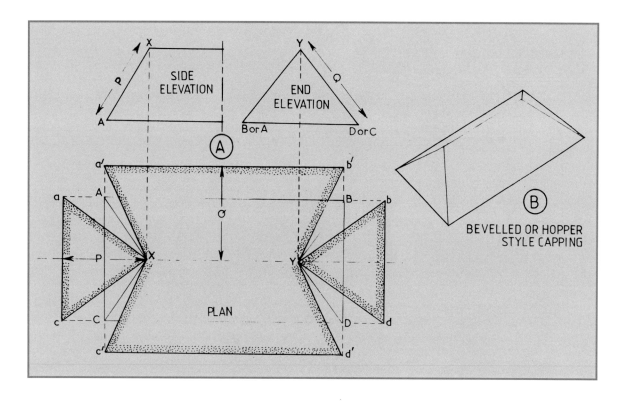

Fig 14:11 Setting out hipped tops

SETTING OUT HIPPED TOPS

These can be tricky because you are dealing with compound angles formed by inclined planes – an everyday example is the hipped roof on a house.

Begin by drawing the side elevation AX, the end elevation BDY, and the plan ABCD; all are shown in Fig 14:11(A). Next, draw the line a-c on the plan parallel to A-C at a distance P (see side elevation) from point X, which is an apex. In the same way draw a'-b' parallel to A-B at a distance Q from line X-Y. The lengths of a-c and a'-b' are determined by extending the lines A-B and C-D, and A-C and B-D respectively.

This gives you, in effect, a flattened version of the capping shown in Fig 14:11(B) and, when marked on the timber and cut out, the pieces can be assembled.

SETTING OUT A BASKET OR CADDY TOP

In principle the basic setting out is the same as for a hipped top but there is the added complication that the straight line, a'-X in the illustration, has to be converted into a curve, and the method is shown in Fig 14:12(A).

Begin by dividing the line a'-X into a convenient number of equal spaces. Seven are shown, but you could use six, eight, or more. Next, draw vertical lines from each of these points to intersect the curve A-X shown in the side elevation. Then draw a series of parallel horizontal lines through the intersections.

Next, divide the straight line a-X on the plan into the same number of equal parts and draw vertical lines upwards from the points. The intersections of these verticals with the horizontals previously drawn will give you a series of points that you can join up freehand to form the required compound curve. The same curve can be used for the other three corners; (B).

PLOTTING ENTASIS IN COLUMNS

Columns are usually slightly tapered from bottom

Fig 14:12 (opposite top) Setting out a caddy top

Fig 14:13 (opposite bottom) Determining the amount of entasis in a column

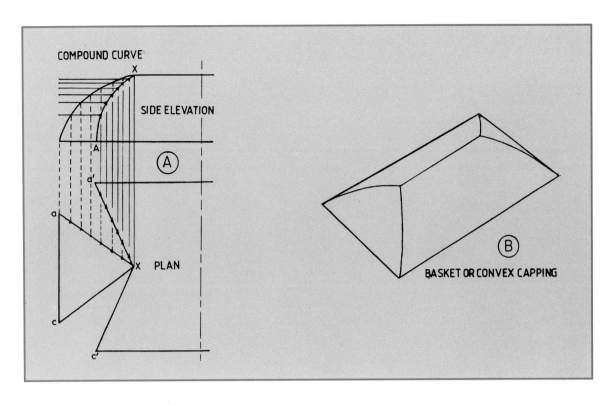

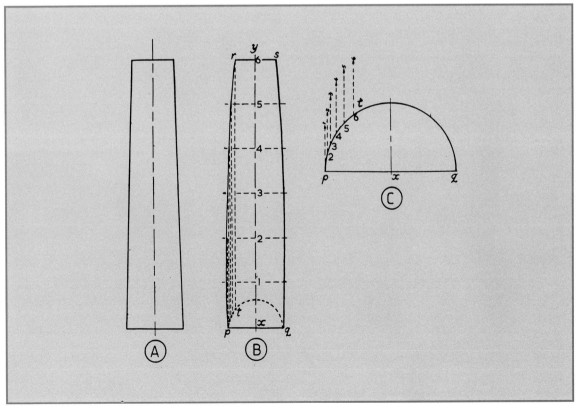

to top, and if they are left as tapered cylinders they tend to look awkward like the one shown in Fig 14:13(A). The ancient Greeks recognised this and introduced a feature called 'entasis' to improve the appearance of columns by incorporating a slight swelling towards the base. Fig 14:13(B) shows how the amount and position of the entasis can be plotted.

First, draw a vertical centre line x-y, and draw in the ends p-q and r-s at right angles to it. Then, with x as its centre, draw a semicircle using p-q as its diameter. Now, drop a vertical line down from r to cut the semicircle and create the arc p-t; this is shown enlarged at (C). Divide the arc into any convenient number of parts – six are shown – and then divide the centre line x-y into the same number of equal parts and draw horizontal lines at each point. Draw vertical lines upwards from the numbered points on the arc to intersect with the corresponding horizontal lines. Thus, point 4 on the arc should intersect with horizontal line No 4. This will give you a series of points that can be joined up freehand to create the curve of the entasis.

Fig 14:14 Details of a true piecrust top

APPENDIX B
MISCELLANEOUS DETAILS
OF TABLE CONSTRUCTION

'PIECRUST' TOPS

A true piecrust top is shown in plan in Fig 14:14(A); 'true' because there are many variations that have been, and are, produced in attempts to make the job easier, and none of them has the crisp beauty of the original pattern.

The plan illustrated is for a 20in (510mm) diameter top, and the purpose of the dotted lines and angles quoted is to enable you to reproduce either a larger or smaller plan easily. Obviously a much larger plan may need the inclusion of an extra repeat of the pattern, or even two, and this has to be left to your discretion. The small hollows can be drawn with compasses, their centres being on a circle just outside the circumference of the top. You will have to draw the serpentine shapes by hand. Once the plan has been drawn, you should make a card template of half of the entire repeat pattern with lines showing the inner and outer edges of the moulding.

To be authentic, the top should be carved out of the solid. If you have enough room between the centre and the bed of the lathe you can turn

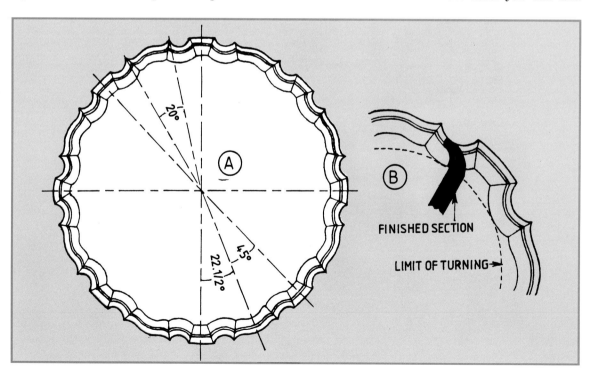

the top by fixing the blank to the face plate, and you can at the same time take out the recess with scraping tools up to the limit shown in Fig 14:14(B).

An alternative method is to use a bandsaw, a powered jigsaw, or a bowsaw to cut the outside circular shape, and the small hollows and serpentine shapes as well. The inner recess can be removed to the limits as shown by means of a powered portable router mounted on its trammel. Because the latter has a point at one end about which it swivels, stick down a small piece of waste wood with double-sided adhesive tape so that the point does not actually enter and mark the top. The remainder of the work falls into the province of the woodcarver.

DRAW-LEAF TABLE TOPS

The draw-leaf table probably has a longer history of unaltered construction and appearance than any other piece of furniture, and some sixteenth-century designs are obviously the precursors of tables you can buy today. There is usually a specimen of the breed at every second-hand furniture sale that needs only a few repairs to convert it into a perfectly serviceable table.

Fig 14:15 shows the 'working parts' of a typical table. There is a sliding leaf at each end, with a pair of bearers screwed to it from below. The bearers slide in notches cut in the end frieze rail, and diminish in shape so that as the leaf is drawn outwards it eventually rises to become level with the main top. The two most usual faults are (1) that the locating blocks on the underside of the main top are broken or missing, and (2) that the stops that prevent the bearers from being pulled out too far have been broken off. This happens especially on modern designs because they are often merely dowel pegs. The repair work is obvious and straightforward and really needs no description.

The lever shown at (B) was incorporated in some of the oldest antique designs but is not often seen today, which is a pity. Without it, when you need to close the leaves you have to stand at the end of the table and reach over to lift the main top so that the leaf can slide under it. This can be avoided by fitting a lever centrally at each end of

Fig 14:15 Details of the working parts of a draw-leaf table

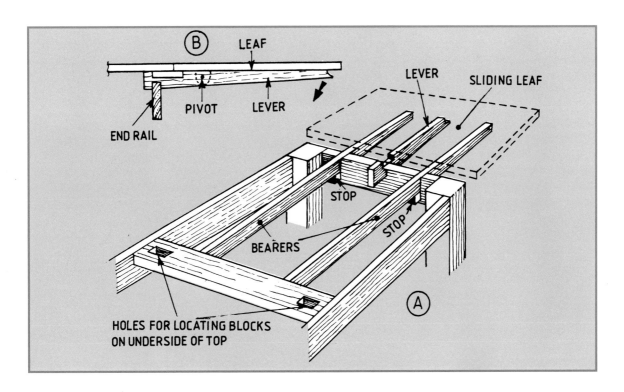

203

the frieze rail; when its end is depressed, it lifts the main top so that the leaf can be slid under it.

'CONCERTINA' EXTENDING CARD TABLES

This type of card table is one of the most sought after but, unfortunately, it is also the one most likely to be damaged because there are several hinged parts that are put under stress by continual opening and closing.

Fig 14:16(A) shows the general construction, and when fully extended, the slide is pulled outwards in its grooves and holds the whole thing rigid. Backflap hinges are used at the joints indicated, but the middle joints can use either proprietary centre hinges, or hand-cut knuckle joints. The latter have to be adapted to take into account the acute angle.

Fig 14:16 How a 'concertina' extending table works

Another point to note is that there are halvings at the middle joints so that the rails can lie perfectly flat against each other when the table is fully extended. The wooden spring (B) holds the legs when closed.

PIVOT POINT FOR A SWIVELLING TOP

Fig 14:17 shows the position of this, which is determined by the following formula. Distance y = half the length of a, minus one-quarter of the length of b. Distance x = half the length of a, minus distance y. The shorter side of the top is a; while b is half the length of the longer side.

METHODS OF FIXING TABLE TOPS

The way in which a table top is fixed on can be a help when judging its age. The methods used are as follows.

Up to the middle of the seventeenth century, and later in country districts, holes were bored through the top and down right through the frieze

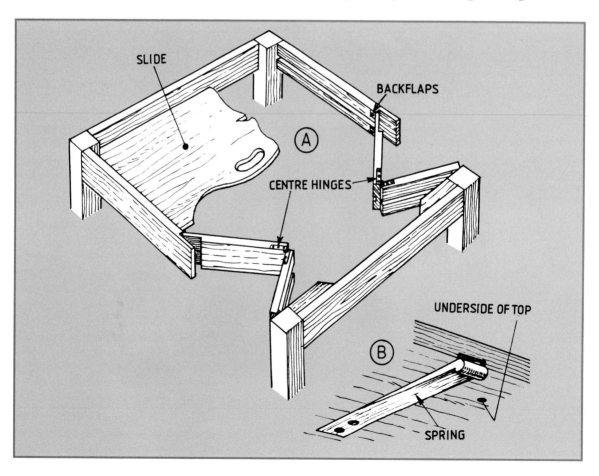

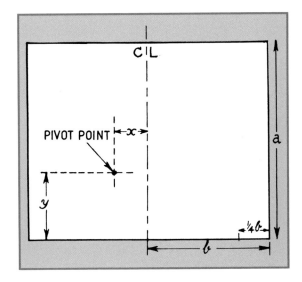

Fig 14:17 Finding the pivot point for a swivelling top

rails, and wooden pegs were driven into them. This meant that the pegs showed at both ends, namely on the top and also under the frieze rail. While the upper end was planed off, the lower end was chopped off with a chisel. These pegs were made from the same wood as the rest of the table, which in most cases was oak. Pegs were always riven and never sawn.

The next development was to use glue blocks instead of the wooden pegs; these are illustrated in Fig 14:18(A). These were simply small blocks of wood that had glue brushed on two of their sides and were rubbed into the angle between the top and the rail. The rubbing expelled air between the surfaces and ensured better adhesion. Country-made tables, however, often had the tops simply nailed on.

By the middle of the eighteenth century, improved lathe-made screws were becoming more widely used, and pocket-screwing as at (B) became standard practice. A gouge was used to scoop out sloping holes on the inside of the frieze rail and the screws were driven through them up into the top. A later variation shown at (C) was formed by two chisel cuts. This method was used in the late nineteenth century.

One modern way to fix solid table tops is by means of the 'buttons' illustrated at (D). A long strip of them can be prepared and the individual buttons sawn from it. Their tongues slide into grooves cut on the inside of the frieze rails. If these tongues can be tapered slightly from one side to the other, a wedging effect is created that will hold them more firmly. Their great advantages are that they can be disengaged so that the top can easily

Fig 14:18 Different ways to fix table tops

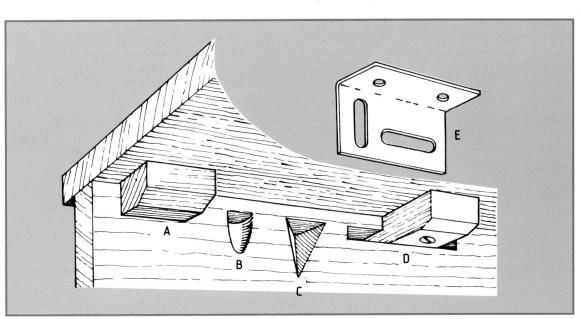

be removed, and they allow the top to shrink or swell freely.

Fixing tops made from man-made boards is best accomplished by using the kind of shrinkage plate shown at (E). The plain circular screw holes are attached to the top (which will not shrink), while the slots are screwed to the wooden frieze rails with round-headed screws. These should not be tightened down too hard or the rails will not be able to move.

WOOD SCREWS AND NAILS

Very little is known of the history of the wood screw, and hopefully you will find the following information useful, bearing in mind that the kind of screw used on a piece of antique furniture can be a guide to its age.

Screws and bolts have been used since time immemorial for joining metal parts together, usually as armour, and almost all of them had slotted heads, thus presuming the existence of screwdrivers. Wood screws were certainly known to the Romans about AD250, and they were used on the European continent in the middle of the sixteenth century. The earliest date of their employment in British furniture seems to have been during the late seventeenth century. They were then made of brass (which was not produced in England until 1568), with hand-filed, practically horizontal threads, slotted heads, and a conical shape.

The thread and the shape were the two characteristics which meant that they had little holding power, and each screw was usually accompanied by a pin driven alongside it. Because they were hand-made, if you have to remove any of them, you must identify each one so that it can be replaced in its own individual hole. One way to do this is to make a rough sketch of the piece and number the position of each screw on it; the screws themselves can be kept in numbered envelopes to avoid confusion.

About 1760, a method of turning the threads on a lathe was discovered by Wyatt, and screw threads became more like the modern pattern. The spiral diminishing became more regular but the ends were comparatively blunt and lacked a gimlet point. This kind of screw was still being produced by home-based 'screw-girdlers' in the Black Country until the modern factory-made screws with gimlet points were introduced about 1850.

NAILS AND TACKS

There are historical records showing that these were being made in homes in England by women and children in the fourteenth century. The nails they produced were similar to the deck-head nail in common use among boatbuilders until recently, with square, tapered shanks and faceted heads.

APPENDIX C
MAKING TWIST, OPEN BINE, AND FLUTED OR REEDED LEGS

TWIST LEGS OR COLUMNS

Before describing how to make these, it would be as well to define the terms 'lead', 'pitch', 'bine', and 'swash'.

Imagine a nut being turned and travelling along the threads of a bolt. The distance covered by the nut in one complete revolution is the 'lead', while the 'pitch' is the distance between two adjacent ridges or 'bines', and the angle of these is the 'swash'. There are two historical features to bear in

Fig 14:19 Barley-sugar and open-bine twists

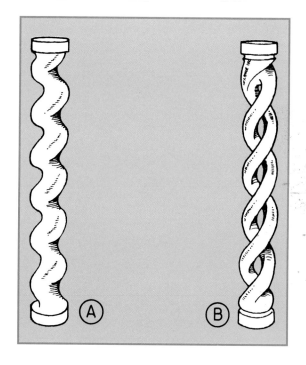

mind. The first is that in seventeenth-century pieces, the swash of continental legs was at a more acute angle than that of the English. And secondly, that the angle of the swash was almost always the same on all the legs and columns of any one piece of furniture. It was not until the Victorian period that they were 'handed' or paired so that the angles were inclined to oppose each other.

The 'bine' is the ridge or spine round the piece that forms the spiral; Fig 14:19(A) shows a typical 'barley sugar' twist, and (B) an open-bine twist. These can be elaborated to incorporate three or even four bines. It's interesting to note that in the 1680s a John Ensor of Tamworth invented a machine for doing the work twenty times faster than by hand. Although there are twisting lathes today for mass-producing quantities, the following method utilises hand work and is for those who occasionally have to make a few.

You do not need a lathe to do twisting but it can be a help in turning a square blank into a cylinder, particularly if the cylinder has to taper or be shaped for entasis. It can also be very convenient

Fig 14:20 Stages in making a single twist

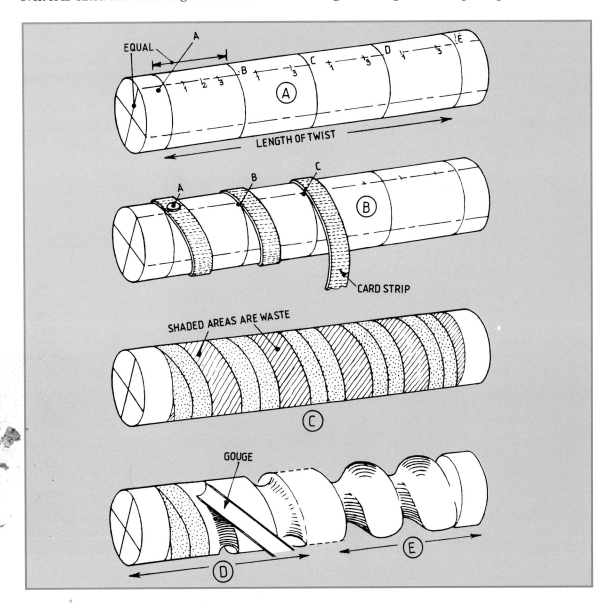

for the blank to be held in the lathe while you are working on it.

Assuming that you have turned the blank to the correct length and diameter, mark on it the two ends of the section to be twisted. The best proportions for a single twist are achieved by making the pitch equal to the diameter of the cylinder. For a double twist, the lead is twice the pitch; for a triple twist three times, and so on.

Because we are dealing with a single twist, the next stage is to mark a series of rings round the cylinder, the distance between each of them being equal to its diameter – see Fig 14:20(A). A piece of thin card cut to length makes a good template. Make sure you mark these rings in heavy pencil because the sections between them have to be subdivided later. To complete this stage, mark in the four longitudinal lines as shown, which run the whole length of the twist.

Next, mark in the centre of the ridge or bine. You can do this by taking a long strip of thin card about ⅜in (10mm) wide, which has one true straight edge. Fix this edge at the intersection A with a drawing pin and wind the strip round the cylinder so that the same edge is located at the intersections B, C, and so on; the process is shown in illustration (B). Pencil along the edge to mark in the centre of the bine.

Returning to illustration (A), the next job is to subdivide the lengths A-B, B-C, etc into four equal parts. You will only need points 1 and 3; point 2 can be ignored because it is only put in temporarily for marking out. With the true edge of the card strip, pencil a spiral line joining all the points marked 1, and then another line to join those marked 3. You should now have a cylinder, marked out as at (C), and the spiral can be made clearer by scribbling on the parts to be cut away.

From now on, you will have to use an assortment of gouges, chisels, rasps, and/or Surform-type

Fig 14:21 Stages in making a double-bine open twist

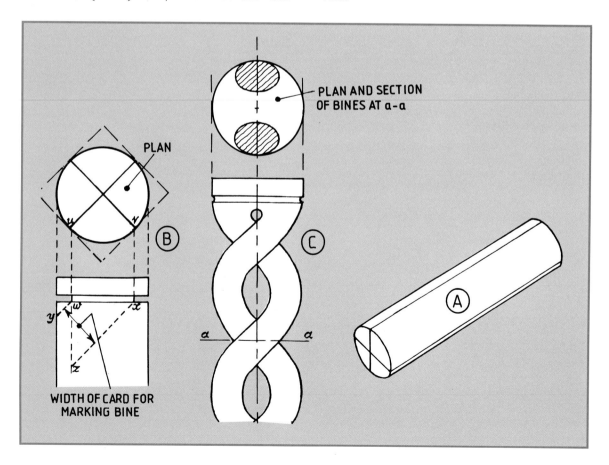

PLAN AND SECTION OF BINES AT a-a

PLAN

WIDTH OF CARD FOR MARKING BINE

shapers. A woodcarver's small gouge, followed by a larger one, are probably the best tools to start with, followed by a chisel to start the rounding of the bine. Then use a rasp or shaper tool, followed by glasspaper, to finish the work.

DOUBLE-BINE OPEN TWIST

Having turned the cylinder, mark out two diameters at each end at right angles to each other, and mark pencil lines joining them as shown at (A), Fig 14:21. Next, draw out the diagram shown at (B) full size, consisting of a section of the cylinder with the diameters marked, and one end of the cylinder. Note that the diameters are opposed at 45° to the centre line of the cylinder.

Drop vertical lines from u and v to the points w and x, and from these latter points draw lines at 45° to points y and z. This will determine the pitch and width of the strip of card for the bine, as shown. For a triple bine, the angle would be 60° instead of 45°. Fig 14:20(B) shows how the card strip is attached to and wound round the cylinder for marking the first bine. The second bine is marked similarly from the opposite sector.

Shaping the bines (C) follows the same general pattern as for the single bine design but, in addition, you may be able to use a drill to clear away some of the waste. A sharp penknife is invaluable for much of the final smoothing before finishing with glasspaper.

FLUTED OR REEDED LEGS OR COLUMNS

You can use the method described here for either fluted or reeded legs, depending on the profile of the router cutter.

Turn the leg or column to the desired shape, leaving a projecting pin on each end. Make these pins of the same diameter because this will make it easier to hold the work in the jig, the base of which can be made of an offcut of timber, plywood, or chipboard. The two sides should be spaced slightly farther apart than the diameter of the workpiece, and be about 6in (150mm) longer.

The two end clamps are solid wood blocks, and before they are fixed between the sides, a hole of the same diameter as the pins on the workpiece should be bored through the centre of each. The blocks are then sawn across at a point that is at a distance of one quarter of the hole diameter down from one side. The larger portions are then screwed between the sides and act as cradle ends to support the pins, while the smaller portions can be screwed down to hold the workpiece firmly. Two further jobs complete the jig. First, fix some stops on the outer faces of the sides to limit the travel of the router so that it can only cut the length of the flutes or reeds. Second, make a sawcut register mark at the exact centre of the top of each end block so that the mark is precisely over the centre of each pin.

The spacing of the centre lines of the flutes or reeds is critical and they must be equidistant from

Fig 14:22 Off-centre turning a chair backfoot

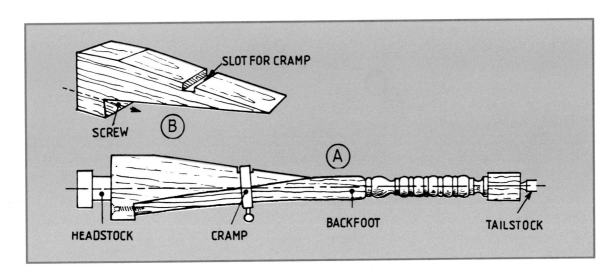

each other and marked on the top and bottom of the workpiece. You can do this accurately by winding a strip of thin paper round it to find the exact circumference, then removing the paper and dividing it into the required number of divisions. They can then be transferred to the workpiece by rewinding the paper strip round it and marking them off.

Having fitted the cutter into your router, you can arrange its fence or guide so that the cutter will be located exactly over the register mark. Start routing with a shallow cut and increase the depth in easy stages until you achieve the correct size.

DECORATIVE SPIRAL REEDING
From the end of the eighteenth and throughout the nineteenth centuries, decorative turning was very popular and was widely used on chair and table legs and the pillars of tripod tables. At that time, there was a great deal of interest in accessories and devices that could be added to an ordinary lathe to transform it into one that could also undertake ornamental turning in metal, wood, and ivory.

There are still such devices and attachments on sale today, and several utilise a portable power router as the cutting agent. In principle, the workpiece is mounted between a headstock and a tailstock, and is turned slowly (usually by hand) while a router travels on a carriage alongside it at such a distance that its cutter describes a cut in the workpiece. By varying the three factors involved, namely, the shape of the cutter, the speed at which the router travels, and the speed of rotation of the workpiece, different and very attractive patterns can be created.

As such patterns would be difficult if not impossible to make by hand, you will need either to buy the attachments (which are advertised regularly in magazines devoted to woodwork), or make your own. A comparatively straightforward design for a lathe on which you can do twisting or ornamental turning and which you can make yourself, largely from wood, was given in the August 1957 edition of the *Woodworker* magazine, and it could easily be adapted to incorporate a power router. Most large public libraries stock *Woodworker Annuals*, which you could consult, or no doubt the magazine could supply photocopies.

OFF-CENTRE TURNING
Those who are interested in conventional woodturning will find that this is an intriguing variation, and one that is useful for turning some kinds of shaped legs.

Fig 14:23 shows a typical club foot chair leg that can be turned by this method. There are six stages. (1) Mark the centres on the ends of the blank, which is then mounted in the lathe with the end which is to be the club foot towards the tailstock. (2) Turn it in the normal manner to a cylinder, and shape the club foot, leaving a slight hollow on the shank side of the foot. (3) Remove the leg from the lathe and mark a second centre on the club foot end halfway between the first centre and the edge. (4) Remount the leg in the lathe with the new centre at the tailstock end, the centre at the headstock end being the original one. The shank of the leg will then be eccentric to the tailstock chuck. (5) Turn it and (6) finish it off with a rasp, a spokeshave, or both.

Fig 14:23 Typical club foot leg

The same style of turning can be used for turning a chair backfoot with a splayed end, Fig 14:22(A). You will need to make the jig shown at (B) which has a slot cut in it to accommodate the arm of a small thumb cramp. A screw is inserted through the end so that it can be tightened to hold the work in place. The work can then be mounted in the lathe as shown, and turned.

APPENDIX D
STEAM-BENDING WINDSOR CHAIR BOWS
This has to be undertaken methodically, because if you do not have all the equipment ready to hand, or try to take short cuts, the result may be poorly shaped or ruptured bows.

Ash is the traditional wood, and it is best for steam bending when it is 'green' – that is, freshly sawn. This proviso also holds for other woods.

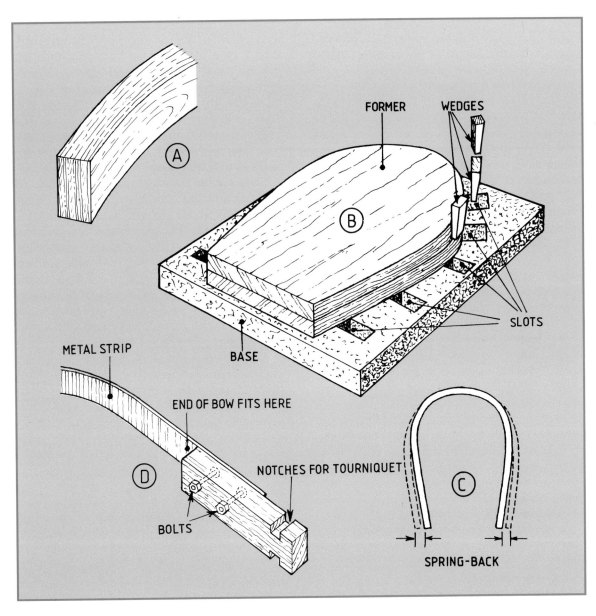

FORMER WEDGES

(A)

(B)

SLOTS

METAL STRIP

BASE

END OF BOW FITS HERE

NOTCHES FOR TOURNIQUET

(D)

(C)

BOLTS

SPRING-BACK

Fig 14:24 Stages in bending a bow for the back of a Windsor chair

Generally, kiln-dried timber tends to be brittle, while air-dried stuff will bend but needs care. The rule-of-thumb reckoning of the time required is about one hour per inch (25mm) of thickness. Home-grown timbers such as ash, beech, oak, and yew respond well to steam bending, but imported hardwoods and most softwoods do not.

The wood to be bent must be straightgrained and free of all knots, even 'pinhole' ones, which can cause distortion. It is much easier to bend strips of rectangular section than those which have been pre-rounded or moulded, so all shaping should be done after steaming. Fig 14:24(A) shows the best alignment of the annual rings on a strip that is to be bent.

The wood strip has to be bent round a 'former' or template which will give it the required shape, and this former needs to be fixed to a base; Fig 14:24(B) shows the general arrangement. The base should be about 1¼in (32mm) thick and can be made up either by jointing boards together, or gluing and screwing two sheets of plywood together. Its size should be about 6in (150mm) larger all round than the former. The latter can also be made from two pieces of plywood fixed together and cut to a shape that follows exactly the inner curve of the bow at the top, but with the open ends inclined towards one another more than is necessary to allow for the 'spring-back' on the bow when it dries out; see Fig 14:24(C). It must also be appreciably thicker than the wood strip to be bent. There is no need to use good quality plywood – strength is what is needed, not appearance.

The former is screwed and glued centrally on to the base, but before you do this, slots that penetrate right through the base have to be cut. You will have to decide the number of slots and their sizes, remembering that wedges are driven into them to tighten the bow round the former.

The last requirement is a metal strap that has to be wider and longer than the wood strip being bent. A handy size is 66in by 2in by 18SWG (1,675mm by 51mm by 1.5mm) and although stainless steel is the perfect (but expensive) material, ordinary mild steel or even a piece of galvanised sheet are suitable alternatives. The strap is located round the outer face of the wood strip to prevent the fibres from fracturing because of the tension they are subjected to in the bending process. You will find it a great help to bolt an end block to each end of the strap, so that the wood strip can be fitted snugly between them as in Fig 14:24(D). They also act as useful handles during bending.

You now need some form of steam generator, plus a steam-chest in which to place the wood while it is being steamed. An empty two-gallon (9 litres) metal paint tin or something similar forms the basis of the generator. The water in it may be heated by an electric kettle element or the tin can be supported on bricks and the water heated by a small camping gas heater. The tin must have a lid that has had a hole cut in the centre of it. A short length of 1in (25mm) diameter metal or plastic tubing is fixed into this hole and connects the generator to the steam-chest at its higher end. As a result, the chest slopes slightly so that condensed water will drain away.

The steam-chest is simply a long box open at both ends. One with internal dimensions of 40in by 4in by 4in (1,015mm by 102mm by 102mm) should do for most jobs. You can make it of BR (boil-resistant) or WBP (weather and boil-proof) plywood, both of which can withstand the heat and the steam. For occasional use, it could be built up from ordinary softwood. In all cases the parts should be nailed together with galvanised nails. Nail a few blocks to the floor of the chest as well to support the wood strip so that the steam can permeate all round it. Bore a small hole near the lower end to drain off condensed water.

Because the steam-chest needs only to be long enough to deal with the portion actually to be steamed, there are often lengths protruding from each end, and the easiest way to close the ends to stop steam escaping is with pieces of rag stuffed into them. Don't worry if some steam does escape because there is no question of its being under pressure – in fact, pressurised steam neither helps nor hinders the actual bending.

Now we come to the sequence of stages in the bending process. First, fill the steam generator about three-quarters full with water, which should be enough for about 1½ hours' steaming.

Next, fit the wood strip to be bent between the end blocks on the metal strap, and tie the two together with string. Make sure that the strap is clean and free from loose rust, which could stain the wood. Put the assembly into the steam-chest and start steaming. While this is in progress, cramp the base firmly to the workbench so that when the wood strip and the strap are taken out of the steam-chest and bent round the former, the ends will protrude over the edge of the bench. This will enable you to slip a loop of strong cord (such as sash cord) over the notches in the end blocks and insert a piece of dowel allowing the cord to be twisted like a tourniquet.

Once the assembly is out of the steam-chest, you only have a minute or two to produce the bend and, if you can recruit a helper, so much the better. Both of you should wear heavy industrial-type gloves because the wood will be hot. Locate the wood strip and the strap at the centre of the curve on the former and pull them round, knocking the wedges into the slots as you go. Finally slip on the tourniquet and tighten it up. If you need to apply even more pressure, use a sash cramp. After fifteen minutes or so, the bent wood bow with the metal strap and tourniquet still attached can be lifted away from the former and left to dry in a warm room for at least two days – longer if possible.

If you intend to make a large number of bows, you could replace the tourniquet mentioned above with a metal rod, hooked at both ends. It should be long enough to drop over the ends of the metal strap and hold them at a predetermined distance.

By modifying the sizes of the steam-chest and the generator, the equipment could be adapted to deal with other shapes and sizes of wooden components that need to be bent. By using a taller, slimmer steam generator and hanging the wood to be bent from a hook in the lid, so that it is clear of the boiling water, small pieces can be bent without the need for a steam-chest at all.

APPENDIX E
MAKING CABRIOLE LEGS

These were so frequently employed in furniture of the late seventeenth and eighteenth centuries, that a description of how to cut and shape them becomes almost obligatory.

The overriding consideration is that the shape should look right and not suffer from bandiness (usually caused by the knees being too low), or poor proportions. The illustrations in Fig 14:25 are drawn on a 1in (25mm) grid, and this allows you to enlarge them with no loss of shapeliness. The sections through the legs at strategic points should also help. Always make up a set of legs together, bringing each one to the end of a stage before going on to the next, to make matching easier.

Generally, the size of square required for a table leg is 4in (102mm), and for a chair leg 3in (76mm); but you may have to allow a little extra if there is carving – for instance, on the knee or the foot. The first stage is to draw and cut out a full size template on to hardboard or thin plywood, making extra allowances for any carving. Sketch in the details of this, and also of the club foot shown in drawing (A).

Lay the template on the square on one side and mark round it; then on the adjoining side, so that you arrive at (A), Fig 14:26. Note that the knees point towards each other. If the leg has a club foot, now is the time to turn it while the square can still be centred in the lathe. Next, cut out the shape on

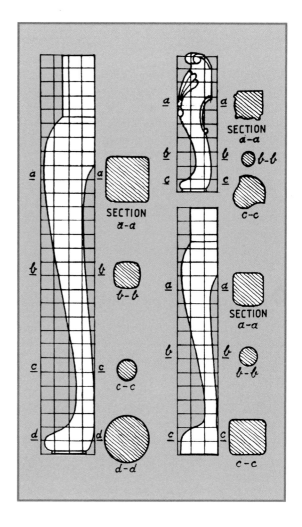

Fig 14:25 Patterns for various cabriole legs drawn on one-inch grids

one side of the square as shown at (B). There is only one machine that can do this quickly and efficiently, and that is a bandsaw, although in the old days it was done with a 'Betty' or chairmakers' saw, which resembled a large bowsaw.

Doing this removes the marking out on the adjacent side, so you will have to re-fix the offcuts temporarily with small pins before you can cut the second shape. This will give you the result shown at (C). The rest of the shaping is done with a spokeshave, supplemented by rasps and glasspaper. Pay particular attention to the ankle because quite a lot of wood has to be removed to achieve a flowing line.

APPENDIX F
GLOSSARY OF TIMBER TERMS

To do justice to all the information relating to timber would require a book on its own, and many such have been published. The following list should help you to understand the most commonly used terms.

Air-dried Timber seasoned in a stack in the open air. The rate of seasoning is reckoned to be one year per inch (25mm) of thickness. The boards are stacked with strips of wood (called 'sticks' or 'stickers') between them to create air gaps. If possible, the sticks should be of the same timber, and are spaced vertically one above the other. Never use softwood sticks because the resin they often contain may ooze out and mark the timber.

Annual rings Rings which appear on the cross-section of any tree that has been felled, and each ring indicates one year's growth. The rings relating to the early growth of the tree are very close, but later ones are wider apart; Fig 14:27(A). Counting them will tell you the age of the tree.

Bark The outer mantle of the tree. Its chief function is to protect the tree from extremes of weather and temperature; Fig 14:27(A).

Batten Strictly speaking, any length of timber from

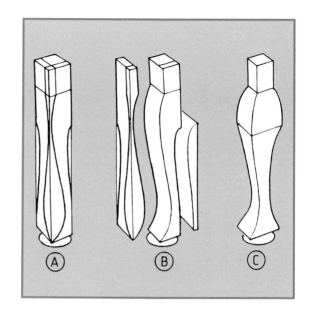

Fig 14:26 Stages in cutting out a leg round a template

5in to 8in (127mm to 203mm) wide by 2in to 4in (37mm to 102mm) thick is a batten, but today the term is usually reserved for 2in by 1in (50mm by 25mm) softwood.

Boule A butt (*qv*) that has been sawn from end to end into boards which are reassembled in the same sequence as they came from the saw.

Fig 14:27 Illustrations of some terms used in the timber trade

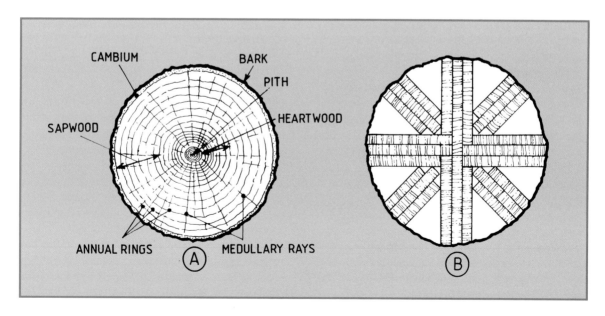

Butt The part of a tree from ground level to the point where the first branch occurs.

Cambium The zone immediately beneath the bark, which contains the current year's growth of the tree. It is also the part through which a starch/sugar solution passes down from the leaves to the roots; see Fig 14:27A.

Case hardening Condition that can afflict kiln-dried timber when the outside sets hard while the inside is still wet. It is a result of kilning too quickly.

Check A split or crack in the length of a board. It can be either shallow and merely on the surface, or penetrate the full thickness.

Clash The silvery flecked figure in oak, also called 'felt', 'flash', or 'silver grain'.

Deal Strictly speaking, a piece of square-sawn softwood from 2in to 4in (51mm to 102mm) thick by 9in to 11in (228mm to 279mm) wide. The word is commonly used today to describe ordinary pine.

Figure The grain pattern created by the growth of the tree itself combined with special methods of conversion. See Fig 3 (Chapter 9).

Hardwood Broadly speaking, timber obtained from deciduous trees that shed their leaves in winter. More scientifically, it refers to wood in which the cells are open-ended and conduct moisture, as opposed to softwoods in which the cells are closed and absorb moisture. Softwoods are obtained from coniferous trees with needle-pointed leaves. There are exceptions such as yew, which is classed as a hardwood but has needle-pointed leaves, but the definition is good enough for working purposes.

Heart wood See Fig 14:27(A).

Honeycombing Wood fibres that have ruptured with consequent severe splitting; caused by incorrect kiln seasoning.

Hoppus Measurer A ready-reckoner that enables the cubic content of a tree trunk to be calculated from its length and girth. The majority of timber merchants still use it, although the calculations are in feet and inches.

Interlocked grain Condition found in several tropical hardwoods (sapele is a good example) and caused by interlocked growth in the annual rings. In one year, the wood fibres incline to the right, the next year, they are straight, and in the third year, they incline to the left. This makes planing the timber very difficult because no matter in which direction you plane, it will always be across the grain in one part or another.

Kilning The modern timber-drying kiln has a system of heating, usually by coils of steam pipes, plus a means of introducing humidity by steam jets, and a controlled circulation of fresh air. The progress of the seasoning is recorded on circular graphs, and is regulated by balancing these factors against each other. The kiln will dry timber down to 9 to 12 per cent moisture content for use in centrally-heated rooms and offices. Air-drying is dependent on the weather, and on average can only reduce timber down to 17 per cent.

Medullary rays Rays, shown in Fig 14:27(A), consisting of very thin, flat bundles of cells that radiate from the pith outwards to the bark between the vertical fibres.

Moisture content Ensuring that the moisture content (often abbreviated to MC) of the wood is correct for its eventual use is one of the most important factors in successful woodwork. The definition of MC is the weight of the moisture in a piece of wood expressed as a percentage of the dry weight of the same piece. As the MC of freshly cut hardwoods can reach 100 per cent, and in softwoods 200 per cent (elm is frequently over 300 per cent), you can appreciate that proper drying is essential.

Battery-powered moisture meters are used in the trade to ascertain the MC, but you can adopt the following method in the home. Start by cutting a sample piece from the wood to be tested; a piece about 6in by 3in (150mm by 76mm) should be suitable. Choose its location carefully about 9 or 10in (230 or 255mm) inwards from the end of the board, because this area is liable to be drier. If you can remember to do it, insert a test piece in the middle of the stack while you build it, and use this to get a truer reading.

Weigh the test piece, which contains moisture, on a set of kitchen scales and note its weight. As an example, suppose it is 8oz (0.28kg). Dry it in an ordinary electric or gas cooker oven set at 100°C (212°F) maximum, and leave it for an hour or so. Then take it out and weigh it. Return it to the oven for another hour and repeat the process and, if the weights are the same, the test piece is dry. If not, continue drying until the weights are equal.

Let us suppose the dry weight is 6oz (0.17kg). By multiplying the amount of water lost – in this example 2oz (0.06kg) – by 100 and dividing the result by the dry weight, the answer will be the percentage MC. Thus, $2 \times 100 = 200$ which, divided by 6, gives an MC of about 33 per cent.

In the old days, before central heating, houses were often damp and cold and probably the furniture in them had MCs of 30 to 40 per cent at best. To bring old furniture from such an environment into a centrally-heated atmosphere, where the MC can be as low as 8 to 10 per cent, is to court disaster through shrinkage problems.

Quarter-sawn A method of converting a log to obtain the maximum number of boards with the best figure. Oak is the favourite timber for this kind of cutting. The method is shown in Fig 14:27(B).

Sapwood Part of the tree located beneath the cambium and extending inwards to the heartwood; see Fig 14:27(A). It contains all the food material and is vital to the growth of the tree. Usually it is commercially less valuable than heartwood.

Scantling Term that covers all small stuff from 2in to 4½in (51mm to 115mm) wide by 2in to 4in (51mm to 102mm) thick.

Shakes There is a variety of these defects, as shown in Fig 14:28. (A) is a longitudinal shake; (B) a star shake; (C) a cup shake; (D) a heart shake; (E) a radial shake. There are two more which cannot be seen until the log has been converted,

and even then they may take a little time to appear. They are the 'thunder' shake, which is usually confined to tropical species, and the 'felling' shake, where the stress imposed during felling eventually causes rupturing of the fibres.

Slab The first cut when converting a log is to square off one face so that the log can lie flat. The offcut is called 'slab' and has one flat surface and the other curved. It has little practical use so is often employed to cover stacked timber.

Slash sawn See through-and-through.

Softwood See hardwood.

Squares Square-sectioned pieces of timber, usually from 1½in to 4in (38mm to 102mm) square, sawn specially for use as chair and table legs; the former being 18in (457mm) long, the latter 30in (762mm) long.

Square-edged A board which has either one edge (when it is referred to as 1SE), or both edges (2SE), sawn at right angles to the face.

Through-and-through Also called 'slash sawing'. Refers to boards of equal thickness produced by sawing a log in a series of cuts from end to end.

Fig 14:28 **The different kinds of shakes**

Wainscot The term originally referred to oak that was shipped from Baltic ports; today it describes oak panelling.

APPENDIX G
ADHESIVES

Although the various adhesives have already been partially described, the following summary explains their characteristics more fully.

The best-known of animal glues is Scotch glue, which is made from animal bones and skins. At one time, it was sold in sheet form but today it is generally available in convenient granular form known as 'pearl'.

The old-fashioned double glue pot consisted of two iron pots, one inside the other, and many woodworkers still use them. The larger pot was filled with hot water to keep the glue in the smaller one at the right temperature. There are also modern types where the glue is thermostatically controlled by electricity, but they are expensive. A perfectly suitable glue pot can be made up in the workshop from an old saucepan in which an oven-proof Pyrex jug can stand on a couple of small wooden blocks; these allow the hot water to circulate freely.

To prepare Scotch glue, empty the granules into the inner pot, having taken it out of the larger one, and cover them with cold water. Leave them to stand and soak overnight. In the morning, add a little more water if it is needed to cover them, and replace the pot into the larger one. Fill the latter with water to just below the level of the glue. Heat the water on a gas ring or stove until it is too hot for the hand, but on no account let it boil. Stir the glue continually until it assumes the consistency of a thin syrup. This is the state in which you use it. Keep the water in the large pot hot enough, but do not allow the glue to boil because this considerably weakens it. Also, never use stale glue or add fresh glue to old – throw away any left over from the day's work and start afresh.

By a happy coincidence the optimum temperature for the glue is 160°F (71°C) and most domestic central-heating systems operate between 140° and 160°F, so the water from such a system will need very little heating.

Salisbury glue is of better quality because it is made from animal skins only and, as a result is lighter in colour and clearer. Rabbit skin glue was often used for making gesso. Although comparable in strength to most synthetic adhesives, animal glues have some disadvantages. They are easily broken down by water or dampness; they lose their bonding capacity unless the parts to be joined are warmed first because the glue soon chills and loses its strength; they are not resistant to fungal attack, they can stain light-coloured woods (although a white pigment powder can be added to minimise this risk), and they are difficult to apply to large areas because they tend to chill as you spread them.

Among synthetic adhesives are the PVA (poly-vinyl acetate) kinds. Examples are Evostik Resin W and Unibond. These are probably the most widely used general purpose adhesives for wood-work. The only kind of joint where they are not suitable is one that is subjected to stress or lateral pressure because they may tend to creep. They can be diluted with water to make a good adhesive for laying leather.

Epoxy resins include Araldite, Bostik, and Devcon. These adhesives form an immensely strong bond between a wide range of substances such as wood, most metals (either to each other or to wood), glass, and some plastics. They are, however, expensive to use for general woodwork.

Contact adhesives, such as Evostik Contact, are impact adhesives. When the two parts are pressed together, even if only with the fingers, there is an immediate bond. The chief use is for laying plastic laminates, but they can also bond veneer to shaped surfaces. Resorcinol-formaldehyde (RF) includes Croid Aero. This is an adhesive specially developed for outdoor work such as building, boat-building and the like. It is fully water- and weather-proof, but expensive.

Upholstery adhesives, such as Copydex, are used for bonding plastic foams and upholstery fabrics, either to themselves or each other.

Urea-formaldehyde (UF), is a strong adhesive used in industry for bonding plywood and laminating. It is water-resistant but not water- and weather-proof. It can cause stains round nails or metal fittings in woods with a high tannin content. One great advantage is that it cures without air being present, which is convenient for joints that fit internally.

All manufacturers include detailed information

on how to use their products. This can vary slightly from brand to brand and is therefore not given here. You must follow the manufacturer's instructions exactly.

APPENDIX H
REPAIRING DAMAGE FROM DAMP AND WOODWORM

Unless caused by unusual circumstances such as flooding, damp normally takes a considerable time to affect furniture. It follows that remedying the problem should be a leisurely business which, if it cannot be measured in years or months, should nevertheless extend over several weeks.

There are good reasons for this. One is that animal glue, including Scotch, has the ability to reconstitute itself and re-create the bond in a joint even though damp may have begun to soften the glue. This is always provided the furniture can be dried out gently and slowly and is not subjected to a violent change in temperature because of central heating. A waxed or polished finish may recover from the effects of damp in a similar fashion, but in all cases you must put the furniture in a dry but not a hot or very warm room, and leave all the drawers and doors open for air to circulate.

After this treatment, you will naturally need to check all joints to see that the glue bond is holding. Joints that fail the test will have to be remade. Polished surfaces can be rubbed with a reviving cream on a soft cloth. You can use either a proprietary cream or a liquid reviver made from equal parts of raw linseed oil, methylated spirit, turpentine substitute (white spirit) and a spoonful or two of vinegar. Leave the mixture on the surface for half an hour, wipe it off, and then apply a coat of good quality wax polish.

Wood which has been so badly affected by damp that it has become crumbly and flaky is past repair and must be cut away and replaced. If it is soft and spongy but not actually breaking away, you can try Ronseal wood hardener. Applied with a brush and left for a time, it will harden the wood sufficiently to hold screws or nails. It is colourless, but preferably leave any treated parts for several hours before applying polish.

WOODWORM DAMAGE

The fact that a piece of furniture has woodworm holes does not necessarily mean that it is still infested. In most cases, the woodworms have long since gone, although there is always the danger that a female may return at a future time and lay her eggs in the holes. This is why all holes, no matter what their age, should be treated with the appropriate proprietary spray or cream.

You can test to see if the woodworms are at home by standing the piece of furniture on sheets of newspaper so that any dust (called 'frass') they make falls on to it, thus indicating their presence. You will need to leave the piece for a few days. Examine it every day and tap it sharply so that any dust will fall out.

If the woodworms have done so much damage that the wood is merely an outer shell which crumbles away when touched, there is nothing you can do but replace the affected parts. There will, however, be occasions when the damage is marginal. In such cases you can apply the wood hardener mentioned above, ensuring that it is brushed well into the holes. The holes can then be filled with the special filler, also made by Ronseal.

Alternatively, you could build up the damaged parts with a putty made from epoxy resin that has had fine wood dust well mixed into it. Or possibly you may be able to reinforce the damaged wood with a piece of canvas soaked in Scotch glue. It all depends on how visible the repair will be and whether the job is one of authentic restoration or merely a repair.

List of suppliers

CABINET FITTINGS AND BRASSWARE

J. D. Beardmore & Co Ltd, (Head Office) Field End Rd, Ruislip, Middx, HA4 0QG. Tel 081 864 6811. Shops at: 3-5 Percy St, London, W1P 0EJ. Tel 071 637 7041; 49 Park St, Bristol. Tel 0272 27831; and 120 Western Rd, Hove, Sussex. Tel 0273 71801. Period brassware for furniture, doors, and windows.

Charles Greville & Co Ltd, Willey Mill House, Alton Rd, Farnham, Surrey, GU10 5EL. Tel 0252 715481. Brass finials, spandrels, and hinges.

General Woodwork Supplies, 76-80 Stoke Newington High St, London, N16 5BR. Tel 071 254 6052. General range of cabinet fittings.

Romany Tyzack, 52-6 Camden High St, London, NW1 0LT. Tel 071 387 2579. Comprehensive range of period and modern brassware, including brass and wooden gallery rails. The firm is part of the Tyzack Retail Group which has branches as follows (full addresses in *Yellow Pages*): Parker Tyzack at Catford, London; Parry Tyzack at Old Street, London and Borough High Street, London; Hall Tyzack at Merton, London, and Bath, Bristol, Cardiff, Plymouth, and Taunton.

H. E. Savill, 9 St Martin's Place, Scarborough, North Yorkshire, YO11 2QH. Tel 0723 373032. Probably the widest stocks of all the suppliers of period brassware.

Woodfit Ltd, Kem Mill, Chorley, Lancs, PR6 7EA. Tel 02572 66421. A really comprehensive range of cabinet and kitchen furniture fittings; some period brassware. Their catalogue is indispensable.

World of Wood, The Art Veneers Co Ltd, Industrial Estate, Mildenhall, Suffolk, IP28 7AY. Tel 0638 712550. Some period brassware and cabinet fittings. Their catalogue is well worth having.

LEATHER TOPS

S. Doctors, 5a Lansdown Mews, Farm Rd, Hove, Sussex. Tel 0273 774630.

Dorn Antiques, Tew Lane, Wooton, Woodstock, Oxon, OX7 1HA. Tel 0993 812023.

World of Wood (address above).

FINISHES, OILS, POLISHES, SEALERS, STAINS, VARNISHES, AND WAXES

Fiddes, Brindley Rd, Cardiff, CF1 7TX. Tel 0222 340323.

House of Harbru, 101 Crostons Rd, Elton, Bury, Lancs, BL8 1AL. Tel 061 7646769.

Liberon Waxes Ltd, 6 Park St, Lydd, Kent. Tel 0679 20107 or 21299. Waxes plus general polishing supplies.

John Myland Ltd, 80 Norwood High St, London, SE27 9NW. Tel 081 670 9161. Can supply adhesives and abrasives as well as polishing materials.

Poth, Hille & Co Ltd, High St, Stratford, London, E15 2QD. Tel 081 534 2291. All kinds of waxes, especially rare ones.

Weaves & Waxes, 53c Church St, Bloxham, Banbury, Oxon, OX15 4ET. Tel 0295 721535. Good range of waxes.

World of Wood (address above). Usual polishing materials.

SPECIAL TOOL SUPPLIERS

Alec Tiranti Ltd, 70 High St, Theale, Reading, Berks, RG7 5AR. Tel 0734 302775. Also at 27 Warren St, London, W1P 5DG. Woodcarving tools and equipment.

Ashley Iles (Edge Tools) Ltd, East Kirkby, Spilsby, Lincs, PE23 4DD. Tel 07903 372. Woodcarving and turning tools.

Peter Child, The Old Hyde, Little Yeldham, Essex, CO9 4QT. Tel 0787 237291. Wood turning tools and pyrographic equipment.

Henry Taylor Tools Ltd, The Forge, Lowther Rd, Sheffield, S6 2DR. Tel 0742 340282 and 340321. Woodcarving tools.

World of Wood (address above). Woodcarving, turning, and veneering tools; also marquetry donkeys.

SUNDRIES

A. & H. Supplies, 149 Faraday Avenue, Sidcup, Kent. Tel 0737 554966. Safety wear including masks, goggles, etc.

Liberon Waxes Ltd (address above). Gilding materials.

E. Ploton (Sundries) Ltd, 273 Archway Rd, London, N6 5AA. Tel 081 348 0315. Gilding materials.

Racal Chubb Products Ltd, PO Box 197, Wednesfield Rd, Wolverhampton, WV10 0ET. Tel 0902 455440. Can supply keys to most Chubb locks if the lock is sent to them. They also have archives containing working drawings of old locks.

Sefco Ltd, 8 Gun Wharf, Old Ford Road, London, E3 5QB. Tel 071 981 8161. 'Shortwood' plastic carvings.

J. Smith & Sons (Clerkenwell) Ltd, Tottenham Rd, London, N1. Tel 071 253 1277. Non-ferrous metals in rod, bar, and sheet form.

Vitrex Ltd, Kilnhouse Lane, Lytham St Annes, Lancs, FY8 3DU. Tel 0253 721291. Safety equipment such as masks, goggles, ear defenders, etc.

G. M. Whiley Ltd, The Runway, Station Approach, South Ruislip, Middx, MA4 6SQ. Tel 081 841 4241. Also at Howston Industrial Estate, Livingston, Lothian, Scotland. Tel 0589 38611. Gilding materials and tools.

K. R. Whiston Ltd, New Mills, Stockport, Cheshire. Tel 0663 742028. Brass and other metals in sheet, rod, and bar form; also 'Tufnol' sheet (recommended for making router jigs).

Yorkwire (Leeds) Ltd, 34 Lupton St, Leeds, LS10 2QW. Tel 0532 777472. Brass strip, rods, and wire.

SUPPLIERS OF EXOTIC AND DECORATIVE TIMBERS

Mackintosh Craftwoods, Unit 7, Fort Fareham, Newgate Lane, Fareham, Hants. Tel 0329 221925.

MHL Specialwoods Ltd, Beldray Park, Mount Bilston, West Midlands, WV14 7NH. Tel 0902 353733.

Milland Fine Timber Ltd, Milland Pottery, Milland, near Liphook, Hants, GU30 7JP. Tel 042 876 505.

North East Hardwoods Ltd, Whisby Way, Lincoln, LN6 3QT. Tel 0522 501485.

Palmyre Ltd, Glasson Estate, Maryport, Cumbria, CA15 8NX. Tel 0900 812796. Suppliers of bamboo.

South West Hardwoods Ltd, Blackweir Terrace, Cardiff, CF1 3EQ. Tel 0222 382053.

Timberline, Unit 7, Munday Works, 58-66 Morley Rd, Tonbridge, Kent, TN9 1RP. Tel 0732 355626.

UPHOLSTERY MATERIALS AND TOOLS

Bostock Woodcraft Ltd, 5 Fairfax Mews, Fairfax Rd, London, N8 0NH. Tel 081 341 2511.

Cope & Timmins Ltd, Angel Road Works, Edmonton, N18 3AY. Tel 081 803 6481

Dunlop Ltd, Dunlop House, 25 Ryder St, St James's, London, SW1Y 6PX. Tel 071 930 6700. This is the head office from which you can obtain details of their products and their factories, and also several useful booklets containing technical information.

Romany Tyzack (addresses above).

Russell & Chapple Ltd, 23 Monmouth St, London, WC2. Tel 071 836 7521.

SUPPLIERS OF VENEERS, MARQUETRY DECORATIONS, AND BANDINGS

R. Aaronson (Veneers) Ltd, 45 Redchurch St, London, E2 7DJ. Tel 071 7393107.

J. Crispin & Sons, 92-6 Curtain Rd, Shoreditch, London, EC2A 3AA. Tel 071 739 4857.

Fiddes (address above).

General Woodwork Supplies (address above).

Mackintosh Craftwoods (address above).

MHL Specialwoods Ltd (address above).

Weaves & Waxes (address above).

World of Wood (address above).

Bibliography

BOOKS CONTAINING PLANS AND WORK-
ING DRAWINGS OF PERIOD FURNITURE

Hayward, C. H. *Antique Furniture Designs* (Unwin Hyman, 1979)
Period Furniture Designs (Unwin Hyman, 1956)

Hurrell, John *Measured Drawings of Old English Oak Furniture* (Dover, USA, 1983)

Making Antique Furniture (Argus Books, 1988)

Making Period Furniture (Taunton Press, USA, 1985). American and British designs

Salomonsky, Verna *Masterpieces of Furniture in Photographs and Measured Drawings* (Dover, USA, 1965)

Taylor, V. J. *The Construction of Period Country Furniture* (Stobart Davies, 1978)

BOOKS CONTAINING WORKING DETAILS
AND DESIGNS

Chippendale, Thomas *The Gentleman and Cabinet Maker's Director* (Dover, USA, 1966);

English Furniture from 1574 to 1820 (Roy Arnold, 1989)

Hayward, C. H. *Antique or Fake?* (Unwin Hyman, 1970)

Hepplewhite, George *The Cabinet-Maker and Upholsterer's Guide* (Dover, USA, 1969)

Nicholson, P. & M. A. *The Practical Cabinet Maker* (Educational Productions Ltd, 1973)

Sheraton, Thomas *Cabinet-Maker and Upholsterer's Drawing Book* (Dover, USA, 1972)

Taylor, V. J. *The Antique Furniture Trail* (David & Charles, 1989)

Warne, E. J. *Furniture Mouldings: Full Size Sections of Moulded Details on English Furniture from 1574 to 1820* (Roy Arnold, 1989)

TECHNICAL AND INSTRUCTIONAL BOOKS

Hayward, C. H. *Practical Veneering* (Unwin Hyman, 1961)
Staining and Polishing (Unwin Hyman, 1973)
Tools for Woodwork (Unwin Hyman, 1973). Includes sharpening methods
Woodwork Joints (Unwin Hyman, 1965)

Howes, C. *Practical Upholstery* (Unwin Hyman, 1973)

Lincoln, W. A. *The Art and Practice of Marquetry* (Thames & Hudson, 1971)

O'Neil, Isabel *The Art of the Painted Finish* (William Morrow, USA, 1971)

Phillips, J. *Techniques of Routing* (Building Trades Journal, 1986)

Roubo, J. A. *Le Menuisier Ébéniste* and *Le Menuisier en Meubles*. In French; written and illustrated by one of the greatest French craftsmen of the eighteenth century (Roy Arnold, 1991)

Stokes, G. *Modern Wood Turning* (Unwin Hyman, 1973)

Wearing, Robert *Woodwork Aids and Devices* (Unwin Hyman, 1987)

Wheeler, W. & Hayward, C. H. *Practical Woodcarving and Gilding* (Unwin Hyman, 1973)

Index